Chasing the Past

Geopolitics of Memory
on the Margins of Modern Greece

S O C I É T É S
CONTEMPORAINES

Collection dirigée par Noël Dutrait et Matthew Graves et Constance de Gourcy

Ali Mekki, *De la vallée de la Soummam à la vallée de la Durance. Un siècle d'émigration et d'immigration 1915-2015*. Préface de Monique de Saint-Martin, 302 p., 2017

Stéphanie Latte Abdallah et Cédric Parizot, dir., *Isaraël / Palestine L'illusion de la séparation*, 313 p., 2017

Pierre Sintès, *En présence du passé. Géopolitique de la mémoire aux frontières de la Grèce*, 210 p., 2017

Quoc-Thanh Nguyen, *Le culte de la baleine. Un héritage multiculturel du Vietnam maritime*, 160 p., 2017

Nathalie Chapon, dir., *Parentalité d'accueil et mémoire*, 132 p., 2016

Laurent Mucchielli et Émilie Raquet, dir., *Délinquances, police, justice. Enquêtes à Marseille et en région PACA*, 244 p., 2016

Fabrice Argounès, *L'Australie et le monde. Entre Washington et Pékin*, 268 p., 2016

Ève Bureau-Point, *Les patients experts dans la lutte contre le sida au Cambodge. Anthropologie d'une norme globalisée*, 252, p., 2016

Yannick Duvauchelle, *Les représentations de la réalité. Étude sociologique*, 118 p., 2016

Loïc Le Pape, *Une autre foi. Itinéraires de conversions religieuses en France : juifs, chrétiens, musulmans*, 200 p., 2015

Fabrice Dhume-Sonzogni, dir., *Entre l'école et l'entreprise, la discrimination en stage. Une sociologie publique de l'ethnicisation des frontières scolaires*, 274 p., 2014

Truong Hoang Truong, *La banlieue de Ho Chi Minh-Ville. Bà Điểm (Hóc Môn) et Vĩnh Lộc A (Bình Chánh)*, 258 p., 2014

Véronique Dallet-Mann, Florence Bancaud & Marion Picker, dir., *Marseille. Éclat(s) du mythe*, 240 p., 2013

David Fée et Jean-Claude Sergeant, dir., *Éthique, politique et corruption au Royaume-Uni*, 216 p., 2013

Phuong Ngoc Nguyen, *À l'origine de l'anthropologie au Vietnam. Recherche sur les auteurs de la première moitié du xxe siècle*, 262 p., 2012

Sophie Vallas, Richard Phelan, Sylvie Mathé et Hélène Christol, dir., *San Francisco à l'ouest d'Éden*, 244 p., 2012

Jean-Marc de Grave, dir., *Dimensions formelle et non formelle de l'éducation en Asie orientale. Socialisation et rapport au contenu d'apprentissage*, 260 p., 2011

Marie-Claude Barbier, Gilles Teulié, dir., *L'Afrique du Sud, de nouvelles identités ?*, 256 p., 2010

Isabelle Widmer, Dolorès Pourette, *Les Violences envers les femmes à l'île de la Réunion*, 176 p., 2009

Carmela Lettieri, dir., *Comprendre l'Italie des années 2000. Du social au politique*, 212 p., 2009

Virginie Baby-Collin, Delphine Mercier, dir., *Sud à sud. Dynamiques sociales et spatiales, Amérique latine/Méditerranée*, 316 p., 2008

Pierre Chabert, *Les Cercles, une sociabilité en Provence*, 284 p., 2006

Laurent Sébastien Fournier, *La Fête en héritage. Enjeux patrimoniaux de la sociabilité provençale*, 188 p., 2005

Béatrice Mésini, Jean-Noël Pelen, Jacques Guilhaumou, *Résistances à l'exclusion, récits de soi et du monde*, 386 p., 2004

S O C I É T É S
C O N T E M P O R A I N E S

Chasing the Past

Geopolitics of Memory on the Margins of Modern Greece

Pierre Sintès
(Aix-Marseille University)

Translator: Jenny Money
(with the collaboration of
Samantha Eddison and Caroline Stephens)

Published 2019 by Provence University Press and Liverpool University Press

First published 2019 by
Provence University Press and Liverpool University Press

British Library Cataloguing-in-Publication data
A British Library CIP record is available

ISBN 978-1-78694-089-6

Typeset by Carnegie Book Production, Lancaster
Printed and bound by CPI Group (UK) Ltd, Croydon, CR0 4YY

Contents

List of tables

List of figures

Introduction

Since 2008, Greece has been at the centre of European current affairs due to the financial crisis that has affected its public finances and shaken the whole of the old continent – even the entire world – by threatening the stability of the European Union's monetary system and the economy of all its partners. The development of what is commonly called the 'sovereign debt crisis' is not country-specific, but the reforms that followed in Greece resulted in very significant impoverishment for a large part of the population now living in stark poverty. In recent years, the images that have encapsulated this situation have been widely circulated in the world's media to the point of becoming familiar: strikes and protests, street demonstrations turning into riots, a political crisis, last-chance agreements, misery and violence. The different figures released from the Greek state's statistical services, and estimates from international organisations such as the World Bank and the IMF, or associations fighting against poverty in the country, like Clandestino, Médecins du Monde, Smile of a Child, etc., often seem hard to believe when we realise that this is happening to a state that has been part of the European Union since 1981. The levels of poverty and distress that are suggested seem unbearable. Unemployment has risen to 27 per cent of the working population, but double this figure for young people. The minimum wage has been reduced to 456 € net and may be 10 per cent lower for those under 25. In such a context, the standard of living has dropped by 50 per cent owing to falling incomes and rising public costs, despite there being a reduction in rent and certain other prices. This has put nearly a third of the Greek population below the poverty line. In particular, such an impoverishment followed a period where the high development of consumption was accompanied by rapid economic growth, known as the 'second Greek miracle', and was characterised by an annual increase in the GNP of 6.75 per cent between 1948 and 1962 (Dallègre 2011).

The abrupt end to the improvement in living conditions that had accompanied this growth, their marked deterioration and, especially, uncertainty and the absence of perspective have hit the Greek people for the most part since the end of the 2000s. Symbolically, this is demonstrated by the dramatic increase in the number of suicides in a country which, up to now, has known so few (a 22.7 and 27.6 per cent increase respectively from 2007 to 2009 according to the *American Journal of Public Health*, 18 April 2013) and the appearance of many homeless people on the streets of the cities (20,000 people according to the press). Another symbol of this distress during the winter of 2012 was the abolition of collective heating in most of the buildings due to the occupants being unable to pay for the petrol, which resulted in the illegal felling of trees in nearby cemeteries, parks and forests.

Greek daily life was now marked by this cruel reality, and its impact on the very foundations of society in terms of relationships with family, work and public spaces, etc. will be felt for many years to come. This impact is still difficult to measure as a whole – even if we are already receiving glimpses of it, such as the inversion of demographic indicators, the resumption of migration abroad, the intermittent return of populations to rural areas, the self-organisation of certain sectors neglected by investment and the abandonment of public services, etc. However, what is the most frequently observed from abroad amongst the consequences of this new situation is the sharp increase in radicalism and political violence. This has been particularly evident with the confirmed emergence of a troubling neo-Nazi party – Golden Dawn – since the May–June 2012 legislative elections, where it won nearly 7 per cent of the vote, as well as around twenty seats in parliament. Such scores were confirmed by the following elections, where the party won almost 10 per cent of the vote throughout the whole country. The open affiliation of this political movement with the national socialist ideology of the Third Reich and the violent practices for which it is well-known add, henceforth, to the landscape of poverty and desolation evident in many areas of the country, and amalgamate all the elements of an explosive socio-political formula. Such an image provokes continual concern over the future of social cohesion in Greece, especially if we add to the mix the continual discrediting of traditional elites due to repeated politico-financial scandals affecting the political, ecclesiastical and economic milieus, and implying that little consideration for the good of the people is shown by those in power. One of the most important scandals is that of the 'Lagarde List', which brought to light the extent of tax evasion in the highest echelons of the state, incriminating no less a person than a former Minister of the Economy and the mother of the former socialist Prime Minister, Giorgos Papandreou.

Beyond the country's borders, this new situation has questioned both the feasibility and the strength of the European project on this part of the continent: its development and integration model has indeed been radically undermined, more so than in the other countries in Southern Europe, like Spain or Italy, whose economies are in trouble. Hence, today, all the states of the Western Balkans see their future membership of the EU as threatened in the short term, despite it having already been confirmed by the leaders of the EU summits in Feira in 2000 and in Thessaloniki in 2003. At the same time, the austerity policies that have been developed, due the global *subprime* financial crisis that dampened public finances, may seem comparable to those that Greece has experienced. Throughout the Balkans, as elsewhere in Europe, real supervisory administrative policies – the fruit of IMF injunctions and conditionality policies imposed by Brussels – have assigned a convergent position on the continental chessboard to this group of South-East European countries, despite the wide diversity of situations as regards the EU: member-states, new members, countries applying for membership, or potential candidate countries. Thus, in many ways, Greece proves to be an important place in which to test hypotheses about the future of regional transformations because, firstly, of the strong repercussions of its crisis on the economies of its neighbouring countries, which are linked to Greece in several ways – close trade links, mass migration – and, secondly, because its trajectory can be presented as a(n) (counter-)example or a (counter-)model to validate procedures reserved for other Balkan countries in terms of' 'European engineering' and relationships with the EU. Over and above Greece, it is undoubtedly not just the future of South-Eastern Europe as a whole that has been directly shaken by the Greek crisis, but also the foundations of the European project as it was designed back in 1957.

Shadows and light

The research that I began in Greece before and after the outbreak of the crisis – and that I am still currently pursuing – may seem disconnected with the recent concerns of its people. Some would, without doubt, qualify it as irrelevant given the situation. It is true that, if my work were to document the economic survival of some actors within Greek society, it would mainly concern the Albanian economic migrants from the early 2000s, rather than the new poor at the end of the decade. Rather than studying the economic transformations, the civil-service redundancies and the soundness of the banking sector, I became more interested in the questions of space and identity after examining several case studies that had used both medium- and long-term surveys and observation methodology. My work often sought to document and analyse the formation or the reformation of discourses about 'minorities', 'locality' or, to avoid the connotations of these two words, 'small groups', mostly activated by geographic mobility, migration or a transnational network. This work led me to repeatedly envisage the contemporary use of memory to bring more coherence to the current practices of some people in Greece, whether settled migrants, nationals or foreigners passing through the country.

However, in the new context of the late 2000s, who is currently interested in the dynamics of minority groups or cultural revitalisation policies in peripheral areas of the country when retirement pensions are experiencing unprecedented cuts? Who is still concerned about the multiple identities of some Greek citizens while riots rage in Athens? Even the most sensitive topics like the problematic place of many Balkan migrants in Greek society, which were the subject of much reflection in the 1990s, no longer seem likely to make the headlines, or even attract the interest of my academic colleagues. Only geopolitical questions, like migration on the Greco-Turkish border, within a context of dissemination of nationalist discourses, reveal a tenuous link between my work on border identities and emerging issues in the country. The urgency today seems to reside more in understanding the dynamics of the banking and financial sector than in analysing the construction of social identities within the Greek population. However, when examining the austerity policies and adjustments that affect both the economy and Greek society, we should bear in mind that the effects of these new developments are engraved in the continuity of the previous period's dynamics, and remain essential to understanding these latter.

Undoubtedly, before the traumatic events resulting from the 2008 economic crisis, Greek society had already undergone a number of transformations, although less publicised abroad, which had drawn its population into what could be perceived as a dive into the dark side of globalisation. Thus, the political upheavals of the early 1990s and the collapse of Marxist-inspired regimes prevailing on the other side of the Iron Curtain had already radically transformed the face of the country. Certainly, the opening of a once-closed northern border (albeit closed to varying degrees because differences existed in the cross-border relations between Greece and Albania, Yugoslavia and Bulgaria throughout the Cold War) had two main consequences: the proliferation of Greek investments, mainly in the banking sector (which is not the least of the paradoxes in light of what happened a few years later) in the Balkan countries, and the triggering of a massive migration flow, especially from Albania to Greece. This latter brought in numerous contingents of migrants, whose presence was felt throughout the Greek territory, even in the smallest villages in the Cretan countryside or the Peloponnese. Nevertheless, such a movement created a valuable contribution in terms of labour force, enabling significant achievements to be accomplished in economic terms, such as the structures necessary to the organisation of the 2004 Olympic Games. At the same time it also provoked an infinite number of negative reactions from people, whose image of a happy and peaceful past seemed to have come to a definitive end with the arrival of the migrants, first and foremost the Albanians (Sintès 2010a: 85). It is just such a nostalgic version of the history of the country that was always presented, in both the Greek media and in the narratives of those I met during my first fieldwork in the early 2000s, where the advent of crime was still attributed to this new migratory situation which began in the early 1990s.

Nevertheless, however much these traits were conventional for a new country of immigration, the opening of the northern borders also brought Greece closer once again to the realities that some observers saw as eminently Balkan. These 'new' issues mainly involved border disputes, but also minority issues and national definitions, for which the region was already renowned in the early-twentieth century and which were even stronger by the end of it. These implications led in public opinion to the consideration of a more specific trait about the country itself: its position as a member of the EU, while questioning its singularity or, in a way, its compatibility with 'European values'. Firstly, the Yugoslavian crises which, without having directly affected Greece, gave new impetus to the border disputes that had for many years been frozen by the Cold War. In the 1990s for example, some observers suspected the Greek Prime Minister, Andreas Papandreou, of maintaining secret links with Slobodan Milošević, with the ultimate goal of encircling the Albanian territory by Greek and Serbian forces (Michas 2002). Complications in Greek–Albanian relations were a discrete sign of this situation, which sometimes led to extremely tense moments – such as, for example, the persecution and imprisonment of several representatives of the Greek minority in Albania in 1994 (Sintès 2010a: 211).

Moreover, the independence of the former socialist Republic of Macedonia* in 1991, and the issue of the new name the country had chosen, had a greater impact internationally and brought a feeling of instability to the gates of Greece, in spite of the country's membership of the European Union and the North Atlantic Treaty Organization. This resurrection of the 'Macedonian question', reminiscent of the Balkan wars, gave rise to the return of the ghost of the Slavic groups in Northern Greece who had partially disappeared after the Civil War, and to fear of neighbouring countries' plans to annex Thessaloniki, the second largest city in Greece. Thus, with some disbelief, its European partners saw the Greek government impose a trade embargo in 1993–94 on its smallest neighbour, even though this country did not seem to be in a position to seriously threaten regional stability. This feeling of irrationality over the Greek position on geopolitical border issues surfaced once again during the Imia/Kardak islands crisis in 1996 with, as a backdrop, the presence of a Muslim minority in Western Thrace. The latter is traditionally suspected of being a Trojan horse for Turkish expansionism, which could have been used in an act of force such as that experienced by Cyprus in 1974.

After several decades of stability, these different regional geopolitical tensions contributed, beyond the exotic clichés, to the construction (or reactivation) of an image of otherness, even of isolation, of Greece on the international arena. They also established within Greek society a new experience of marginality, or even a lack of understanding from their European partners, well before the financial crisis and the stance of the Euro-group had increased these feelings for the majority of the inhabitants of the country. Such a movement, which affected the image of Greece from the early 1990s, may also have been analysed more broadly as a kind of 'return' to the Balkans (Yérasimos 2002). This expression could not be fully credited due to the fact that all these topics encapsulated by this expression (i.e. border disputes, minority issues, geopolitical tensions) had without doubt never completely disappeared from Greek society during previous periods. Nevertheless, it is difficult to deny that the conditions for the expression of minority identities in Greece appeared to have been modified at that time, validating to some extent the 'return' to the forefront of such questions. This movement involved increasing the visibility of non-compliant groups to the canons of the Greek nation-state that wanted a Greek citizen to be of the Orthodox religion and Greek-speaking. However, more generally, and quite concordant with what was happening elsewhere in Europe, the question of diversity was omnipresent in the public debate during the 1990s and 2000s, and was often controversial, whether it was about Albanian migration, the conflict surrounding the creation of the Republic of Macedonia or, later, about long-distance and transit migration. The publication of a broad scientific literature testifies to this, bringing awareness and recognition of a long-silenced reality – the diversity of the country's population – to the heart of academic and institutional milieus.

It is true that such themes undoubtedly echo the population's concerns. Besides the international situation and the issue of the country's borders, several events that occurred in Greece were indeed linked with public debates on the notion of Greekness (*Ελληνικότητα*). One such case was the issue of removing religious denomination from identity cards as of the spring of 2000. This aroused fierce opposition from a large part of the population, as well as an extremely strong commitment against this measure by the church (Dépret 2005). In the same year, a young Albanian was given the opportunity to carry the Greek flag during the National Day celebrations on 25 March on account of his excellent academic results, and this led to intensive debates on the meaning of national belonging for the children of migrants, which resulted in the removal of this student from his position as flag-bearer for his class (Kapllani and Mai 2005; Sintès 2010a: 82). In 2009, these debates were resumed with Giorgos Papandreou's accession to power; wanting to be recognised as a moderniser, he proposed an overhaul of the right to citizenship by introducing some aspects of *jus soli* to Greek law. These measures had last been addressed by the following government of Antoni Samaras who, at the peak of the economic and political crisis, seemed to rely on the firmly defined contours of a classic nation-state identity, which was often more exclusionary for migrants and their children. This backward move was made in relation to the new position of the country on the chequerboard of Mediterranean migration that designated it essentially as a transit point for long-distance migration from African and Asian countries, through the Greek-Turkish border *en route* to Western Europe. As was the case after the economic crisis, Greece was also presented as the victim of a wider EU policy that refused to share the burden of migration, forcing the country to manage too high a number of asylum-seekers on account of European treaties destined to regulate the flows on the continent. This is a situation that guaranteed political success for the Golden Dawn Party, along with the emergence of racist violence on the streets of Athens in the late 2000s. The rapid evocation of these different sequences helped to identify a double movement: a movement of compliance and resistance to the implementation of new social and economic norms that, promoted from the outside or proceeding from a movement in which Greek society participated, would impose itself (here as elsewhere) without necessarily gaining the support of the majority of its inhabitants. Even if this trend did not solely concern Greece, during this period there were signs of a quite explicit rejection of otherness (minorities and migrants) in the country, because these groups were seen as raising doubts about the homogeneity of the nation. On the other hand, a second movement shows a kind of opening up of Greek society to 'the world', and more specifically to the European Union, through the application of territorial cohesion policies, the recognition of the diversity of expression and minorities, the preservation of local heritage within the framework of international cooperation programmes… and to other Balkan societies through the circulation of goods and people as well as the development of economic relations with numerous countries on the peninsula.

More generally, without going into detail about what happened after the 2008 crisis, a great number of transformations seem to have affected Greek society in recent decades, with some even changing the frameworks that appeared to be the foundations of its collective organisation. Without returning to the themes of secularisation in a country where religious practices of Orthodox Christianity used to be a common base, or the ongoing disappearance of rural life despite the admirable resistance of visits 'to the village', one can only observe the rise of individualism that can be perceived as the consequence of the rapid urbanisation of Greece from the 1950s, as well as the strong outflow of Greek migrants, mainly to the United States and West Germany up until the 1970s. Moreover, in the classic way, the conditions of individual development permitted by the globalised capitalist society and the establishment of neo-liberalism met with great success in the country. They enabled the Greeks to enter the era of mass consumption, professional and geographical mobility, bank credit and the nuclear family. From the 1980s and the country's accession to the European Economic Community, the transformations in lifestyles once again accelerated, affecting both the demographic distribution and the use of space. Marietta Karamanli's essay on the social roots of the Greek crisis (Karamanli 2013) describes this individualism as a persistent legacy from the former times of frugality specific to the mountain societies of South-Eastern Europe. Moreover, it can equally be seen as a relentless penetration of global *Zeitgeist* of liberal post-modernity, combined with the particularity of a small country with a fragile economy. It should be noted here that it is a paradox of a society whose point of reference and objective timeframe are those of some form of material or societal 'modernisation', which leads to both a form of 'individualisation' and the emergence and intensification of more radical discourses, referring frequently to the past and to authenticity to explain the present. As elsewhere, this leads to the current strengthening of local identities and small minority groups and paves the way to the building of a more radical discourse. Without claiming that it is country-specific, such a paradox seemed important to address for it has turned out to be one of the recurring aspects of the situations that I have been studying in Greece since the early 2000s.

Memory – identity – space as a trinity for observation

In recent years, the observation of different situations in Greece has led me to compare the context described above with the notions put forward by a number of authors dealing with globalisation – such as 'primordialism' by Arjun Appadurai, 'retrovolution' by Jean-Loup Amselle, and the expression 'race backwards' by the anthropologist Ivan Čolović. Such notions describe the strengthening of the discourse of belonging, drawing legitimacy and coherence from a glorification of the past or of traditions. It is mostly seen among groups the dimensions of which are smaller than those of the main national groups produced on the European model in the nineteenth and twentieth centuries. This process supports allegiances, as they existed in the region, that go beyond (or under) the classic state level. This trend is presented in numerous works as one of the movements weakening the nation-state's influence on society, as a local equivalence of the strengthening of supranational players that are one of the other signs of globalisation on power/territory relations. By creating 'invertebrate' or 'cellular' social forms such as diasporic groups or alternative affiliations (Appadurai 2006), these identity networks become modes of allegiance more suited to contemporary processes, due to their greater flexibility and ability to use the modern technological means of communication. At the same time, they take advantage of the generalisation of a post-modern condition of the individual, of the fluid dimensions of the world today, which offer themselves as a potential option for many actors, free to determine their identification from among the different possibilities of allegiance available in an accessible, globalised and competitive 'identity market'.

Despite the disembodied nature of the support mobilised for these new narratives of identity, well expressed by the different neologisms in *-scape* of anthropologist Arjun Appadurai (1991), such discourses can be observed through their geographic implications: they are always taken from a located set of values or are found in a certain relation to space. These invocations of the past are regularly accompanied by an explicit reference to a territory, or to given places, to a real or imaginary geography, or to a number of relationships to space. What, thus, are these special relationships with places when roots, memory and the past are glorified as sources of imprescriptible legitimising virtues? Does this kind of immaterial or ideal relationship with places result in distinct practices like those that are becoming increasingly present for the preservation or enhancement of the material signs of the past? Such questions lead to replacing these values and the social space they produce in nested levels, going from localism – that is to say, the excessive embellishment of the qualities of a place – to a 'global hierarchy of value', as defined by Michael Herzfeld (2004), together with the revitalisation of an infinity of affiliations located at intermediate levels. Such considerations (which entail our perception of the scale of social processes) will lead to a questioning of the relationships between the different 'levels of power' and a return to the hypothesis presented above. Do these new identity statements proceed from forces systematically opposed to the strengthening of national discourses that serve as a legitimacy framework for a nation-state losing speed? This is a question that can be found in some of the anthropologist Michael Herzfeld's works dedicated to Greece, and especially in his book *The Body Impolitic, Artisans and Artifice on the Global Hierarchy of Value*. The author examines the future of the traditional skills of a group of Cretan artisans. It thus emphasises how the enhancement of particular traditions, whether they be those of a country (Greece) or of one of its regions (the north coast of Crete and the town of Rethymno), can be linked to – paradoxically – the implementation of a self-representation which he describes as 'Western' values and, more broadly, to a 'global hierarchy of value.' The latter summons up the past by reinventing it and assigning it a relative value. Simultaneously, this leads to the subjugation of the particularities of places by setting them within a dominant system that is characterised by a neo-imperialist tendency and a global dimension. Thus such hypotheses allow us to consider the possibility that movements to recognise and promote a particular group, however small it may be, would also be in a position – somewhat paradoxically – to strengthen certain aspects of a national discourse, even an internationally recognised vision of identity and territory, and which all refer to the past (via memory), as a source of indisputable legitimisation. Nevertheless, even if the observations presented in Michael Herzfeld's book deal with the logical changes of reference to the past in an age of globalisation (even of neoliberalism), there is always a link to the object of his study – a group of Cretan craftsmen he researched between 1992 and 1994. The political dimension and, more particularly, the subversive and centrifugal potential of the appearance or strengthening of local or minority identities cannot be detected due to this group's particular conformity *vis-à-vis* the mainstream canons of Greekness. Therefore, to enable completion of this approach, the study of groups falling within other defining parameters also deserves to be undertaken in this country.

Nonetheless, to avoid the centrifugal dimensions concealing other aspects of this dynamic, the case studies proposed in the following chapters will be categorised according to their graduated positions, while respecting the 'geopolitical sensitivities' of the observed groups. The diverse situations presented in this book show how the implementation of this global *hierarchy of value* in Greece should be understood in relation to a *hierarchy of Greekness* well established in the mainstream representations in the country, as defined by Anna Triandafyllidou and Mariangela Veikou (2002). Hence, the chosen cases vary between the groups the most stigmatised and distant from definitions of Greekness – like Albanian migrants or minority groups seen as a threat on the Greek–Albanian border – to those where the mechanisms taking place appeared more consistent with definitions of Greek national identity – for instance, the revitalisation of local cultures compatible with the contemporary canons of Greekness on the Greek–Albanian border or in Macedonia, or in the case of the Rhodes Jewish community's return of memory. The study of these different cases will enable measurement of the various processes that evoke the past and memory and thereby strengthening group identities in Greece today. They will shed light on the rapid changes that the country has undergone in recent decades, detailing situations where, on the one hand, mobility and migration were often involved and where, on the other, the effects of international and national dynamics on the formalisation of heritage and memorial policies are confirmed.

Hence, studying these discourses that mobilise the past through the observation of daily life situations will help to evoke the changes that have more generally affected all European territories. From a more theoretical point of view, it will show how local configurations fit into a global context by addressing paired themes through locality: the uniqueness/diversity or, rather, the standardisation/fragmentation frequently invoked to explain current cultural dynamics. In the same spirit, the question of the nation-state's future can be raised through local observation, leading once again to debating the relationship between the areal and the reticular (Lévy 1994). Despite the fact that they can give too simple a viewpoint on a complex reality, these different conceptual diptychs (standardisation vs fragmentation, areal vs reticular) can help to avoid a too hierarchical vision that systematically brings the centre and periphery into opposition – as Michael Herzfeld's (2004) case study suggested – and where social and spatial margins seem hopelessly swallowed up by the dominant discourse, modelled passively by a central power, be it national, continental or global. By addressing these different questions through the study of a deliberately varied set of actors and groups, we can adapt our viewpoint on modern topologies – where liminality or centrality no longer depend on stable criteria. This is due to the increase in the number of power centres and especially the transformation of the different styles of relationship with space. For this purpose, a multisite research has been fruitful. When studying these new power relations through the issue of the *embodiment* of values and norms, Michael Herzfeld always focuses his research to examination of the ways in which his interlocutors present themselves to others and define their position(s) in Cretan society. Yet the paradoxes presented above remain the same if we remain with discursive logic: producing global values seems inevitably to lead to the exclusion or fragmentation of those considered to be marginal (subaltern populations, peripheral nations, minorities, the proletariat, etc ...), while a kind of multiculturalism is imposed as a hegemonic value of contemporary societies. Yet, such processes should be addressed in a more nuanced, but also more complete, way, by focusing on the relationships between the different scales of the social and political reality seen from their material dimensions (as a sum of practices and results) as well as a metaphysical or ideological construction (c.f. the definition of 'territory' in Francophone social geography or 'space' in North-American humanistic geography). The following studies on the relationship of small or minority groups to space bring to the fore, through direct observation, the numerous negotiations that are developed between the different levels and different worlds (or '*régimes*') of legitimacy. These negotiations are based on different interpretive frameworks such as national identity, globalised 'ethnoscapes' or local identities. This hypothesis then helps to modify slightly what initially appeared as an irreducible paradox of globalisation, pitting margin against periphery, nation-state against minority, Jihad against Mac World ...

Admittedly, the transformations and diversification of the ways in which to consider value, in Greece as elsewhere, lead to ruptures between what is accentuated by the mainstream discourse and what is fought against, often precipitating the non-compliant into marginality and exclusion. However, it is interesting to note that tension may work its way not only between global norms and local, traditional and authentic values – between 'ideology' and 'reality', in fact, as many anthropologists seem to suggest – but also within what constitutes the norm due to the proliferation of frameworks of reference now accessible to social actors. It is a game, 'making do' with the diversity of frameworks, rather than a single hierarchy of values, and this appears undoubtedly to be the most obvious sign of globalisation in society. Moreover, this plurality may also be transformed into a misunderstanding or a 'loss of bearings' that paradoxically thrives on this multiplication of references. It may lead to the hardening of discourses too: the rejection of otherness, as shown, for example, in contemporary Greece in crisis. Embellishment of roots and the past, retrieved, reorganised and legitimised, can justify what has been, over many decades till now, merely an illusion: the reversibility of the march of history, and trust in the benefits of authenticity inspired by the past, especially when the future appears worrying.

* * *

This book is the result of several years of field research in Greece, in its neighbouring Balkan countries and in more distant places, the realisation of which would not have been possible without the support of different institutions – first and foremost, the TELEMME Laboratory and the Maison Méditerranéenne des Sciences de l'Homme in Aix-en-Provence. It was also greatly helped by much research that was sometimes collaborative, especially within the framework of the BALKABAS ANR-08-JCJC-0091-01 programme funded by the National Research Agency between 2009 and 2012. More specifically, the exchanges that took place with social anthropologists working in these regions (Gilles de Rapper, Olivier Givre and Cyril Isnart) greatly inspired certain pages to the point of having been fully influenced by their vocabulary, references and expressions. In particular, the pages on the uses of the past in the first chapter and those concerning the construction of locality in Chapter 5 owe much to Oliver Givre and his investment in these themes within the BALKABAS programme. I would also like to thank everybody, both in the scientific domain and in the various places where I conducted my research, who contributed to the writing of this book. The translation was carried out with the support of the TELEMME (Aix-Marseille University–CNRS) laboratory UMR 7303 and the *Laboratoire d'Excellence* LabexMed – *Humanities and Social Sciences at the Heart of Interdisciplinarity for the Mediterranean,* reference 10-LABX-0090 – with financial support from the French government and managed by the National Research Agency, project title *Investissement d'avenir* A*MIDEX, reference ANR-11-IDEX-0001-02. I would like to thank Jenny Money very much for her precise and patient work in the course of the translation of this book. Her sustained benevolence and generosity have helped make this English language version in places a clearer and more understandable text than the original. In the era of automated translation, Jenny's practice of translation as a fine art illustrates for me better than ever Borges' words: once again, *el original es infiel a la traducción* and I am convinced that it is a good thing…

Chapter 1

Understanding Greece in the world

Before looking in more detail at a number of research projects I have carried out in Greece in recent years, I first summarise in this chapter the environment in which they were undertaken, examining the political and social transformations that occurred in this area as well as the academic work that enabled their realisation. In this way, non-Francophones will be introduced to the state of the art concerning study of these issues in France, and the focus will be shifted for those Balkan Anglophone specialists for whom French publications remain a distant province and are often difficult to access. For this reason, I begin by presenting the main themes and bibliography that were instrumental in my understanding of the transformations that have taken place in Greek society and the theoretical tools and themes provided by the social sciences in order to address them. My starting point was the study of international migration in Greece, but the presentation of this earlier work will reveal the positioning of my research which, based on more general reflections with regard to the effects of globalisation on territories, aims at capturing both Greek and South-East European society in their specific forms, while observing the broader transformations taking place. Without necessarily wishing to diverge on every point, this approach will lead to discussion of the proposals that were put forward in Maria Todorova's work, *Imagining the Balkans* (2009), and which have become hegemonic in the field of studies on South-East European societies. If Todorova's work rested on the construction of a dominant Western-European perception of the Balkans, which drew on the literary and political discourses of the nineteenth and twentieth centuries and was greatly inspired by Edward Saïd's (1978) analysis of Orientalism, the implications that such vision has had for contemporary social sciences can, today, disregard the internal power relationships within societies in the region, as well as the economic and political imperatives that govern their position in Europe, and only privilege a theory of periphery and dependence. In spite of the interest such a viewpoint arouses, it could, today, act as a barrier to effective thought processes; the complex, contemporary changes that global processes are imposing on South-East European societies do not portray a comprehensive image of certain changes that may also appear to be local productions of globality rather than the exclusive effects of a unequivocal domination process.

Thus, to present the elements that were of interest to my research over the last decades in Greece means returning to the main changes that affected Greek society in the 1990s and 2000s. Although not exclusive to Greece, they do seem to suggest complex dynamics, bringing certain themes – like migration, economic development, minority expressions, national identity discourses, heritage and the country's relationship with Europe, to the fore. The importance and visibility of these transformations led me to privilege not only certain types of approach but also certain hypotheses.

The geopolitical upheavals of the 1990s

In the early 1990s, the bloody wars in the former Yugoslavian space were the triggers, via the Western media and public opinion, for a new visibility in the Balkans, and Greece found itself indirectly caught up in the turmoil that affected its neighbouring countries. Yet, more than fifty years before, in sealing its attachment to the Western camp, the end of the 1945–49 civil war effectively isolated the country from the regional environment in which it was historically formed. In France, the classic works on regional geography situated Greece from this date in the 'Southern Europe' section (which was the case for *Géographie Universelle* edited by the *GIS-RECLUS* team) or in a strange 'EEC Mediterranean' section (Balabanian *et al.* 1991; Drain 1990). Several decades later, the events of the 1990s indubitably changed this perception, simultaneously with the revival of Balkan realities in Greek daily lives.

The questions raised by the conflicts of creating new Balkan states and the extent of migration flows from other countries of the peninsula affected Greek society as a whole, and forced it to clarify its own identity, even while Greek entrepreneurs were (re)discovering a most propitious investment opportunity. In such a situation, the border areas provided eloquent examples of the resurgence of regional problems for the country. Indeed, Greece has ongoing disputes with its neighbours on virtually all its geographic peripheries, enabling assessment of its potential involvement in the geopolitical tensions throughout the 1990s. Its current political boundaries are the result of successive conquests and annexations, product of the Greek state's irredentist policy since its creation in 1830 (Prévélakis 1997). Its borders with Albania and the Republic of Macedonia result from the 1912–13 Balkan wars, as does the maritime border with Turkey to the north. The border with Bulgaria derives from the annexation of Thrace to Greece after the First World War, whereas the land border with Turkey was established by the Treaty of Lausanne in 1922. In the extreme south-east of the Aegean, the Dodecanese Archipelago, incorporated into modern Greece in 1947, completes the existing contours of Greek state territory. However, it is striking to note that all these boundaries, even if forgotten today, have at some point been the subject of litigation. Although, if these border disputes have been abandoned, at least officially, the new situation arising from the consequences of the fall of the Berlin Wall seems to have rekindled some of them.

The main geopolitical concern arose with the Socialist Republic of Macedonia's Declaration of Independence in 1991, as this new state seemed to pose a threat to certain regions of Northern Greece where the presence of Slavic populations had been carefully concealed following the end of the civil war in 1949. The success of the street demonstrations as well as the increase in diplomatic activity, provoked by hostility towards the new state, highlighted the sensitive nature of this issue in Greece. This is not the first time that the geographical area of Macedonia, shared between three countries, Greece, Bulgaria and Serbia (and later, the Yugoslavian Republic of Macedonia) since the Balkan wars, was at the centre of such conflict between nations claiming a presence and/or a historical, cultural and demographic legitimacy in this area. Initially, the conflicts were very intense between the late nineteenth and early twentieth centuries (Lory 2011), when national borders were being defined, and this continued up until a *status quo* was imposed by the Cold War. In the early 1990s, the independence of Yugoslavian Macedonia produced, or reactivated, a series of political and symbolic differences of opinion between Greece and its new neighbour, its main bone of contention being the name given to a state whose constitutional appellation was the 'Republic of Macedonia', with Greece officially rejecting the latter in favour of the acronym FYROM (Former Yugoslav Republic of Macedonia).

Nevertheless, Greece managed to formally adopt this position at the UN, even blocking the Republic of Macedonia's membership of NATO and the EU, as it suspected the Skopje government of using this name to hide irredentist views on Northern Greek territory. Thus, for this reason, the Greeks denied this new 'Macedonian nation' the use of symbols claimed to be purely 'Greek', such as the historical figures of Alexander the Great and his father, Philip II, King of Macedonia, or the Vergina Sun, the symbol of the Macedonian dynasty in the 4th century BC. Thus, the Macedonian question was one of the first elements in the revival of a militant nationalism in Greece in the early 1990s, highlighted from this moment on by the impressive display of car stickers affirming the Greekness of Macedonia, by the Macedonian flags (the Vergina Sun on a blue background) attached to public buildings and statues glorifying Alexander the Great or other figures of the Macedonian dynasty in many Greek cities. The reality of economic relations between the two countries, however, was totally different, and their fate was clearly linked. Until 2006, Greek investments in the Balkans were estimated at $200 billion and trade with countries in the region accounted for nearly 20 per cent of Greece's foreign trade. The Republic of Macedonia figured prominently among these partners as Greek investments there created employment for almost 10 per cent of its work population.

Although relations with the Republic of Macedonia were highly prominent on the international scene, certain questions were more discreetly raised from 1990 that revealed the conflict-generating characteristics of the other borders of the country. This was the case, for example, for the Islet of Imia/Kardak crisis that led Greece and Turkey to the brink of armed confrontation over the limits of their territorial waters in the Aegean Sea in 1996. This clearly questioned the potential peacemaking abilities of UE policies on the Greek–Turkish border (Athanassopoulou, E. 1997; Rumelili 2004, 2007). Moreover, even more discretely, the Greek–Albanian border had also been the site of significant tensions between the two countries in the 1990s over the question of the Greek minority in Albania. While the Bosnia-Herzegovina War was at its fiercest, and the Greek government maintained close ties with Belgrade, a group, giving itself the same name (MAVI – *Μέτωπο Απελευθέρωσης Βορείου Ηπείρου* or Northern Epirus* Liberation Front) as the armed resistance group of the Greek minority of Albania during World War II, carried out a campaign of violence. In addition to the car bomb that killed the Albanian ambassador in Athens in 1984, the group also claimed responsibility for the attack on an Albanian border post, which killed two Albanian soldiers near Peshkëpi village in the Gjirokastër region in 1994. Although Greek security forces rapidly put an end to this group's activities, some ecclesiastical authorities in Greece expressed their support, thus demonstrating the sympathy that this type of position can engender on public opinion (Michas 2002). Moreover, this incident generated further repercussions in Albania, with the government of Sali Berisha prosecuting several political leaders of the Greek minority and their *Omonia Association* for their involvement in conspiring against state security and in espionage and their possession of prohibited weapons (a charge which could have been punished by the death penalty). The jail sentence came very close to being carried out, but the Greek minority association leaders were released due to pressure from the US and European governments. It was after this affair that the *Omonia Association* left the political scene and was replaced by the Human Rights Party, which had no official ethnic basis but, in fact, became the Greek minority political wing.

These developments with regard to the country's international position also had consequences within Greece, especially the relationships that Greek society had with its peripheries and with a perceived destabilising diversity. This distrust was clearly manifested in 1992 when, at the request of the European Parliament, the Greek government wanted to conform to EU standards by removing the mention of religious affiliation from Greek identity cards, presenting it as a potential source of discrimination for religious minorities in the country like Muslims, Catholics and Greek Jews (Clogg 2002). Hence, an amendment – which initially allowed the individual to choose – was passed by the members of the different political parties. However, in May 2000, this question was raised again by the governmental authority for the defence of personal data, which advocated that certain information, such as a person's occupation, maiden name and, once again, religion, should no longer appear on identity papers. This time, the debate culminated in an open crisis between the government and the Orthodox Church, with the latter holding two mass rallies in Athens and Thessaloniki, and convincing more than three million out of the ten million inhabitants to sign a petition. The Greek Church presented this mobilisation as a significant act of resistance towards a creeping secularisation of society that would lead to the loss of its Greek specificity (Dépret 2005). It also showed the mechanisms of a national construction consubstantially linked to its Orthodox religious affiliations that automatically caused distrust *vis-à-vis* non-compliant citizens. Numerous studies have focused on the issue of discrimination towards minority religious groups in Greek society in these decades. Among the publications in French are those, notably, by Jeanne Hersant (2001, 2008) and Jeanne Hersant and Néphélie Yatropoulos (2007) on the Muslim communities of Western Thrace or by Katérina Séraïdari (2006, 2010) on Catholics in the Cyclades. The collective works co-ordinated by Richard Clogg (2002) represent a significant effort to summarise this new situation within the country. Throughout this period, the link between national identity and the Greek Orthodox religion was accentuated for observers of this society (such as Georges Drettas 2003), due to the divergence between this discursive construction and the social reality of the country because of the persistent presence of different minority groups, both Christian and non-Christian. Undoubtedly, the new context of the 1990s owed much to the renewal of different ways of expressing these alternative identities that had resulted from both the new regional geopolitical conditions, and the very heavy consequences of migration.

A new intensity in international migrations and domestic mobility

In the 1990s, migration in South-East Europe was certainly not a new phenomenon. The early twentieth century had already testified to the importance of migratory mobility in the Balkans as the history of the population of the peninsula demonstrated (Cvijić 1917). Yet from the end of the Second World War, the Balkans drew back from the field of global migration. It is true that, apart from Greek and Yugoslavian workers migrating to Western countries, the Balkan population had been hit by a dearth of border-crossing mobility, even though much internal circulation had taken place within these countries during the second half of the twentieth century (see, for example, Guentcheva 2008). Only Greece, whose geopolitical situation was somewhat unique in the Balkan area, was a country of mass out-migration (Kolodny 1985; Laliotou 2006a; Moussourou 1991; Ventura 1999; Vermeulen 1990), repatriation (Emke-Poulopoulou 1986; Kasimati 1984; Kollarou and Moussourou 1980) and diaspora (Kasimati 1993; Vergeti 1991; Voutira 1991).

The following period was in sharp contrast to this first image. Indeed, since 1990, the entire peninsula had been experiencing a resurgence of mobility and international migration and, from then on, the Balkans became a source of Mediterranean migration. For more than a decade, the Balkan migrants contributed to the diversification of origins and the increase in the number of countries of departure and destination, characterising new trends in international migration at the end of the twentieth century (Simon 2008). Moreover, they were also involved in the affirmation of Eastern Europe's new role in the European migratory game. Figures show that, in 2001, 7 per cent of the Greek population was made up of foreigners (compared to only 1.5 per cent of the total population in 1991) and one fifth of the Albanian population and a seventh of the Bulgarians migrated abroad… At the same time, more than 900,000 people became forced migrants in the Balkans due to the conflicts in the former Yugoslavia between 1992 and 2004. From the 1990s, the main countries of out-migration in the Balkans were Bosnia-Herzegovina, which lost 500,000 people from a population of fewer than five million, and especially Albania. The latter had the highest migratory exodus of all Balkan countries and a negative migratory balance in the 1990s due to 700,000 people (out of three million inhabitants) leaving the country. Romania and Bulgaria were two other countries of out-migration, but at a much lower level relative to their total population: in Bulgaria in the early 2000s more than 700,000 people emigrated out of a population of 8 million; in Romania, 2 million out 22 million inhabitants left the country. These people left their regions mainly for Western countries: 1.2 million to Germany; 600,000 to Italy; 400,000 to Spain; 374,000 to Switzerland, and

345,000 to Austria (Cattaruzza and Sintès 2012). However, the novelty was in the fact that this economic migration (even if the term is debatable) was actually also to certain countries within the Balkans themselves – Slovenia, Croatia and Serbia thus became indisputable host countries, even though, in Serbia, the 8 per cent of foreign-born in the current population are largely determined by population movements from Bosnia-Herzegovina or Kosovo.

Swept up in this movement, the situation in Greece was, once again very unique in the peninsula. In fact, Greece became the main host country in the Balkans, with migrants numbering some 760,000 people in 2001 – some estimates even suggest one million. In less than a decade, the country was confirmed as one of the European Union members whose number of foreigners *per capita* was of the highest order. From this point of view, the country was in the same position as the new host countries of Southern Europe. The proportion of foreigners was superior to that of Italy (6 per cent) and almost equal to that of Spain (11 per cent). Nevertheless, this radical change in the country's role in the international migration game was undoubtedly most striking for the Greek population, and the migratory shock was all the greater as, since the nineteenth century, Greece had been a land of traditional emigration to distant, transatlantic and European destinations. Before the country's independence in 1830, these regions, like all Ottoman territories, had experienced many types of mobility: forced movements, seasonal migration, migration from rural regions to the towns, etc. The Greeks, a population defined by its linguistic and, more especially, its religious characteristics, were present in many parts of the Ottoman Empire. Their commercial networks spread across the whole of the Mediterranean, where they founded small communities, especially in port cities such as Trieste, Marseilles, Venice, Odessa, Ragusa, etc… as well as in commercial towns in Northern and Central Europe like Vienna and Bucharest. After independence and the conflicts that affected the country in the nineteenth and twentieth centuries (the Balkan Wars, World War I, the Greco-Turkish War of 1922, World War II and civil war), the Greeks were increasingly impacted by massive migration flows and other types of mobility. The most striking in mainland Greece was the installation, in 1923, of nearly 1.3 million refugees from Asia Minor who, following the population exchange between Greece and Turkey, settled mainly in the northern rural areas of the country and the biggest cities like Athens and Thessaloniki.

At the same time, between 1890 and 1940, some 500,000 Greeks migrated long-distance to the United States and Australia, as well as to Egypt, West Africa, Romania and Russia, moving notably from regions where the introduction of mercantile capitalism was well advanced, such as the Aegean Islands. Nevertheless, this trend changed after the Second World War. Thus, Western Europe, in particular the Federal Republic of Germany

(FRG), became an important destination for Greek migrants. Between 1945 and 1975, more than one million people left the country, with two-thirds going to industrialised Europe (mainly the FRG and Belgium). This time, the migration movements came more from the north, the 'new Greece', which was politically less stable and had been more affected by the civil war. This situation resulted in Greece having a very large national community outside its borders: today, according to the figures published by Greek embassies and consulates abroad, the size of this Greek diaspora is estimated at more than 6 million people, for a country of 10 million inhabitants. The United States is the leading host country for Greeks, with 1.3 million migrants, followed by Germany with 400,000 Greek nationals. It is important to note that, in light of this history, international migration terminology in Greek was contrived from essentially two concepts that designated the migrants' motivations: *προσφύγης*, meaning the Greek refugee of 1923, driven out of Asia Minor due to the defeat by Turkey, or 'exchanged' at the Treaty of Lausanne, and *μετανάστης*, defining an economic out-migrant, thereby encompassing those in Greece and the diaspora. These two terms show that, up until the late twentieth century, the migratory reality was alluded to in an unequivocal way, only taking 'forced migration' to Greece and economic out-migration to wealthier countries into consideration.

This situation gradually changed from the 1970s on, with migrants essentially from distant countries taking up Greek space. The presence of these newcomers was relatively unobtrusive, and therefore did not question Greek identity as later migrations flows would. This first wave of immigration had already moved into the segments of the labour market where there was a real shortage of manpower due to the high levels of out-migration abroad and the exodus from rural areas to cities. Domestic jobs were thus attributed to those from the Philippines, whilst the Poles and Egyptians sought seasonal agricultural work or factory work. In 1972, the situation was worrying enough for the Association of Greek Industrialists to announce that it was looking to hire 10,000 contract workers, based very much on the German *gastarbeiter* system and, at the end of the same year, the country was host to 20,000 foreigners. These first migrations to Greece were complex and involved differing migratory patterns: the Filipinos began by using domestic networks while maintaining close links with their home country, as their objective was to eventually return there, whereas the Poles used Greece as a springboard to other destinations (Ptéroudis 1996). Thus, this initial phase gave the country its first experience of a limited in-migration consisting exclusively of workers for what was often only a short period.

Over the course of the following decade, the country was fraught with massive disruption – as was the whole of Southern Europe. Greece entered the European Economic Community in 1981 and, from then on, its economic situation improved, due to the support granted to the industrial and agricultural sectors, which increased openings and opportunities for unskilled migration. In addition to this new appeal, the country also benefited from the carry-over effect of migration flows that had been denied access to Western European countries (i.e., their former colonial tutellages) where a zero migration policy was then applied. Thus, this was how communities from West Africa (mainly Nigeria), North Africa (Morocco and Tunisia) and the Indian subcontinent (Pakistan, India and Bangladesh) became established in Greece. At the time of the 1991 census, the arrival of these new groups had led to an increase of no fewer than 117,000 foreigners in the country. In fact it was the new geopolitical situations in Central and Eastern Europe which radically transformed Greece into a massive host country in the 1990s. Indeed, large groups of migrants from neighbouring countries, or farther afield from the former 'Eastern bloc', arrived in Greece, attracted not only by the work that they so badly needed, but also by the political stability and idyllic images of a way of life that Western television conveyed. Thus, large contingents of Georgians, Romanians, Bulgarians and, especially, Albanians, sometimes the descendants of ancient Greek communities like the Pontic Greeks (as studied, for example, by Michel Bruneau 1998) that had been dispersed in the past throughout the Ottoman and Russian Empires, settled in Greece. They featured strongly in the 2001 population census results and contributed essentially to the presence of 762,191 foreigners on Greek soil, more than 7 per cent of the country's total population. The Albanians were by far the most represented nationality among them: the 500,000 migrants counted made up almost 60 per cent of all foreigners in Greece. The true value of these figures can only be seen when one considers that, between 1961 and 1991, foreigners only accounted for a small fraction of the country's total population.

However, in the 2000s, the country's situation changed once again, almost to the point where the dimensions of the Balkan migratory movement and how it had affected the country previously – both inside and out – had nearly been forgotten. From then on, Greece appeared exclusively in the media as the area of passage for illegal migration from Asia and Africa to other countries in the European Union. This image was taken up by numerous Greek and European political figures, and the Aegean border thus became the main stage for this new narrative, with striking images, similar to those of the Canary Islands or the Strait of Gibraltar, showing migrants aboard light crafts flocking to poorly patrolled border islands (Sintès 2011a). This presentation undoubtedly corresponded to a new reality, with many migrants reaching the country's coasts clandestinely before continuing their journey elsewhere in Europe. The increase in the number of victims reported from the Greek borders in the 2000s was a persuasive testimonial to this as were the makeshift camps that were regularly erected around the ports on the Ionian Sea coast (Patras and Igoumenitsa) from where these migrants continued their journey to Italy. This was the consequence of the country's geographical position, sharing the borders of the major geopolitical entities of the Middle East, Eastern Europe and the European Union at a time when 'The transit function became a new piece of data in the global migration system' (Simon 2002: 44). Indeed, restriction policies gave the states surrounding the main destinations of migrants (in this case, Western Europe) the role of a buffer zone, a zone in which the migrants had to live, find accommodation and organise their travel arrangements whilst waiting for the opportunity to continue their journey to the West. However, the 'bouncing' from one country to another became less and less easy and the 'antechamber of the West was being transformed into a *de facto* immigration region' (Morokvasic 2002: 25).

Hence, just like countries such as Serbia, Romania and Bulgaria, albeit to varying degrees, Greece has irrefutably become a country of 'long-term transit' migration or, to put it another way, a country where the settling of long-distance migrants is underway. For all practical purposes, and until the migrant crisis of summer 2015 totally changed the situation, it seems probable that these migrant flows arriving by sea initially only represented a small proportion of a group numerically dominated by migrants from the Balkans. Even if the former have increasingly tended to supplant the latter in terms of image, often because of the tragic fate that accompanies them, it was at that time difficult to obtain accurate information about this new phenomenon. The Aegean Sea and Thrace were, nonetheless, already recognised passages for migrants from further afield. At most, the flow of illegal migrants was officially estimated at 250,000 by the Greek authorities in 2009 and, according to the European Agency FRONTEX deployed along its borders, this figure established Greece as the European country the most affected by illegal migration. Among these illegal migrants, 150,000 were arrested by the Greek police according to information supplied by the Ministry of Public Order in 2008. If such figures suggested an increase in migratory pressure on the country, it was difficult to see it as an undeniable sign of the changing circumstances on its eastern border as, once again, they related to a large majority (over 60 per cent) of Albanian migrants who had entered Greece via other regions. During 2012, figures published by ELIAMEP researchers at the Hellenic Foundation for European and Foreign Policy reported that 270,000 people had entered via the eastern borders of the country, although this was still significantly lower than the quasi-million migrants from the Balkans in previous decades (Maroukis 2012).

During this period, and a long time before the 'migrant crisis' of summer 2015, Greece became a country whose entire society was marked by the forces of migration. Spatially, the migrants were present throughout the territory, from the centre of major cities to the smallest village. As will be discussed in more detail later, it was the Albanian migrants who were mainly involved in this dispersion; they were the only ones who settled and worked in the remotest regions of the country, owing to their greater familiarity with the traditional activities of the Greek countryside. Nevertheless, substantial numbers of these migrants also settled in peri-urban areas, working in sectors such as market gardening and logistic service areas, which had become repellent to Greek nationals. Conversely, the migrant groups in the big cities were more cosmopolitan and there was often a wide variety of foreigners from different origins. Although it may have been difficult to identify real ghettos in these cities, the working-class areas in Athens, as in Thessaloniki, sometimes had an extremely strong foreign presence. For instance, the central municipality of the capital registered a high proportion of foreigners (more than 17 per cent) at the 2001 census for some areas in central Athens, like Patissia and Kipséli. This was also the same for the peripheral working-class neighbourhoods, such as Kalithea, where 14 per cent of the registered population were, at that time, foreigners. This massive spatial and social presence of migrants had, for many years, been illegal. Indeed, Greece had been slow in bringing its legislation into conformity with its new host-country situation. What was even worse was that migration was often managed depending on the country's diplomatic relations with Albania, the Greek electoral calendar and the media coverage of various facts. Thus, the long absence of a legal framework resulted in diverse relationships between the migrants and the authorities, ranging from the latters' complete tolerance – due to the need for a labour force for entire sections of the economy (i.e. the construction industry and seasonal agricultural work) – to total rigidity, with operations of mass expulsion to migrants' countries of origin. It was only in 1997 that the first measures to regularise the status of many illegal migrants were launched almost a decade after the start of mass migration. Since that time, migration laws have been revised in 2001, 2005 and 2010 – modifying the conditions of access to the country so as to allow for a selective migration chosen according to the needs of the labour market. It was not until 2010 that legislation addressed the issue of the migrant second generation – of whom there were more than 100,000, all born and educated in Greece – and lifted the taboo of naturalisation in a country where national belonging was strongly associated with the principles of *jus sanguinis*.

Migration Studies in the Balkans: a multiplicity of perspectives

As presented in the following pages, the importance of migration in Balkan societies, especially in Greece, has led to an increase in academic work on the topic. Nevertheless, they are still few and far between compared to studies of other Mediterranean and American migration flows. The first studies on migration in the Balkan area relied heavily on traditional methodologies, merely exploring the economic implications of the different migration flows. Focusing initially on the logics of social exclusion, these studies seemed blinded to other issues involving cultural and political outputs of the migration movements in the different Balkan countries. In the late 1990s, however, when the French Association of Balkan Studies (*Association française d'études sur les Balkans*) received support from the Ministry of Foreign Affairs and organised its first interdisciplinary symposium in 2002, a few studies on the Balkan situation were published in France, enhancing what was known about this area. Publications like *Le Nouvel Islam Balkanique* by Xavier Bougarel and Nathalie Clayer (2001), and more general geopolitical works like those of Georges Prévélakis (1994, 1997) were conducive in bringing new elements of knowledge on the area after 1989 to interested academics and the general public. Nevertheless, during the 2000s, the public authorities, academic work and editorial publications gradually seemed to lose interest in this area. There were very few French texts to be found on Balkan migration, and what was available was usually restricted to highly specialised publications. Aside from the general work of Mirjana Morokvasic (Morokvasic 2002; Morokvasic-Müller 2001), the sole synoptic work in French on migration in the Balkans – *Migrations, Crises et Conflits Récents dans les Balkans,* published by the Demobalk Network (Parant 2005) – only presented demographic dynamics. In general, therefore, with the exception of international relations and geopolitics, French publications on social transformations in the Balkans remained relatively scarce compared to those from Great Britain or Italy. This gap is a contributing factor in the way in which the Mediterranean region is conceived or constructed within the field of French research, a construction which is largely dominated by a 'Euro-Mediterranean' vision and strongly influenced by North–South relations rather than East–West.

There were many more publications in the UK and within the English-speaking academic milieu on the issue of migration in the Balkans, and these were thanks, first and foremost, to the researchers and students from the Sussex Centre for Migration Research at the University of Sussex, under the supervision of the extremely prolific Professor Russell King, whose many works on this subject have been cited and highly regarded since the early 1990s. However, these publications were still of a more general nature, evident in the literature that existed on the effects of migration on countries of origin. The Albanian situation was by far the most studied, aside from forced migration in the former Yugoslavia, the 'development paradigm' remains one of the most influential (King 2005) and migration was predominantly viewed through an economic lens. Thus, in spite of the difficulties in obtaining reliable data, migrant remittances were at the forefront of these studies (Arrehag *et al.* 2005; Conti *et al.* 2003; Kule *et al.* 2004, *inter alia*). Emigration was also envisaged via the concept of brain drain (Gedeshi 2006; Memaj *et al.* 2003) as was return migration (Labrianidis and Lyberaki 2004), with some researchers predicting a reverse trend of Albanian migration to Greece (Labrianidis and Hatziprokopiou 2005). Publications on the cultural transformations that affected these countries of migration were rarer. Generally researched from a *cultural studies* perspective, they were supported by studies on gender (King and Vullnetari 2009) and the younger generation (King and Vullnetari 2006; Orgocka and Jovanovic 2006). Migration in itself, and more specifically the movement within space or the forms of mobility and networks, were only exceptionally the object of study, and very few are the publications dealing with these specific modalities (although see Arrehag *et al.* 2006; King *et al.* 1998).

As for the situation in the host countries, nearly all the studies on migrant groups in the Balkans were exclusively in English. These studies concentrated primarily on the social and cultural integration of migrants, following an economic methodology and applying the inclusion/exclusion theory. They rarely considered the relationship migrants kept with their countries of origin or with other places in the world. Many of these studies focused on Greece, as the main host country in the Southern Balkans in the 1990s. Firstly, they addressed migration from a comparative perspective, looking for similarities and differences between the Greek situation, other countries in the European Union and the EU's political orientations. The question of integration is raised explicitly in several publications (Cela and Moretti 2008; Hatziprokopiou 2006; King and Mai 2004) and, as such, characterisation of the migrant group as a social minority led to measurement of the degree of the group's insertion, especially from an economic (Baldwin-Edwards 1998; Baldwin-Edwards and Salifios-Rothschild 1997; Memaj 2008; Vgenopoulos 2000) and educational (Fragoudaki and Dragona 1998; Gogonas 2009; Hatzidaki 2005; Paleologou 2004; Tsokalidou 2005) point of view. Nevertheless, nuances appeared which would provide a more cultural dimension to the study of migration, and enable the effects of displacement on the migrant way of life to be studied, and therefore be of interest in the territorial organisation created by these social actors. From this perspective, questions concerning identity and otherness often came to light in the numerous studies on migrants' legal status during, for example, the wave of regulatisations which occurred (Cavounidis and Chatzakis 2000; Fakiolas 2003; Kontiadis and Papatheodorou 2007; Lazaridis and Poyago-Theotoky 1999; Skordas 2002). This reflection generated a veritable questioning of the changes brought about by migrants, seeking to position them in relation to the notion of 'Greekness' (Kaurinkoski 2008; Petronoti and Triandafyllidou 2003; Triandafyllidou and Veikou 2002). This more analytical perspective, which sought to highlight the way in which migration can be used in practice to examine collective identification processes, even appeared to be a way of analysing migration in Greece. It was the most evident when the authors approached the topic, once again, from a cultural studies perspective, or when their theoretical concerns were associated with the study of transnationalism (Michail 2008; Petronoti 1998) or the spatiality of migration (Iosifides and King 1998; Kasimis *et al.* 2003, Kokkali 2008). From this same perspective, all of the publications by the Minority Group Research Centre (KEMO), whose objectives were often based on public intervention in Greece, focused on defending the rights of minorities, refugees and immigrants in Greece (Marvakis *et al.* 2001; Pavlou and Christopoulos 2004), integration policies through education (Emke-Poulopoulou *et al.* 2007; Kyprianou and van Boeschoten 2006; Mavromatis and Tsitselikis 2004), the second generation (Karydis 2004) and the reconfiguration of nationalism and racism in Greece following the new migratory flows (Ventura 1994).

Compared to these different publications, the contribution based on the work I carried out during my PhD research on Albanian migrants in Greece (1999–2005) was intended to be both consistent with the general movement as well as relatively original. Initially having more of a descriptive bias, especially in the early years, my contribution was centred on inclusive data and statistical results (Sintès 2002, 2003), as was the case for other researchers studying Albanian migration to Italy and Greece at around the same time (Campani 1992; Ptéroudis 1996). During the 2000s, the publication of new statistical data allowed me to continue in this direction, enabling me to update my knowledge on these issues and offer these initial results to the French academic milieu (Sintès 2008a). In addition to this, I started on more original research, building on the fieldwork that I had carried out at the same time in Corinth, the Aegean Islands and Athens. It quickly took me to the areas on the Greek–Albanian border, and even within Albania, from where the migrants I met in Greece departed or to which they returned. Thus, through direct observation of the migratory phenomenon in all the places concerned (settlement, departure and transit areas), I was able to comply with the perspective that dominated the study of international migration in France at that time, even though these approaches did not often concern the Balkans. This way of proceeding considered migration as a true spatial circulation, thus illustrating the complexity of new international mobility and going beyond the duality/dichotomy that marked the literature presented above and whose approaches focused uniquely on host societies (questioning the social integration of the migrants) and the places of origin – underlining the economic (lack of) development generated by an out-migration from these places. This research position reflected a concern to take into account both the multiplication of places affected by migration and the escalation in migrants' movements between different areas, the flow of materials (goods, services and remittances) and the ideals (values, representations) that they implied. Thus, my aim was to continue and further the pioneering work carried out in France by Roger Béteille (1974), Gildas Simon (1979), Yves Charbit, Marie-Antoinette Hily and Michel Poinard (Charbit *et al.* 1997).

Studying Albanian migration in this way enabled me to highlight the development of relationships to territory stemming from the more general processes in which this migratory movement was involved. Study of the daily practices of migrants and their justification at an individual level enabled me to illustrate, within the Greek and Balkan context, the latest tendencies in social science research on mobility (Appadurai 1991, 1996a; Kaufman 2008; Knafou 2004; Stock 2004, 2005) which perceived contemporary societies as having entered a new era, characterised by the hyper-mobility of people and information. Indeed, in accordance with the conclusions of these different authors, it appears that technical (development in transport and communication) and political developments (the 'opening' of borders) challenged classic analytical categories of geographical mobility, favouring incalculable 'mobile spatial practices' (Appadurai 1996a; Castles and Miller 1993; Wihtol de Wenden 2001) that were difficult to classify due to their sheer numbers and complexity, but which still revealed a new relationship with places. In addition, the transformations embedded in the new spaces of circulation revealed by the migrants will facilitate the maintenance and development of 'transnational communities' – i.e. groups who are maintaining a shared social functioning across the distances that separate them in space. The study of these new group logics leads to a two-fold observation: challenges to the borders of the nation-states concerned, and the rising ease of maintainance of the links between people beyond sometimes very long distance. Studies also highlight the concept of transnationalism (Glick Schiller *et al.* 1992, 1994; Kearney 1995; Kivisto 2001; Levitt 2004; Mintz 1998; Vertovec 1999) in relation to theoretical frameworks such as the critique of 'methodological nationalism' (Wimmer and Glick Schiller 2002) and of the binary (national) approach to migration. They also accentuate the 'de-territorialisation' (Appadurai 1991) of social relationships and identities, and the interest in the vernacular meanings of migration. The first implications of these different studies reveal a strengthening of the trend towards community functioning (Brettell 2003) in contemporary migration. The ties and social relationships remain as well maintained as ever between people from the same region settling in the same country, and even between people from the same country or region who find themselves in far-away places. This type of hypothesis would explain the great success of diasporic models, the study of which has truly exploded onto the academic scene since the 1990s (Anteby-Yemini *et al.* 2005; Brah 1996; Bruneau 1998; Clifford 1994; Cohen 1997; Ma Mung 2000; Vertovec and Cohen 1999).

Considered within these new analytical frameworks, Albanian migration to Greece seemed to me to produce a flow of exchanges, both material and immaterial; it also appeared to function within an area thick with historical, cultural and symbolic background that would be one of its fundamental determinants. During my fieldwork, this background was frequently recalled to explain how certain of the migrants' networks were constituted. Such an hypothesis enabled me to query the future of the identity frameworks constructed during the historical formation of the two nation-states. This then led me to describe a process of identity fragmentation as a consequence of the functioning of these new migration networks, reliant on historical connections between inhabitants of both countries, which have been dormant for nearly half a century. During my investigations I watched, in effect, the (re)forming of bonds uniting both Greek nationals and Albanians. On that occasion, the people I met recounted surprising stories, often referring to common, regional, denominational and ethnolinguistic belonging. This drew me to studying alternative memories and minorities, especially on the Greek borderlands, as well as discretely questioning traditional legitimacy that sometimes led to tensions and fragmentation processes. These buried memories pushed me to focus my attention on minority phenomena, such as the 'Greeks of Albania' (Nestoropoulou and Sintès 2007) or the Albanian-speakers in Greece (Sintès 2010b). This approach, following on from the previous one, facilitated an explicit reading of the complexity of transnational links induced by migration that had been studied on other borders in the southern region of the Balkans (de Rapper 2004; Mai and Schwandner-Sievers 2003; Monova 2002; Schwandner-Sievers 1999; Sintès 2008b). Thus I felt compelled to emphasise that these Albanian migrants suffered from a strong negative stereotype whilst moving/settling in Greece (Nestoropoulou 2008), resulting from the fact that they were the holders of a memory and competing legitimacy for certain areas belonging to Greece, but which were historically claimed by the Albanians – Chameria*, for example – or for regions in Albania claimed by the Greeks – the 'Northern Epirus'. This trace of past disputed territories, of once competitive national groups, seemed to have stayed (or was rather re-established), as an 'engram' of these territories, in the minds of the population. These mutual stereotypes weighed on the Albanian migrants' daily lives in the form of a tacit 'ban' on any demonstration of their presence that was too visible (Kokkali 2008; Sintès 2002). Moreover, they also proved to be very influential in how the places were managed by these new migrants.

It was not until the late 2000s that the related methodologies were adopted more widely so as to study migration in Greece and the rest of the Balkans. In Greek universities, this new work led essentially to the study of immigration through research in the field, addressing the taboo question of otherness in the country and raising the issue of a redefinition of Greek identity in the face of the presence of immigrants (Agelopoulos 2006; Papataxiarchis 2005, 2006). These studies also emphasised the immigrants' discourses through qualitative surveys often conducted with the support of students who were, themselves, of Balkan immigrant background. The resulting publications also bear the hallmark of social anthropological methodologies, favouring long-term immersion in the research. Occasionally, these studies also focused as much on the migrants' practices and strategies in the host country as on cross-border practices (Nitsiakos 2010) and, for the first time, addressed the issue of representation and stereotypes on the Other, the neighbour and the Self, involving both the immigrants and Greek citizens (Angelidou 2008; Lauth-Baccas 2002; van Boeschoten 2006). These recent trends sometimes tried to link the immigrant presence in Greece to the conditions that occurred following the regime change in their countries of origin, as Aliki Angelidou's (2008) work on Bulgaria portrayed, and included life histories and memory of the recent past (Papailias 2007; van Boeschoten 2007). Affected by the Greek crisis, other work elected to measure the implications of the presence of migrants on issues of neighbourliness and social mobilisation, for example through looking at gender, especially in domestic work (Vaïou 2002, 2007; Vaïou and Kalandides 2009) and at the redefinition of relationships between the genders and generations (Angelidou 2008; Laliotou 2006b; Papataxiarchis *et al.* 2008; Stiliou 2004, 2007; Topali 2005, 2006, 2008; van Boeschoten 2007).

Towards new fields of research

In Greece, the approach to migration seems to have radically changed in the last two decades. It has ultimately become the support used for studying the identity reconstruction of individuals and communities that has been taking place in the country since the 1990s, and for analysing the relationship between society and nation-state in an era of globalisation. This position, while remaining in line with analyses of migration processes, has opened up a wider field, allowing the fundamental movements currently traversing Greek society to resonate. As in many other parts of Europe, with the new situation after the fall of the Iron Curtain and the political changes that followed, representations and allegiances that had previously been hidden or erased became 'flavour of the day' once again, as though testifying to a 'return to a censored past' (Dimitrijević 2004). Such considerations questioned this transformation of relationships with the past, moving, instead, closer to issues of memory and heritage. As we will see in more detail in subsequent chapters, this new situation sometimes gave new prominence to a minority or alternative memory, i.e. a memory that differed from that of the main nation-state's narrative, and which led to the creation of (or return to) new ways of thinking the 'common' in which people are called upon to reassess their vision of the past, history and the sometimes antagonistic relationships which united them.

From the 1990s onwards, one common interpretation of these processes was to put forward a form of 'return from/to the Balkans' (Yérasimos 2002), seen as a negative construction of 'Europe', in which was labelled 'Balkan' anything that did not fall within the legitimate representation of democratic society, and was therefore stigmatised as belonging to folklore, custom, at best localism and at worst communitarianism and nationalism. The main criticism that could be levelled at this perspective was that it did not take into account the interpretations of these changes generated by the inhabitants themselves. So, without totally abandoning the classic interpretative frameworks of the transformations that strongly affected the entire region in the 1990s – governed by notions such as ethnicity, minorities and the nation – which had all contributed to a vision of the Balkans through the concept of 'permanence', or even 'inertia', it now seems more pertinent to admit that these terms cannot be used to describe who the people and social groups are, but rather what they do and how they perceive the society and the places that surround them, sometimes restoring former interpretative frameworks that enable them to understand these new situations.

For example, in those Balkan countries which had already experienced socialism, it was noticed that the social frameworks inherited from the past were frequently called upon to manage the transformations imposed by the present (Giordano 2001). Initially, this was the case for the mode of functioning inherited from socialism, although, at the same time, these frameworks were rejected as an undesirable re-emergence of the previous system. Old situations can often appear more stable when compared to recent turmoil, and thus be seen as a kind of regretted reference point when the present is uncertain. This 'lost' stability is thus invoked in opposition to the changes of the 1990s, which were experienced as ruptures that created a certain form of emptiness, chaos even, and evoked a nostalgia for an 'order of things' long gone. In Albania, the years under Enver Hoxha can thus be presented now in a positive light, although the actual period, with its whirlwind of transformations, in fact worried a large part of the population (de Rapper 2008). This same process also occurred in the former Yugoslavia, and is customarily referred to as 'Yugo-nostalgia' or 'Tito-nostalgia'.

Considering the construction of memory from the anthropological perspective of Joël Candau (2005) leads, nevertheless, to maintaining that this period did not ultimately lead to 'regaining memory' after the eclipse of socialism, but rather to the emergence of new processes through the reinvention and reclamation of certain versions of the past. Heritage, in the institutional sense of the word, is a good example of this since, evolving from a sense of rupture, it attempts to fuse new links to old realities, both material and immaterial – places, objects, traditions, languages – and by giving them new values, and thereby justifying their protection and enhancement. This statement illustrates one of the mainsprings of the link between past and present that should not be based on a radical distinction. Cultural and social values, as well as identity processes, should not be taken at face value for what they are, but rather as resources in the new regional context of economic scarcity and politic uncertainty. Insofar as the changes that affected Balkan societies during the 1990s led to redefining identities and positions, we need to step back from the contrast between suddenness (ruptures and events) and the long term (family genealogies, historical memory, cultural models, heritage and traditions), or the classic opposition between culture and society, erudite and popular, tradition and modernity …

In Greece, of more concern than the radical policy changes that were unlike those in the other Balkan countries were the issues related to immigration and the geopolitical tensions that had surfaced in the 1990s, for these questioned again the stability of the frameworks that had been developed around the notion of Greekness. If their effects could be seen as an increasing tendency towards the 'ethnicisation' of social and economic relationships in the country (Sintès 2010a: 138–52), they could also be seen as a factor of transformations in some perceptions of the past. After the 2008 crisis, the economic and financial agenda greatly monopolised the attention of Greek citizens, with this new situation seeming to reduce the sensitivity of migratory issues and border disputes. With regard to migration, it is true that, from that moment on, out-migration prevailed once again in Greece, owing to the country's unattractive economic situation. The first results of the 2011 census demonstrated this: net migration had a deficit of nearly 200,000 people for the 2001–2010 period, whereas it had exceeded 700,000 during the previous decade. For the first time since the Second World War, the population decreased in Greece and, even though Albanian and Bulgarian workers, affected by the lack of employment, were the first to go back to their country of origin or elsewhere in Europe, the nationals, and especially young graduates, were also tempted to leave Greece. However, it was striking to note that the questions of ethnicity and migration reappeared on the Greek political stage during the 2012 elections, and the way in which they were handled was exacerbated within the political arena due to the confirmation of the far right and neo-Nazi party Golden Dawn's electoral success. The appearance of this party was accompanied by discourses presenting migrants as a real threat to Greek national identity. If this accusation was initially directed towards Albanians due to the border disputes which pitted nationalists from the two countries one against the other, from then on it was the African and Asian migrants who became the targets of the far right. They were accused of being behind the rising insecurity in the streets of Athens and of taking advantage of the economic measures the state had set up to accommodate them, while Greek citizens had been hit by the harshness of the crisis. Moreover, the most radical group did not hesitate to take action alongside far-right thugs. In 2009, the residents' committee of Agios Panteïlemonas, a neighbourhood in Athens heavily infiltrated by the Golden Dawn neo-Nazis, for the first time took the lead in expelling Afghan and Pakistani migrants by force from a public garden, resulting in a cycle of violence in this quarter. Since the 2012 legislative elections and the entrance of Golden Dawn to parliament, the number of violent acts against foreigners has continued to increase in the country. For instance, according to the Greek press, in the first six months of 2012 nearly 500 migrants were the victims of varying degrees of violence. Today, these events are accompanied by a discourse that presents the history of Greece and the Greeks, thereby reviving memories of the authoritarian regimes that the country lived through during the twentieth century and, despite its extreme radicalism, also recalling a general tendency that had appeared in the country, and elsewhere, to resort to the past in order to legitimise the present. For a significant number of inhabitants of the Greek peninsula, finding themselves face to face with foreigners due to geographical mobility and the (relative) opening of the borders to international migration became their daily reality, generating new relational models and creating new positions implied by the vision of the country, region and national group with which they identified themselves.

Observing such political phenomena raised the question of what heritage and national and local affiliations actually meant in a world that seemed simultaneously more globalised yet more localised. Without necessarily going as far as validating Georges Prévélakis's hypothesis of a 're-Balkanisation of Greece' (Prévélakis 2011), we should recognise that the trends observed in Greece were comparable to those that were developed by other authors concerning other Balkan countries in the 1990s and 2000s. Even if Greece was not a post-socialist state, the period that began in 1989 also raised, though sometimes in different forms, the question of the state's legitimacy over the different groups that made up society. Now, this theme was a fundamental area of study enabling light to be shed on the transformations that had been taking place throughout the Balkan countries (and in other European countries), following the political changes they had experienced in the 1990s – the rebirth of nationalism and minorities, armed conflicts, the process of state-building, etc. Likewise, through association with this theme, that of the political legitimacy of group identity was also at the forefront of debate and the ethnicisation of social and political relationships was often presented as a relentless process throughout the region (Ragaru 2007: 5). This focus on ethnicity as a sole and systematic explanation was a sort of collateral damage for the treatment of the Yugoslavian crisis by the media and by international authorities. Under the 1995 Dayton Agreements and the 2001 Ohrid Agreement in the Republic of Macedonia, the partition of Bosnia-Herzegovina led to the inclusion of ethnic principles in the legislation of these countries. The ex-Yugoslavian wars – and their resolution – led the way for this type of 'solution' by imposing the issue of minorities on the international agenda as from the 1990s (Deets 2006). European institutions reacted rapidly and introduced legal processes for their recognition from texts such as the Convention for the Protection of National Minorities (1991) and the European Charter for Regional or Minority Languages (1992). Nonetheless, as Florien Bieber (2007) noted, these dynamics were not solely confined to being institutionalised, as was the case for Bosnia-Herzegovina, where all areas of public life seemed to have been affected. These dynamics may therefore have led to a legitimisation of demands for minority rights within the political framework with regard to their international recognition, thus contributing to their (re)constitution as a political issue, and leading to the emergence of pressure groups, supporters and ethnic parties. Political science analysts were divided in their interpretations: some saw them as a springboard for political action, ultimately reinforcing loyalty to the new state under construction, while others feared the consolidation of dangerous centrifugal forces. For Nadège Ragaru, such a process 'tended towards self-sustenance up to the point of subverting the entire political space and, more importantly, reconfiguring each social issue as an 'ethnic' problem (Ragaru 2007: 8), i.e., reducing everything to an issue almost impossible to negotiate, or at least one where the consensus would often be difficult to find.

Without claiming to exhaust this debate, it is clear that this kind of mobilisation for minority group recognition seems well established in the Balkan Peninsula and Greece, as in many other contemporary societies. As Nadège Ragaru reminds us, caution should be the rule when addressing these issues. Since the 1990s, many experts have asserted – maybe too quickly – that stigmatising the Balkan region, the sole explanation of the conflicts that struck the peninsula would have been a kind of endemic ethnic nationalism.

This type of reasoning once again presents South-East Europe as essentially different from Western Europe, and this also led to cultural and social diversity being seen as a threat to peace and democracy or to the democratisation of societies in general (Ragaru 2007: 6). Other approaches to the lived experiences of the inhabitants of the Balkans offered more nuanced ways in which to analyse such processes. For example, Dejan Dimitrijević-Rufu (1998) presented these identities as contextual narratives in Bosnia-Herzegovina, while Amaël Cattaruzza integrated political discourse into the dynamic processes of construction of collective indentification in Montenegran society (Cattaruzza 2010). More generally, though, my methodology followed the path set out by Jean-François Gossiaux (2002), who had already proposed this type of approach for declarations of ethnic identity, and who saw in them the result of power relationships across societies, in the Balkans as elsewhere. The concept of 'identity entrepreneurs' which he developed proposed such a vision of the process of ethnicisation, which should be based on the social and political actors involved. In scientific debates, this type of observation has led to a growing reflection, through challenging notions such as ethnicity, religious affiliation and nationalism, on how social groups can establish themselves in the long term. Following Rogers Brubaker's study on identity (2001), both the ethnic group and the nation should thus be seen as discursive notions, concealing and homogenising identification dynamics that are always contextual, fluid and plural when envisaged at the level of those social actors whose agregation can be seen as short-term and often instrumental. Note, however, that the movement to mobilise the past, based on the evocation of ethnic and national identities, is also relevant on a global level. These new dynamics, which affect both identity experiences and practices of space, are, in fact, absolutely in no way a Balkan prerogative. They raised the question of macro-historical frameworks, heavily hit by the changes that globalisation had provoked on the entire planet (Sassen 2007; Abélès 2008). Nevertheless, it is clear that the references to the past that have been raised, be they ethnic identities or regional belonging, like the focus on cultural heritage (Amselle 2010), are used to build positions and reference points in a world which is so rapidly transforming. This is, therefore, how we can understand the revitalisation of a specific heritage in a place affected by mobility, like affiliation with cultural entities (for example, a 'European civilisation' for the Greek far right). Within such a framework, heritage is no longer perceived solely at the national level; it concerns both local and global spaces (from small places to the whole of Europe), and generally shared or more circumscribed values.

Locality as an indicator of globalisation

One of the spatial effects of these variations of scale would be the re-establishing of the frameworks of locality, which represent not only a sub-division of national and international frames but also a particular level of construction, analysis and social representation (Gupta and Ferguson 1997) involving specific forms of historical and territorial narratives. The 'production of localities', as invoked by Arjun Appadurai (1995, 1996b), is multiscalar and simultaneously includes a territorialisation and a de-territorialisation based on both material and non-material resources. Far from threatening localities, mobility and migration, on the contrary, can be perceived as an increasingly frequent way of building these local scales (Clifford 1997) for they lead to the co-presence (peaceful or antagonistic) of varied populations (migrants, tourists, foreigners) who attribute different values to one and the same place. Furthermore, this production of the local increasingly implies the coexistence of different values, identities and memories. The memory processes of the various migrations that have marked the Balkans' modern history are good examples of this plurality. Such memories, whose specificity is to cover varied spaces and times, blur both the legitimate (national) historical narratives and the geographical, political and cultural frontiers between national groups, thus questioning the univocal sense of space, territory and time usually advocated by the nation-state.

However, such an approach also allows us to move away from the ideology of hyper-mobility in force today that, through mobility, leads to the minimisation of the grounding processes often associated with nation-state discourses or with outdated historical or cultural depths. This could inappropriately lead to the implicit reifying of ahistorical subjects with a supposed total freedom of action, which is obviously not the case of all those who are held apart from these practices of mobility for economic reasons or their lack of connectivity (Le Breton 2004; Martucelli 2004). Thus, the repositioning of my work (presented in the next chapter) led me to integrate it into my analysis of more general processes habitually attributed to globalisation, understood as the disruption of certain hierarchies, and especially the introduction of a new discourse or new dominant discourses that exceed that of the current nation-state (though without always running counter to it). These inputs were used to rediscover the determining place of memory in the particular formation of nowadays Greece. Fundamental background, heritage, but above all permanent reinvention and interpretation, social memory in the country can sometimes give rise to the reversal of prevailing stereotypes or to their most rigorous applications, indicating the variability of this type of reference point. In the different cases presented in the following chapters, these processes will be discussed based on certain specific forms of mobilisation of the past in this country.

To describe the contemporary relationship between society and places, this work takes up Teresa Gowan and Sean O'Riain's thematic project of embodying the global in 'the ordinary, the marginal, the daily' (Burawoy 2000: 12), even though globalisation is more often signified by the transfer of capital, the flow of people and goods, and the spread of Western cultural productions. This principle is therefore much closer to the goal of proposing, via the observation of spatial practices of specific groups, a 'global ethnography', to use Michael Burawoy's (2000) oxymoron. Yet these 'bottom up' perspectives, i.e. the direct observation of individual trajectories, speeches and perceptions, are also able to tell us about more general processes. They enabled me to deal with the realities of marginalisation and diversity in Greece, at a time when their coverage by the media often led to them being perceived as elements of disorder. These objectives resulted in the adoption of methodological perspectives based on surveys and observation in extremely localised contexts and configurations, as described in the following pages. In the Balkans, the radical changes that affected Eastern Europe after 1989 were often seen as a massive and global fact, leading to the setting up of a 'transition' paradigm which has since been rejected. Ethnologists were among the first to denounce the deterministic and reductive character of this paradigm (Burawoy and Verdery 1999; Verdery 1996) as this approach effectively took very little account of the multiple modalities of its reception and impact. They have since been joined by the very economists and political scientists who had initially contributed to the imposing of the paradigm (Michel 2006). This reversal confirmed the notion that societies should not be perceived as complete entities in a state of constant global transformation (whether through 'globalisation' or 'transition') but, rather, that we should consider the multiplicity of experiences that are encountered through the study of situations and concrete experiences (Givre 2008).

In this conceptual and methodological framework, the focus of the '*eccezionale normale*' (exceptional normal) proposed by the Microstoria approach (Grendi 1977), and applied to my fieldwork in Greece, had the aim of documenting this complexity while proposing a new interpretation of the dichotomy between centre and periphery, which involves globalisation (and its corollary of fragmentation) and their implementation in specific places. I therefore chose to study them through the dynamics of Greek geographical peripheries. Indeed, for reasons specific to the history of modern Greece, the changes initiated in the 1990s led me to wonder if this society would unfold according to dynamics that were more specific to its margins than to its centre (this was the case in many of the Balkan countries and undoubtedly this explained the increase in scientific studies and workshops on the dynamics of border societies in the region in recent decades). The territorial formation described above was, in fact, characterised by the progressive integration of new peripheries during an annexation and assimilation process that finally ended in 1947 with the annexation of the Dodecanese Archipelago. After several decades of political stability, the political transformations of the 1990s led to the rediscovery of this heritage through the new relationships with the neighbouring countries. Moreover, due to this particular history, the peripheral regions of Greece were therefore places where homogenisation processes through national policies were the most recent, and where their incompleteness today is part and parcel of the new fragmentation processes produced by increased mobility, migration and the circulation of information, as described in the preceding pages.

Through this approach to the study of geographical margins, this research on the impact of globalisation on Greek society aims to document the changes in the hierarchy of power that dominates the space in relation to the appearance of new actors implicated in the regions' geographic mobility and migration. All the examples invoked link these peripheral spaces with a migratory movement or more global mobilities. The conditions that produced these movements, however different they may have been, are also indicative of globalisation processes and the fragmentory dynamics of society and space, linked to issues of margins and marginality. These latter issues are finally a way in which to rediscover a common theme in the study of South-East Europe, as already mentioned earlier. The vision of a marginal, dominated space is indeed commonplace both inside and outside the region, whether in popular discourse or in academic circles. However, this domination 'stigma' can, nevertheless, sometimes be reversed, in order to see in these Balkan situations the determining spaces of Europe's future.

Chapter 2

Conflictual memories and migration between Greece and Albania

Albanian migration to Greece was the subject of my first research in this region in 1999. Extension of this work was important for addressing the transformations taking place in Greek society in the 1990s and 2000s. By the time I started this research in 1999, the main migratory wave of the early 1990s, which followed straight after the fall of the Iron Curtain, had passed and the second had arisen as a consequence of the violent outbreaks in Albania after the collapse of the pyramid schemes in 1997. By the early 2000s, migration seemed to have stabilised and appeared increasingly to have become a permanent settlement of whole families, even if the representations forged during the previous period were still present. The scale of this phenomenon and the great rapidity with which it took place were enough to explain the quasi-stupor that still prevailed in the country and the sensation of deluge which its inhabitants had felt in wake of the Albanian migratory wave. Such a feeling was well summed up by the daily newspaper *Elefteros Typos*' headline of 31 December 1990: '*Η Αλβανία μετακόμισε στην Ελλάδα*' (Albania moves to Greece). However, seen at first hand, the effects of this migration were that some original trends appeared which led to the emergence of new discourses and practices that could be described as transnational. Nevertheless, these practices could not be considered as completely unprecedented in Greece insofar as they seemed to rely on elements of a past shared by the inhabitants of both countries or on their remobilisation in certain forms.

Migration seen from above

Initially, in order to understand its impact, this flow had to be reinstated within the context of the veritable migratory revolution which had affected

Greece in the early 1990s, a period during which the country had become one of the most sought-after migratory destinations in Europe. During this decade, this migratory phenomenon increased dramatically, as the figures from the 2001 census highlighted. Among the very many immigrants who arrived in the 1990s, the Albanians formed by far the largest group, with nearly 440,000 immigrants registered in Greece. They accounted for 57 per cent of all foreigners and settled throughout the whole of Greece. Arrival data from the 1990s revealed the exponential nature of this migration and tended to confirm the eruption of a veritable two-country migration system at the heart of Europe at a time when this kind of pattern had seemed to have disappeared from the global geography of migration. The numerous migrants who arrived in Greece benefited from the geographical proximity and the permeability of a long and mountainous border that was very difficult to control. In Albania, a major event in the late twentieth century was the migration abroad in of almost one million people, out of the country's population of three million. The extraordinary strength of this flow was the cause of the decrease in the Albanian population, which dropped from 3.2 million in 1989 to 3 million in 2001, then to 2.8 million in 2011. Among the upheavals affecting the country, the acceleration of urbanisation, (Albanian towns accounted for 40 per cent of the total population in 1989 and 54 per cent in 2011), and feminisation (the proportion of the male population dropped from 51.5 per cent to 50 per cent over the same period), could also be seen as direct or indirect consequences of the opening up of the country to the rest of the world and the immense force of out-migration.

Table 2.1 Number of Albanians in Greece

Year	No.
1987 (police)	1
1988 (police)	7
1989 (police)	17
1990 (police)	800
1991 (police)	54,000
1991 (census)	20,556
2001 (census)	438,036

Source: Miletitch (1998) and various censuses

In the 2000s, despite the most fanciful estimates in the press or in public opinion, the number of Albanian migrants in Greece did not exceed 720,000, according to estimations taken from the 2001 Albanian demographic data (Sintès 2005) and later corroborated by more recent studies by the Greek think-tank IMEPO of illegal immigrants in the country (Lianos *et al.* 2008). Beyond the mere proximity, the strength of this flow was also related to a socio-demographic context that favoured the development of a low-skilled labour migration between the two countries. In fact, like the rest of Southern Europe, Greece experienced a real demographic revolution in the last decades of the twentieth century, marked by a significant drop in its fertility rate. The Greek population was thus characterised by a marked sluggishness that was best expressed by the total fertility rate of 1.3 children per woman. These demographic characteristics and the mass emigration of previous decades led to the onset of manpower shortages in the Greek labour market in the 1980s, which particularly affected the construction industry and seasonal agricultural work. Thus, the inflow of foreign workers played a part in the nationwide shift of national workers towards the tertiary sector and better qualified jobs, arriving at just the right moment to compensate for the demographic weakness of a population which, without the arrival of the migrants, would have been on the decline and rapidly ageing. The 1991 and 2001 census figures confirm this: the increase in the country's population was based entirely on these migrant settlements given that the intercensal increase of 720,000 inhabitants for the total population reflected the 762,000 foreigners enumerated in the 2001 census. Lastly, the characteristics of the Greek economy were also relatively favourable to this migration due to the hypertrophy of seasonal touristic services, a supported agricultural sector in need of a workforce and an industry that concentrated on the simple tasks. In such a context, Albanians and other foreigners occupied, indeed amplified, socially accepted niches of pre-existing precarious work. This relationship between economic characteristics and migration is seemingly confirmed by examination of the distribution of these Albanian migrants throughout the country in the 2001 census. Studying the major spatial patterns of migration by means of this statistical system showed how its geography (in the most trivial sense of the term) was largely conflated with that of the Greek economy, since Albanian migrants found themselves essentially grouped in major employment areas in the country.

Indeed, there were extremely high concentrations of Albanians in certain areas of Greece, a distribution that was reflected by all foreigners in the country. The regions of Athens and Thessaloniki received the highest numbers. However, a closer examination highlighted the points of divergence from the geographical distribution of the Greek native population and tended to reinforce the idea that this migration had had a massive impact on the entire Greek territory. The first observation appeared after calculating the number of foreign residents per inhabitant, which allowed the migratory impact on the resident population to be estimated. This indicator established some specificities, notably that the first suburban areas encircling the centres of Athens and Thessaloniki were very attractive to migrants due to their affiliation with national-level urban organisations. But more importantly, the study of these proportions gave rise to two new facts: the migrants were relatively more present in island municipalities and dynamic peri-urban areas than in the two largest cities of the country. Consequently, it was not in the cities that the highest proportion could be observed. The only places where foreigners accounted for over 40 per cent of the total population in 2001 were two small ones close to the Albanian border where 44 per cent of the population were foreigners, an even greater percentage than on the large island of Mykonos, where migrants 'only' represented a quarter of the total population. The municipality of Athens was much further behind with 17 per cent; Thessaloniki slightly exceeded the national average with only 7 per cent.

This nuance was further confirmed by measuring the migratory impact according to population dynamics. The general coinciding of the distributions presented at the beginning of this chapter did not in fact allow an affirmation of similitude in the dynamics. At prefectorial level, if the results of intercensal growth for nationals and that of the total population recorded in the country are compared, the extent of the migratory phenomenon in certain areas becomes evident. Certainly, if the total population in 15 prefectures out of 54 decreased between 1991 and 2001, the Greek population decreased in a far more extensive way in 36 prefectures. Thus, the tendency towards demographic sluggishness – already highlighted by the overall figures for the country's population – was established, resulting in a net difference between the overall development of the country's population and that of its national population (Sintès 2008a). At municipality level, it became possible to highlight the different spatial types shown below: (1) areas whose development was consistent with the spatial tendencies of the Greek population, and (2) areas where the overall picture was the complete opposite, due to the massive influx of foreigners. In addition to this first distinction, the general evolution of the population of each municipality should be taken into account. Thus, for areas where the Greek population was in decline even while global figures were increasing, we can but conclude that this was due to an extremely strong migratory impact. Areas whose population was stable and where the number of Greeks had decreased, and those areas whose population had increased whilst the number of Greeks remained stable, evidenced a strong migratory impact. On the other hand, for regions where the dynamics of the total population and of the Greek

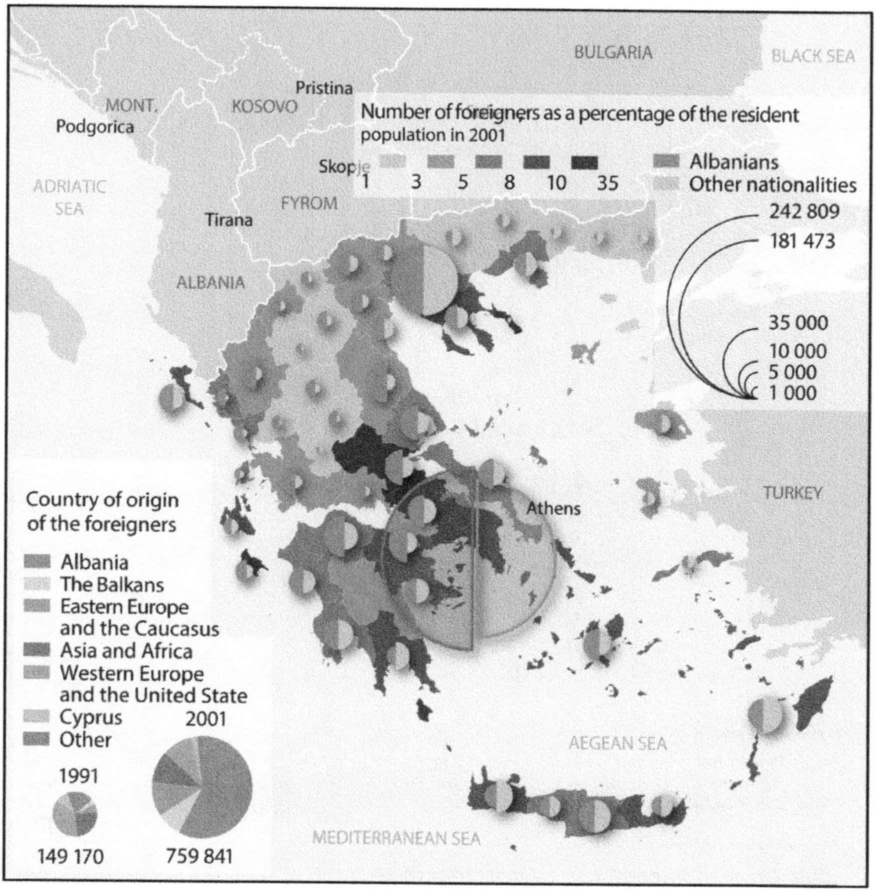

Figure 2.1 Migrants on Greek territory in 2001: preponderance of Albanians and widespread impact
Source: Cattaruzza and Sintès (2012)

population were broadly comparable, the migratory impact was considered to be medium to low.

Examination of the relative impact of migration, as described above, confirms the weight of large metropolitan areas in the way in which migrants were disseminated. Peri-central zones appeared within the urban areas of Athens and Thessaloniki and it was here that the migrants maintained the population's demographic growth. Moreover, the active areas that were directly related to the development of large cities also experienced the same kind of dynamic. Along an axis that goes from Athens to Volos, all along the coast of the Evia Channel, the Phthiotis coast, and the southern shore of the

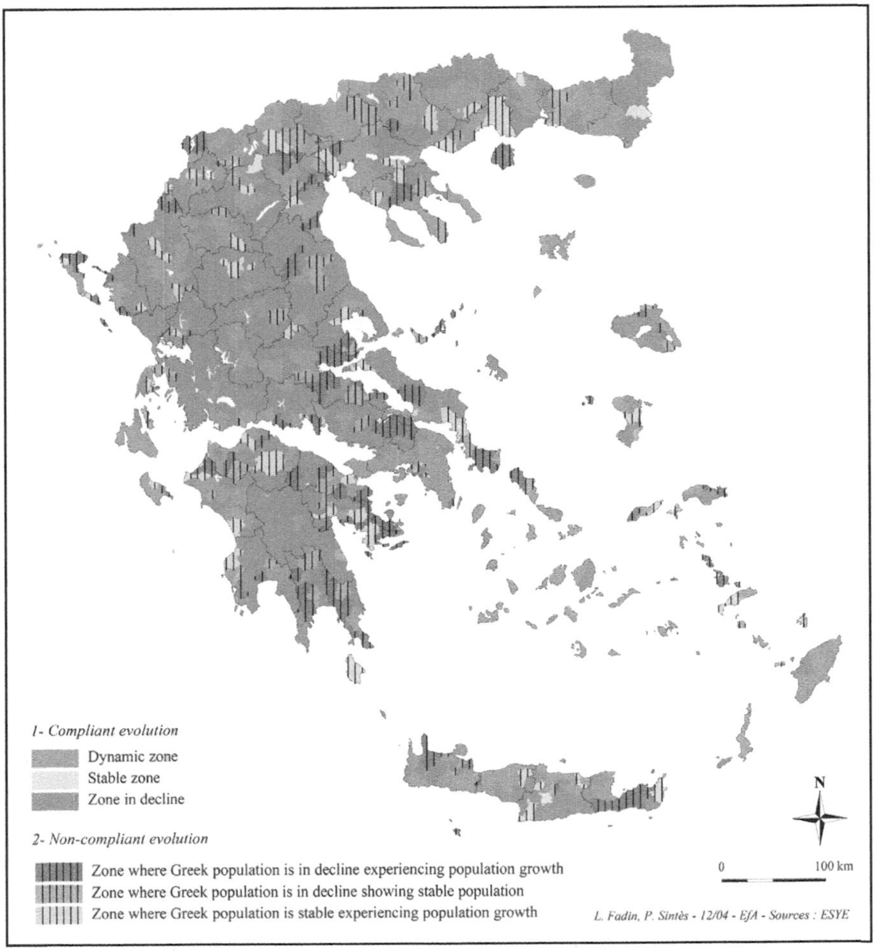

Figure 2.2 Relative migratory impact on the regions of Greece
Source: Sintès (2005)

Saronic Gulf, the settlement of foreign migrants reversed the population's tendency to diminish. Similarly, in Northern Greece, this trend was mainly found in the greater Thessaloniki region, whose population was increasing, despite the declining national population. In general, this inversion of demographic dynamics can be considered to be related to all the factors that attracted migrants to the outermost regions of the two large cities: both a varied job market (construction industry and agriculture) and easy access (since these areas are always located along major routes of communication). The prevalence of work would also help to explain the distribution of these spaces whose dynamics were contrary to those in the rest of the country. The surrounding areas of secondary urban centres seemed engaged in similar processes to those of the coastal regions of 'Old Greece' although, in both the Western part of the country and in the Greek islands, areas bucking the development trend were rarer. However, this does not mean that the impact of migration should be considered invalid, as it reflects the contrast between those regions in sharp decline and the dynamic areas across the country, a contrast that marked the western areas on the Greek mainland. In both cases, the values of migration only had a marginal and non-determining influence and the few circumstances where migrants could have reversed the trend in the country were either located at border-crossing points such as the villages of Kristalopigi and Pogoniani, which are in close proximity to Albanian territory, or areas being developed for tourism, such as the small seaside town of Parga.

Thus, in spite of its recognised importance in urban areas, the massive influx of Albanian migrants in Greece from the early 1990s had, in its own way, strengthened the organisation of Greek territory through the development of peripheries around the two major cities. The Albanians blended into this spatial organisation without really transforming it, but their settling in areas that are today deserted by the Greeks is a measure of the complementarity that developed between foreigners and national citizens on the labour market. Gradually, productive peri-urban and working-class suburbs of the inner urban ring became undesirable areas for national citizens, who preferred the more-distant suburbs of Athens and Thessaloniki or provincial town centres. This reading of the impact of migration on Greek territory therefore appeared stronger than merely understanding the distribution of migrants, and explained in a sense the magnitude of the shock that it represented for Greek society. Indeed, the two spatial areas which made up the most active part of the country (the active rural areas on the coastal plains and urban centres) were the most affected by the phenomenon with (1) the presence of a high proportion of migrants relative to the total population and the reversal of demographic dynamics for the active rural places, and (2) the establishment of several-thousand-strong groups of people in the big cities. Hence, the Greek territory and its different dynamics seems undeniably to be a provider of resources for migrants who settle there, as their patterns of distribution show. Thus, in order to understand how migrants used these resources, and how they were prioritized and exploited along the way, I decided to complete this first approach through fieldwork. Between 1999 and 2004, therefore, I found myself confronted by the reality of migration on a totally different level: that of the migrants themselves and the relationships they had with each other. This change of perspective, no longer the zenithal viewpoint, the famous view from Nagel's *nowhere* (established after analysing the census results in my office), was rather that of the migrants and of those whom they met. This pushed me to consider a whole new series of resolutions, of causalities that gave quite different explanations for the forms taken by Albanian migration to Greece, thereby leading me to distance myself from questions of spatial distribution and economic determination.

Discovering relational space

Effectively, changing perspective enables us to see that Albanian migrants were not engaged in a movement that was uniquely reducible to these figures. The indications given by the police during the early years of their presence were indeed paradoxical: throughout 1991, 54,000 Albanians were recorded entering Greece, while the authorities said that 85,000 had been expelled (Miletitch 1998: 198). This suggested back-and-forth movements and double counting, implying frequent circulation between Greece and Albania. Moreover, if the migratory environment is regarded as the construction of individual networks, it also implies an infinity of relationships between migrants and non-migrants, between Greeks and Albanians, and therefore offers a new perspective on the upheavals that this phenomenon could have caused on other levels.

A summary description of the logistics which appeared to govern construction of these migratory networks indicates that the first migrants from Albania were often temporary or seasonal, attracted as much by curiosity as by necessity. Without denying the great distress and destitution in which the Albanians lived, it is true that other motives could also have impelled some migrants to move: for instance, young people saw it as a way to free themselves from the burden of a family environment. As King and Mai (2008) demonstrated, televised images of the West also encouraged Albanians to look elsewhere. Secondly, working conditions in the fields or the construction industry, which rapidly became the main sources of employment, contributed to the shaping of hybrid, seasonal and temporary migratory patterns – circular movements between the workplace in Greece and the region of origin in Albania. This, for example, is what 193 migrants declared in 2001 to the Voha municipality near the city of Corinth (Sintès 2007); their work was indeed very varied throughout the year depending on the different phases of the agricultural calendar, with maximum employment in this region during grape and orange harvesting, and the workers leaving as soon as the season was over. Such rhythms were also found in popular tourist areas such as the Cyclades, where seasonal variations of activity were as diverse as in agricultural areas. The overwhelming majority of short-stay visitors arrived during the summer months, resulting in a high temporal concentration of seasonal work for the migrants. This concentration was also found within the territory, as illustrated by the following figures: 32 per cent hotel occupancy in the southern Aegean regions, 21 per cent in Crete and 13 per cent in the Ionian Islands during the period June to September 2006. In addition, a succession of veritable cycles of activity could also be observed: the winter period when activity was at its lowest, the preparation period that began during the week before Easter, a mixed time when domestic weekend tourism would take precedence, and finally the summer season when tourism was at its peak. So, for the migrant, it was the space/time of the activity that would dictate migration patterns, which enables the figures given in the preceding pages to be put into perspective, as migrant stocks varied according to geographical characteristics and a seasonal activity calendar. This was apparent in the narratives of many of those undertaking these return trips, at least initially.

> Mihail comes from a village near Leskovik in southern Albania. The first time he came to Greece was in 1995, when he spent three months on the Corinth plain during harvest time before returning to the University of Elbasan, where he was studying mathematics. During the early years he only came for the agricultural season during the school holidays. In 1998, he decided to spend the whole year in Greece despite the absence of official documents: in July he finished teacher-training college in Elbasan and was unable to be in Greece for the first regularisation process. He therefore crossed the border on foot, illegally, via the Grammos Mountain, at the level of the Sarandaporos River. Once in Konitsa, he found acquaintances with whom he could stay. He changed and shaved 'to look more Greek' and then took the bus to Lechaio, near Corinth. On arrival, he was able to rely on the contacts he had made in previous years. His usual employer found him accommodation so he did not have to spend the autumn and winter months in the cabin he had lived in previously. As he now knew many people, he was certain of being able to obtain work almost all year round, and was no longer afraid of being thrown out of the country by the police.

Nevertheless, Mihail's testimony raised the issue of the progressive installation process of these same migrants. Such an interpretation would be reminiscent of certain perceptions of migration that had been promoted in the 1970s and 1980s in the academic work on migration, like Abdelmalek Sayad's (1977) 'Three ages of Algerian migration to France'. According to what can be seen today as a normative or even teleological position, he suggested that migration is a succession of phases that would push the

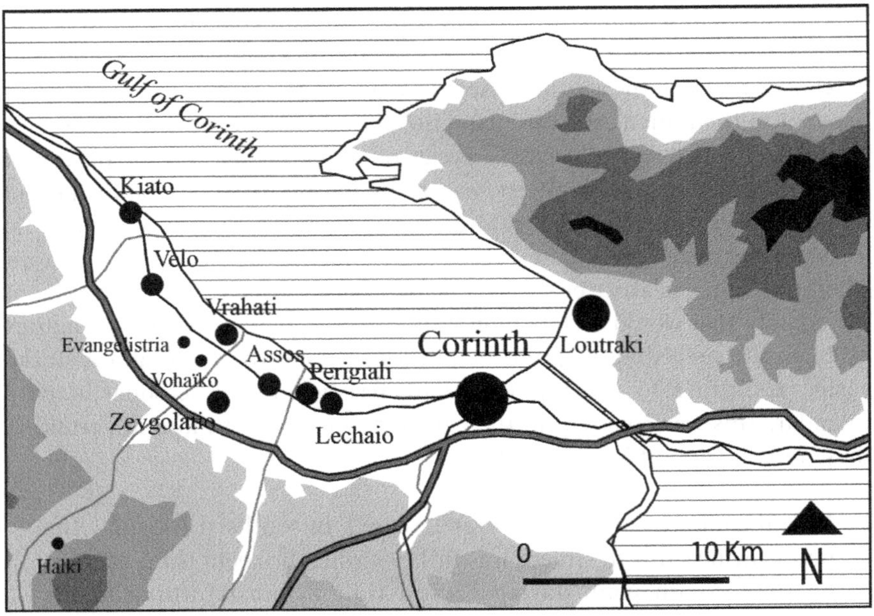

Figure 2.3 The villages on the Voha Plain, west of Corinth

migrants to finally settle more permanently in the host country, having once acquired sufficient knowledge of the places where this seasonal work is based. These temporary movements are considered here as the precursory signs of a permanent migration, with the tipping point occurring when the idea of returning home is abandoned. There may be many reasons for this. For instance, it may be due to children starting school or a new school year, a family event such as a marriage, birth or death, or even a social or political event. From that moment on, the 'base-residence', to use the concept of demographers Hervé Doménach and Michel Picouet (1987), reverses and moves to the host country. Albanian migrants to Greece often demonstrated this type of process, even though, in the early days, Greeks perceived this migration as a sporadic and reversible movement. In the beginning, migrants, especially Albanians and Bulgarians, appeared mainly at harvest time or over the summer, when activity on construction sites was in full flow. However, from 1997, with the collapse of the financial pyramid schemes in Albania, the reality of Albanian migration to Greece changed and veered increasingly towards a majority of couples with children. Could the willingness of the Greek government to regularise the situation for hundreds and thousands of illegal immigrants in the country in 1997 have been a sure sign of a change in the nature of migration during this period?

Table 2.2 Relationship between the provision of social resources and the probable migratory behaviour of Albanians interviewed in Greece (1999–2004)

Probable territorial behaviour	Resources in Albania: farming, assured trade, family imperatives	Network, composed of migrants and natives, assuring reception for migrants in Greece
Remaining in Albania	+	–
Circulating between the two countries	+	+
Settling in Greece	–	+
Reclusion or wandering	–	–

Source: Sintès (2007)

Nevertheless, the majority of the migrants encountered in the field did not follow this simple pattern. It became obvious that many people were, on the contrary, 'settled in mobility' between Greece and Albania because, for some, seasonal migration was just supplementary income. This occurs when migration to Greece is coupled with strong ties in Albania: the moral necessity of caring for an ageing parent, the pursuit of further education, or the ownership of an asset to be made more productive (a business, fields), etc. Thus, the possibility to go to Greece for a few months also became the means of maintaining an unprofitable activity – 'leave to remain', to use Abdelmayek Sayad's (1999) expression once again. In order to organise their movements, the migrants used the networks of those who had already settled in Greece or who had previous migratory experience. According to this hypotheses, economic mobility can be also coupled with leisure travel, thus bluring the analytical categories at this level. Conversely, for others, the limited length of their stay in Greece was due to a lack of support from the Greek side, and therefore took the form of seasonal rather than permanent migration. This was the case for people stuck in a non-migrant sibling group, or those who were already in a marginal position in the origin society. For those whom I interviewed several times in Southern Albania, this intermittent migration was sometimes the result of the weak family ties linking them to a kinship group established in Greece. Finally, when the living conditions in Albania were such that not all family members could be fed, some of its members found themselves wandering between their home country and Greece, moving as opportunities arose, or remaining reclusive in Greece owing to the clandestine nature of their stay and the lack of social ties in the host country. The wording of these different types of mobility (see Table 2.2) illustrates the main tensions surrounding mobility, but may also over-simplify the complexity of the individual trajectories. Effectively, the situations observed in the field showed that, in general, the migrants went through different phases depending on the circumstances. For instance, the rapid flow of information, the (relative) opening of borders and the rapidity of movement reduced the distances for migrants and brought remote locations into one living space. Thus, the migratory styles mentioned above, built on the reversibility of movement, were not always relevant to the description of the practices that evolved from the opportunities that materialised in space and time.

> The first time Dimo came to Greece was in 1991. He went from Elbasan to Kastoria, where he had family. He went to find his cousins and stayed with them for three months before leaving. The second time he went to Edessa, near Thessaloniki, to work in the fields with other friends from Elbasan. He spent some months there before going back to Albania. Each time, he had a visa. His third trip in 1993 was more organised for it was a work trip organised with 60 other Albanians and they were travelling by bus. An employer from Edessa advised them to go to Argolide for several months to pick oranges if they wanted to work over the winter, and they took a Greek bus there. They earned 5,000 to 6,000 drachmas per day (15–20 euros), with board and lodging included. In Argos, a Greek man whose family lived in Hydra advised him to go and work there. He therefore took a boat from Nauplie, near Argos, and arrived on the island without knowing anybody. He found some work fairly quickly in a tavern, and remained there for the next seven months. Then he spent three months in Tripoli harvesting olives before returning to Albania to spend a further three months with his family. His home was therefore Hydra, Tripoli (where he always lived with the owner) and Albania! Today he is 50 and evidently works less. Since 2000, he has stopped going to Tripoli. His two sons are with him in Hydra and work in the tavern in summer. His family arrived in 1995. In winter, the tavern closes and they go back to Albania for four months. They do not work there, but take the opportunity to rest.

Depending on the nature of the resources (administrative, physical, relational, economic), this narrative portrays how a real strategy of circulation has been set up; how its networks and smugglers help the migrant to see the movement as more familiar and routine. In this context, access to information is essential, and the migrant, for whom the cell phone is indispensable, must also be well 'connected'. Yet, as the account illustrates, the resources employed at the beginning very rarely allow the migrant to get to grips with all phases of the journey. For instance, the seasonal migrant will never have enough time to transform opportunities into resources. For Dimo, mentioned above, his first network took him from his home village to different destinations where he knew he was expected, but he was only able to achieve this once he had understood how to transform the new opportunities that appeared on the way into a resource that could supplement his project. With regard to this latter idea, some migrants demonstrate an ability to use the different types of resources and to accept the new forms of 'nomadic' life, which are to some degree characterised by the multiplicity of the places involved and built in a way that is far removed from the classical sedentarity, their original starting ground.

> In 1993, Servet spent 7 days in Larissa, Greece, but the police arrested him and sent him back to Albania. He returned to Greece almost immediately and spent three months in Athens, then in Chalchis, where he worked in the construction industry before going back to his village. The following year, he walked with 15 other people to Tirnavo, where he found work as a shepherd because there was no other work. He then went to Larissa again, where he spent 5–6 months working in the building industry.
>
> Thanks to his new green card, he was able to go through customs for the first time in 1997. He went to Larissa for 5 to 6 months and lived in the same house with other Albanians. One of his friends had come to rebuild the port of Loutra on the island of Kithnos. He was well paid and advised Servet to go and join him. Once the port was finished he found work easily in the construction industry, where he stayed for five months. Since then, he spends some time there every year. He always goes through Larissa for his papers because that is where his situation was first regularised. And it is easier as it is closer to Albania. 2005 was his fifth annual visits to Kithnos. His wife and child live in the house he had built in the village of Cipan, southern Albania near the city of Korçë. He spends the rest of his time there and is able to live on the money he earns in Greece during the working period.

Servet's practices demonstrate an evolving journey from which emerge places that are territorialised and frequented to different degrees by the mobile individual. In his case, the organisation would appear to be bi-local, linking the place of origin in Albania (his family, his home) with his place of work in Greece. It accurately reflects a dichotomy between domestic space and the workplace – at least in the migrant's own representations and discourses – as, in practice, the intermittent or seasonal worker truly has several homes. Nevertheless, he does not confer the same emotional value on the different places, which explains the distortion observed between the discourse generally maintained by migrants when examining the circumstances of the migration, their views concerning their future and the practical reality. Undoubtedly, this perception of the country is also linked to a set of widely extended new practices such as going on holiday in the place of origin. Accessibility (especially in southern Albania) favours this type of circulation, as does the opening of new road crossings and the development of a transport network (Dalakoglou 2017). Moreover, the migrants' children also spend the holidays with the older generation in Albania, while the parents continue to work in Greece. An identificatory to-ing and fro-ing (*le va et vient identitaire*) is how Yves Charbit, Marie-Antoinette Hily and Michel Poinard (1997) described the circulation of Portuguese migrants in France, highlighting the fact that migration is only very rarely a one-way movement, one which also induces many contra-flows. These exchanges are clearly visible in the number of houses that were built by Albanian migrants in their home country. According to the 2011 census, there were 1,075,881 dwellings in Albania whereas, in 2001, there were only 785,515 (an increase of 37 per cent), while the population declined during the same period by 7.7 per cent due to out-migration and a drop in fertility. It would seem that migrants characteristically hold onto the idea of returning home, and adapt the house for a large family and a life together. Besides their economic and investment value, Albanian migrant housing projects in their home villages are also ways of remaining part of their home communities and affirming this 'double presence' invoked in Dana Diminescu's work (2005).

Since 2008, the economic crisis that rocked the whole of Greek society has heavily affected the migrants' lives, and daily and seasonal workers have been severely hit by the slowdown in activity in the country. Nevertheless, the considerable flexibility of this workforce, despite being an asset when seeking alternative ways of earning a living, did not prevent the crisis from having a significant impact on migration. For the moment, it is not possible to distinguish, from the results of the latest 2011 Greek population census, the specific effects that this difficult period had on the presence of Albanian migrants in Greece, as no figures by nationality have yet been published (in addition, the collection of census data also raises questions, given the current status of some migrants who have resorted to remaining illegally). However, the provisional results suggest a reversal in the net migration balance, with almost 190,000 people leaving the country in the decade between 2001 and 2011. The Greek population also fell for the first time in recent history to

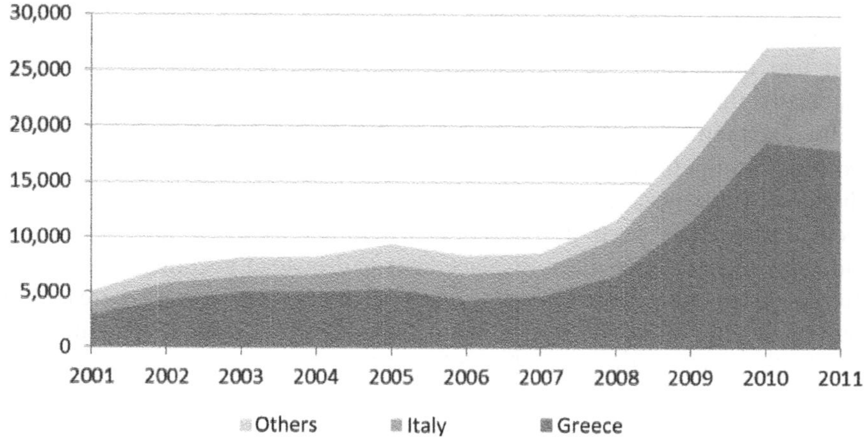

Figure 2.4 Albanian returnees from a foreign country, 2001–2011
Source: Albanian census (2011)

reach 10.7 million inhabitants, compared to 10.9 million in 2001. As such, Greece conforms to current patterns to be found throughout the Balkans and seems to have ceased being a regional pole of attraction despite still being a transit route for migration flows to other countries in the European Union. For its part, the 2011 Albanian census gives more precise data on the return of emigrants from Greece. Indeed, nearly 140,000 returned to live in Albania during the last inter-censal period, of whom more than 86,000 came from Greece. Among the latter, more than 63 per cent chose to return in the years following the 2008 economic crisis – i.e. during the last three years of that period – clearly demonstrating the impact of this event on the migrants' lives.

Yet this number is far from constituting the entirety of Albanians who had previously migrated to Greece, thus confirming the inertia caused by a settlement there of more than fifteen years, due to the many implications a return would have had on daily life (children's schooling, change of language, investments in the host country, and loss of property or support in the country of origin, etc.) Nevertheless, these last movements confirm the complexity of Albanian migration to Greece. In effect, it produced an irregular cross-border context that is subject to permanent change depending on the different situations in which the migrants find themselves. Hence, their project should not only be seen as a transition from one territory to another but, rather, is conceived of as a backward move, as places of transit, and as varying lengths of waiting and returning. Thus, this new type of migrant wove together migration spaces that were more complex than ever before. This kind of project no longer necessarily led the migrant to migrating in the traditional sense of the term, for often he/she circulated back and forth. These conclusions correlated with the outcomes of other numerous works that had questioned the conventional definitions of geographic mobility, especially the supposed contrast between normal mobility, in which the individuals remain in the same living area (labour mobility, leisure, itinerant working, nomadism), and migration (extended stay often defined by a change of residence, or compromising the possibilities for return). It would seem, rather, that, even if geographical mobility on every level continues today or, indeed, intensifies, displacement will instead become increasingly diverse, both at a spatial level (greater distances are travelled, reaching ever-increasing numbers of regions, to the extent that the entire planet can now be integrated into cycles of mobility, migratory strategies or the creation of diasporic networks) and as with other mobility. One migrant can, in effect, be involved in both permanent displacement (international labour migration, return or retirement migration) and seasonal movements (study trips, seasonal agricultural work, etc.) and in yet other reversible mobilities. This observation of new trends in contemporary migration, already mentioned above, seems to make the link between spatial mobility and social fragmentation because, if these new kinds of migrant are increasingly imprecise due to the sheer volume of migratory or mobility motives, they also seem to adopt a multiplicity of strategies for migration. The example of Albanian migrants in Greece bears witness to this process. This multiplicity (and/or fragmentation) of Albanian migrant trajectories seems to justify a questioning of habitual definitions of alterity in the host country, as the following section aims to show.

(Re)discovering the link beyond otherness

This first overview of the Albanian presence on Greek soil has resulted in some expected conclusions. It is, above all, a labour migration flow towards the country's large urban centres, which are also the major employment centres. However, the highly urban nature of this migration should be put into perspective by observing other data, such as the number of Albanians per resident, which confirm that rural areas relative to cities are extremely appealing. Other criteria come into play in explaining this geography. The reciprocal adaptation of the labour market and of migration are appropriate areas for study, as the criteria for the distribution of labour between Greek workers and Albanian workers cannot be the same. Quite simply, they perform different activities and, thus, conform to Michael Piore's (1979) theory on the dualisation of the labour market in times of heavy migration flows. Following these initial results, I decided to examine the modalities of Albanian migration to Greece – particularly the formation of migratory networks – to see what more I could learn about the spatial nature of this migration. This revealed another, quite unexpected, side to this population movement. Indeed, Albanian migration seems to have benefited from relationships inherited from the past that may have opened up many opportunities for the migrants, on this occasion through reviving ancient (and discrete) cross-border or transnational links.

In the villages on the plain of Corinth already mentioned above, the Albanian migrants whom I met several times between 1999 and 2004 seemed to have formed very distinct groups, some of whom had come to Greece in the early 1990s from southern Albania (the border region around the town of Gjirokastra). These groups differed from other migrant groups originating from more northerly Albanian regions in that they tended to be composed of complete families, with an equal ratio of men to women, who lived in quite comfortable conditions, rented houses, spoke good Greek, and enrolled their children in school. To me they appeared to have overcome any potential obstacles to their successful social and economic integration; social by their frequentation of the 'Greek' bars in which other Albanian migrants were implicitly not allowed to eat and drink; and economic, owing to the confidence that the inhabitants had in them, since they were more readily hired in periods of underemployment. They explained that this complete and relatively unproblematic integration was due to their common origins in southern Albania and their appartenance with the Orthodox faith, although not all were members of the Greek-speaking minority in southern Albania that was recognised by both governments after the Protocol of Corfu in 1914. *Vis-à-vis* their Albanian compatriots from other areas, they often kept their distance and did not seek to socialise with them. For example, it was possible to surprise them by speaking Greek when meeting them in public. Above all, they had all settled in this village in the wake of a relative who had left Albania during the Enver Hoxha era and settled in the region.

These findings provided me with the first hint of an original migration from the border areas between the two countries; subsequently, the information gathered during my different stays in these border regions clearly confirmed this. A variety of links had an undeniable effect on the very modalities of migration for some of these Albanian citizens, as they were able to count on relational capital derived from a cross-border history dating back to the period between the two world wars. Thus, despite the long separation of the Cold War years, some had preserved the memory of family or friendly links with Greek citizens whom they fervently tried to find again after 1990. Those stories that had been collected on the reopening of the border in 1991 also described a mutual impetus rather than an exodus, allowing for enthusiastic reunions for families, friends and neighbours separated for fifty years. The following quote describes the first moments of the border opening around the village of Molivdoskepastos, in the Konitsa area:

> Thus, on a path that winds along the mountainside in the Avios valley between the villages of Psiloterra and Molivdoskepastos, the families met up again. How surprised was Dimitri that morning when, on the path that had always been forbidden during his childhood because of the Albanian border guards, he heard the clarinet? He did not believe it, but it truly was the people from Psiloterra, the Greek-speaking village on the Albanian side of the border, winding their way to the monastery. When they drew level with Dimitri, it really was like a celebration for all. One of them introduced himself and handed Dimitri a piece of paper with three names scribbled on it. One of these names was that of Dimitri's mother. He was a cousin. He had never seen him before.

Once in Greece, the assistance provided by the re-establishment of a cross-border link was substantial. Firstly, of course, with the provision of administrative support but, above all, with the enabling of access to a network of relationships that was an undeniable factor facilitating migration. This was in place even before the 1997 law granted migrants from southern Albania more advantages, provided they were Greek-speaking or even simply Orthodox. In material terms, this support was perhaps a determining factor for those who wanted to settle; the importance of these contacts is clearly depicted in Giorgo's account, below, as he undoubtedly relied on the presence of cousins in Greece to migrate and especially to live and work in Athens:

> We meet Giorgo in his modest apartment in Patissiôn Avenue in Athens, and he explained how he came to Greece from his southern Albanian village:
> 'My father's cousin came to Athens before the war and today his children have a café in Maroussi. They helped us to find a job in Athens when we arrived in 1994 from southern Albania, even though we did not know each other. We even spent a whole month in my aunt's house at the beginning. In my wife's family, too, some relatives settled in Athens as from 1940, and searched for family members who had left Albania for Greece between the two world wars. Although these relatives had died in 1994, she still managed to find her cousins, who also lived there and whom she had managed to contact by letter from Albania before coming to Athens.'

Such a situation, which encourages the renewal of links between Greek and Albanian citizens, is somewhat paradoxical in terms of belonging compared to frameworks of national discourse. Sometimes migrants come across these contradictions, though multilingual studies reveal how a simple linguistic shift is sometimes the way to manage such a polyphonic identity in this new framework of migration. For example, an interlocutor (a migrant from southern Albania) can declare him/herself 'a Greek from Albania' (*Βορειοηπειρώτης* i.e. 'from Northern Epirus') when speaking Greek, yet will take a far stronger canonical position *vis-à-vis* the national Albanian discourse when speaking Albanian with his or her friends. The emphasis on local identity can also be a convenient way to get around the difficulty and resolve this paradox.

> S. left her village of Pogon, on the Greek side of the border, after the Second World War. The people of her village (Agia Marina) all went to Athens. Her father was from Agia Marina and her mother from Longo (a Greek-speaking village that had remained on the Albanian side of the border since 1913). In 1990, many relatives came from Albania and looked for her. She managed to help them out as and when she could. She owned a 2-storey building with 14 rooms in Athens, where she accommodated 40 families from her mother's village (Longo) and the nearby villages of Kousovitsa and Vrissera, until they could manage alone.
>
> 'When my daughter told me that the Vlachs* in these villages were from Romania, I replied that they are now Greek, or *ντόπιοι* (locals) … even if they came from Romania a long time ago. It is they themselves who want to keep their own characteristics, like their language. Undoubtedly their persuasion is Vlach, but their conscience and mentality are totally Greek.'
>
> *PS* – But are there Albanian Vlachs?
>
> 'Yes there are, but to be Vlach is like belonging to a local community … Some say "I'm Epirote", others say "I'm Vlach". They are Vlachs from our region, even if they are also Albanian citizens'.

Cross-border – and transnational – relationships appear to quickly disappear from the classical framework of national identity, as the narratives of those we met and interviewed in 2002 in the village of Sopik on the Albanian side of the border illustrate:

> But now we are very happy to be members of the Greek minority in Albania: we can go back and forth to Greece without any problems, as can our children. But, in Greece, we are treated like foreigners. We

> are like gypsies; our country is neither there (in Greece) nor there (in Albania) but here, in our village.

Through these different examples of unexpected solidarity on both sides of the border, this migration appears clearly as a factor of fragmentation owing to activation of the transnational ties and strengthening of the local identities which seem to feed one on the other. The question of migration is therefore also shaped by the encountering of otherness, which reveals, through its different forms, the mechanisms of its social construction. In all the countries of the world, migration gives birth, to varying degrees, to the seemingly contradictory double movement that, on the one hand, leads to a strengthening of the differences whilst, on the other, producing a process of 'metissage' (i.e., cultural hybridisation). Thus, the issue of ethnicity can be addressed through migratory mechanisms according to the particular cases in question.

Migration, transnational relationships and minority issues in Greece

From this point of view, due to their linguistic and religious characteristics, most Albanian migrants in Greece would seem to be condemned to an immovable otherness because of the historical Greek nation-building boundaries based on the distinction between Ottoman Islam, with which the Albanian nation is often associated on the one hand, and the conflation of orthodoxy and loyalty to Greekness on the other. Yet through pursuing the migrants' lifepaths as presented above, it was possible to understand that certain elements from the past or current interpretations of them, would not lead uniquely to a separation of the people of these countries into two completely hermetic groups since the dormant links which migration reawakened would appear to have already existed. More broadly, these links between Greek and Albanian citizens can even be (re-)established thanks to support networks that rely on alternative histories which contradict, in detail, the encompassing narratives of nation-states, and that migration has helped to recover.

To account for this, we can look at the different issues which, throughout history, may have brought closer certain groups located on either side of what would or had become the Greek-Albanian border, and seeing how these memories were able to be revived from the 1990s onwards. Very briefly, the history of Greece and Albania is that of two neighbouring countries on the Balkan Peninsula which have had geopolitical disputes concerning two types of issue: borders and national minorities. Paradoxically, the disputes that pitted these two states against each other may also, depending on the perspective from or level at which they are perceived, have brought some of their inhabitants closer. The demarcation of the borderline was established in 1913 in a patchwork region made up of many groups distinguished by their different religious and linguistic practices. Prior to the hermetic closure of Albania that began in 1945, Epirus and Western Macedonia were in fact places of intense exchange between these groups. Not only did border-crossings not present a particular problem, but the interweaving of lifestyles, languages, religions, properties and families created a space which, in some respects, was well integrated despite the political division. To the south, on the Greek side, Albanian-speakers were to be found in the coastal region of Thesprotia, around the towns of Paramithia, Margaritis and Filiates, and in the villages in the region of Kastoria. One by one, these groups disappeared, the latter in the population exchange between Greece and Turkey in 1923 and the others in the wake of the Second World War. At that time, those known as Chams* were accused of collaborating with the Italian and German occupation forces, and of supporting the massacre of Greek populations in the region. They fled or were expelled to Albania after the war (see the following pages).

Today, several groups tied to Greece by both language and history still live north of the border on the Albanian side. Firstly, there is the Greek-speaking minority from southern Albania, officially recognised by the Greek and Albanian governments in 1914 and found in areas that are relatively well signposted (the group varies in size between 60,000, according to the 1989 Albanian census, and 400,000 according to some of the more radical associations). The Aromanians from southern Albania, descendants of the semi-nomadic transhumant shepherds present throughout Epirus and Macedonia in earlier centuries, also identify with Greek culture to the point where they adopted the Greek language for some of their activities. In addition, they are recognised by the Greek authorities as having a Greek 'national conscience'. The Orthodox Albanians are the final group, which may appear to be bound to Greece because of a common religion. As a whole, this group, far greater in size than the other two, is currently thought to represent 20 per cent of the country's total population (though barely 6 per cent according to the last Albanian census in 2011). It is through this set of representations and realities that many Albanian migrants were considered to be *Omogeneis** – in other words, members of the Greek nation, following passage of the 1997 law concerning them. According to the Ministry of Foreign Affairs, which handled the issue, there were between 100,000 and 150,000 *omogeneis* from Albania in Greece in the early 2000s, and this simple status gave them many rights and better access to the territory and residence in Greece.

On the Greek side, further from the border, other groups may also have characteristics in common with Albanian migrants. Might it not be possible, therefore, that some among these communities, which differ from average Greek-speaking Orthodox citizens, may have instinctively felt a link to the Albanian newcomers when they arrived in 1990? Could it not be the same, we might ask, for other cross-border groups like the Aromanians* and Catholics, both of which are small minorities in both countries. Nonetheless, of all the communities in Greece, it is the Arvanites* – Albanian-speakers who have lived in southern Greece (more specifically in Attica, the eastern Peloponnese and the Argo-Saronic Islands) since medieval times – who might feel closest to the Albanians because of their common language, even if they speak a dialect which is fairly distinct from standard Albanian. It is true that, without questioning their belonging to the Greek nation, research has revealed how discretely this particularism – which applies to hundreds of thousands of people in Greece – is expressed, The use of the Arvanite language up until the second half of the twentieth century, however, is a proven fact (Athanassopoulou 2005; Guefou-Madianou 1998, 1999) though encounters with some Arvanites revealed an awareness of a linguistic otherness that was 'to be concealed' (Baltsiotis and Embirikos 2007; Sintès 2010b). So, how could Albanian migration to Greece contribute to reviving these alternative memories or to conveying a vision of the original Greek nation different to that presented by official narratives? In response, we can only speculate on the influence that these different groups had on the course of migration.

Firstly, it would appear that, for certain of these cross-border groups, their memory was reawakened in 1990 by the urgent need to migrate. Undoubtedly, if the Albanian migrants encountered in Greece frequently evoked 'pure chance' or 'the will of God' to explain why they had ended up in that particular region of Greece, it was not uncommon to find, after further investigation, that it was not luck which took some of them – especially those from Southern Albania – to that area. For instance, some were able to follow in the footsteps of a relative who had settled in Greece before World War II, or of a family friend with whom they had remained in contact despite having been unable to leave their country for fifty years. For many migrants from the regions closest to Greece, the first trip was therefore not undertaken blindly but was an opportunity to reunite with family members from whom they had been separated for fifty years. Thus, those who wanted to migrate often depended on these contacts and visited Greek relatives in villages on the other side of the border. In general, and no matter what welcome they received from these mostly unknown hosts, their village was invariably used as a first step or first base. For example, the village of Kefalovriso became the focal point for Albanian Aromanians from the Gjirokastra region. Migrants often stayed there for some time (between one month and one year) before finding other destinations, for there is always a lack of work in this peripheral and mountainous region of Greece, which had then one of the lowest wealth indices in the whole of the European Union. Immigrants therefore moved to places where they were likely to find acquaintances or family and traced people who had left Kefalovriso or other border villages in previous decades. Whatever impression this experience leaves on the migrants (bitterness or enthusiasm), the assistance given in the border villages is substantial, not least in the administrative field. The existence of these networks is an undeniable factor facilitating migration, and it was no surprise to find that the members of these cross-border groups were those who had mostly migrated '*en masse*'. These examples reveal that the activation of this interrelated solidarity would appear to be an original element facilitating an understanding of migration, and a revitalising factor for relationships that have been in abeyance for 50 years.

Conversely, links between the more distant groups (mainly the Arvanites) and the Albanian newcomers are without doubt more abstract and less based on pre-migratory family or interpersonal relationships due to the great distance from the border. However, during the 1990s, it was clear that mutual identification through their common language could link the Arvanites and the Albanian migrants, thus bridging the gap which separated the Greeks from the Albanians in the dominant discourse. Thus, a great many of the life narratives about the Albanian migrants' settlement on the Plain of Corinth spoke, at some point or another, of the involvement of an Arvanite. One of them, the first migrant from a very large group of siblings from Lunxheri, in southern Albania, made his way to the house of relative who had fled communism in the 1950s and had settled in a village in the region of Corinth, before setting off again to look for work. Along the way, he met 'an Albanian-speaking Greek', who advised him to go down to plain, to the village of Vohaïko, where he should find work, and to give the Greek's name as a reference. Another migrant, from the region of Peshkopi in northern Albania, criss-crossing the country in his search for work, was given some advice by an old lady he met on a train who spoke Albanian. 'She told me to get off at the station at Vrachati and walk straight to Vohaïko.' At this level, these interventions appear to be the result of happy coincidence, but they provoked very heavy flows of people to these villages because of the greater flexibility brought about by the presence of these few Albanian speakers within the Greek population, at the time when Albanians had not yet learned the Greek language. This flexibility was often mentioned when looking for work or carrying out administrative tasks.

However, these facilities – essential in the early 1990s – were no longer needed by the 2000s, though the link still exists. We encountered Arvanite families who had established relationships with Albanian migrants more easily through this common language, thus creating a certain feeling of closeness. 'We also come from there, from Albania' said some of the Arvanites. However, measuring the impact of these meetings is a delicate issue. Nevertheless, it is true that they paint a different picture of these arrival areas for Albanian migrants, as the following anecdote shows.

> For several days, we had seen Christos on the Place de Zevgolatio or in the café, but we hadn't managed to talk to him. We knew he spoke *Arvanitika* because the Albanians from the village had told us. Yet this evening, we were able to visit him with a friend. He wasn't at home when we got there – he had gone out with a certain Roland, we were told. After an hour's wait, he finally arrived. It was no longer the preoccupied man we had seen over the past few days but a beaming Christos, really happy with himself. What had happened? Who was this Roland whose brother was now with us?
>
> 'Roland is a young Albanian who has worked with me in my fields for several years' Christos explains. 'He and his brother have been living with me. I went to help him find a house in the area because he has just returned from Albania with his future wife. He went to his village near Lushnjë to 'kidnap' the girl he was in love with, for the girl's father refused to give her to him. They're getting married in Greece in three months' time. They will be able to return to Albania in a few years when things have cooled down a bit'.
>
> We already thought of Christos as something of a philanthropist but this story confirmed it magnificently. Vezir, Roland's brother, has known him for seven years now: 'He is like my father. When I arrived, I did not speak a single word of Greek. It was he who has taught me everything: the language, the work... We can communicate; him in Arvanite, me in Albanian. I will take him to Albania whenever he wants.' Christos is delighted with these declarations. His face shows the immense satisfaction he feels in helping Vezir and Roland's family. He tells us that he feels close to them; his story resembles theirs. Exiled from his home village in the mountains of the Argolid to the Corinth area in the 1950s, and then ... he also ran away with his future wife by returning quietly to his village one summer evening. That was in 1962. He was 27 years old and she was fourteen.

However, it is difficult to accurately decipher the real issues that arise in such situations. Indeed, the Arvanites whom we met never questioned their belonging to the modern Greek nation; they always claimed to be Greek without any hesitation and saw Albanian migrants as non-Greeks and therefore as foreigners. However, they told us that they were received like foreigners ('like Albanians') when they first arrived in the Plain of Corinth, even if this no longer true. In these statements it is easy to see that otherness can also be measured locally at the level of the 'little motherland' rather than at the national level of belonging. Even if these exchanges between Albanians and Arvanites do not confirm the eventuality of a potential resurgence of a minority consciousness for the Arvanites in Greece, they at least enable us to note a certain discrepancy between the nation-state's all-encompassing discourse, and the way this discourse is reinvested in practice by the inhabitants. Albanian-speaking Greeks, for whom integration within the nation had never been in doubt, now find themselves in a peculiar position; one in which migration seems to have been a catalyst, generating a new type of self-representation which encourages them to look back at their history. These mechanisms enable researchers to better understand how Albanian migration was part of what Alexandra Nestoropoulou called 'the panic for identity', which emerged in the 1990s in the country. Instead of reinforcing perceptions of national identity, the presence of Albanian migrants in fact challenged them by proving that relationships clearly existed between the two populations (Nestoropoulou 2008). This same interrogation was examined in Filippos Tsitos' film 'Ακαδημία Πλάτωνος' in 2009, which evoked, through comedy, identity issues generated by the discovery, post-1990 migration, of previously hidden family ties between Greek and Albanian citizens. Moreover, this work of fiction links back to the 'stranger within ourselves' that Julia Kristeva (1988) borrowed from Freud, reminding us that the foreigner's otherness is all the more disquieting in that it reveals the stranger within us. In this way, Albanian migrants served to remind the very heart of the country of the complexity of social reality in modern Greece.

A new survey deep within the margins

Although my work on Albanian migration to Greece ended with the defence of my PhD in November 2005, my research continued for several years in other areas of Greece (Rhodes – which resulted in the next chapter – and Belgium, South Africa and Israel) as well as on other topics. However, I never abandoned Greek-Albanian issues and resumed my work on the border between the two countries a few years later, under the 'Young Researchers' Collective Programme funded by the *Agence Nationale de la Recherche,* with a project – coordinated by Gilles de Rapper and started in 2009 – entitled *Les Balkans par le Bas* (The Balkans From Below). Within the framework of this programme, I decided to return to my analysis of cross-border relationships, focusing in particular on memories of a very specific area – the coastal region of Epirus known as Thesprotia. I had chosen to avoid this area during my PhD due to its political sensitivity: it had been inhabited by a large Albanian-speaking community, better known here as Chams, who had disappeared after the Second World War in debatable circumstances. Yet, half a century after the violence of the war, and nearly 20 years after the deadly border incidents at Peshkëpi, which had renewed tensions between the two countries, relations between Greece and Albania appeared to have improved by the late 2000s. Though the ending of the war was not made official until 1987, it was finally confirmed in 1996 by the signing of the Friendship, Cooperation, Good Neighbourliness and Security Agreement, which put an end to the earlier period of tensions. Today, anyone who follows or crosses the Greek–Albanian border will see a calm interstate line. Nobody appears to claim its modification officially. This situation is echoed in Thesprotia, even if it still remains one of the most disputed areas in the minds of the people in both countries. Since 2004, the opening of a border-crossing point at a place called *Mavromati* (in Greek) or *Qafë Botë* (in Albanian) has in fact enabled easy contact to be resumed between the two sides of the border, achieved by opening what is now an important area of access to Albania with the completion of the road that joins Saranda and Igoumenitsa, the first port in the region, and *Εγνατία Οδός* the highway that goes from this city through northern Greece to Thessaloniki and the Turkish border. In this region, the border section is composed of two meridian geographical features. The easternmost space is a high-altitude mountainous area with isolated valleys and difficult access: the Mourgana Mountains, part of the Western Pindos mountains and largely depopulated during the twentieth century due to sustained migration to other places in Greece, the German Federal Republic and the industrial and mining cities of Belgium. The second feature consists of the Kalama Plain, with its small coastal river whose course had been controlled in the 1960s. It is mainly the inhabitants' discourses about this second feature, collected from surveys conducted between 2009 and 2011, which were used to compose the following pages.

Heading north from the port of Igoumenitsa the landscape opens up – after a series of small hills – onto a plain that leads towards the Greek–Albanian border. The lower valley of the Kalama River and its delta had long been a swampy and repellent area. Today, the bulk of the population is settled in this region, which is divided up into large villages that live off mandarin-orange farming, while the mountains that rise more to the East and separate Thesprotia from the rest of Epirus and the Ioannina region, are now largely empty due to outmigration. The context of settlement is comparable to the rest of Epirus where one only has to look back to World War II and the Greek civil war to capture the most significant shifts in population, those which still deeply mark the landscape even today. These areas, in fact, suffered from both

Figure 2.5 The Kalama Plain seen from the village of Smerto, to the West

their occupation by Italian and German troops during the Second World War, and from the ensuing atrocities. The violence continued throughout the Greek civil war up until 1948, when the remaining pockets of the democratic army in hiding in the heights of the Mourgana Mountains were eradicated less than a year before the end of the conflict. This troubled period resulted in a population shift and the abandonment of many villages. Some people went to Albania, whilst others had to abandon their homes and move elsewhere either within in the region or in Greece as a whole. If we look at these situations in detail, they are quite varied, but they all lead to movements that are actually quite traditional when placed in the Mediterranean context as described by Fernand Braudel (1977): in other words, the conquest of the plains and their intensive exploitation resulted in the abandonment of the mountain areas and their agro-sylvo-pastoral systems.

This 'downward movement' occurred at a number of levels. For instance, at the regional level, many mountain regions were abandoned, as was the case for the villages in the Mourgana mountain range that were almost entirely depopulated in favour of the plains, the cities and even of migration abroad. Moreover, these displacements sometimes occurred over very limited distances – for example Sagiada, where the current village is separated from the old one by only a few kilometres – but all took place at periods that were directly related to the conflicts of the 1940s. In Sagiada, it was initially the partial destruction of the village by the Germans on 23 August 1943 which led to the population first abandonning it. The Sagiadinis fled across the border *en masse* and took refuge just on the other side in the Albanian

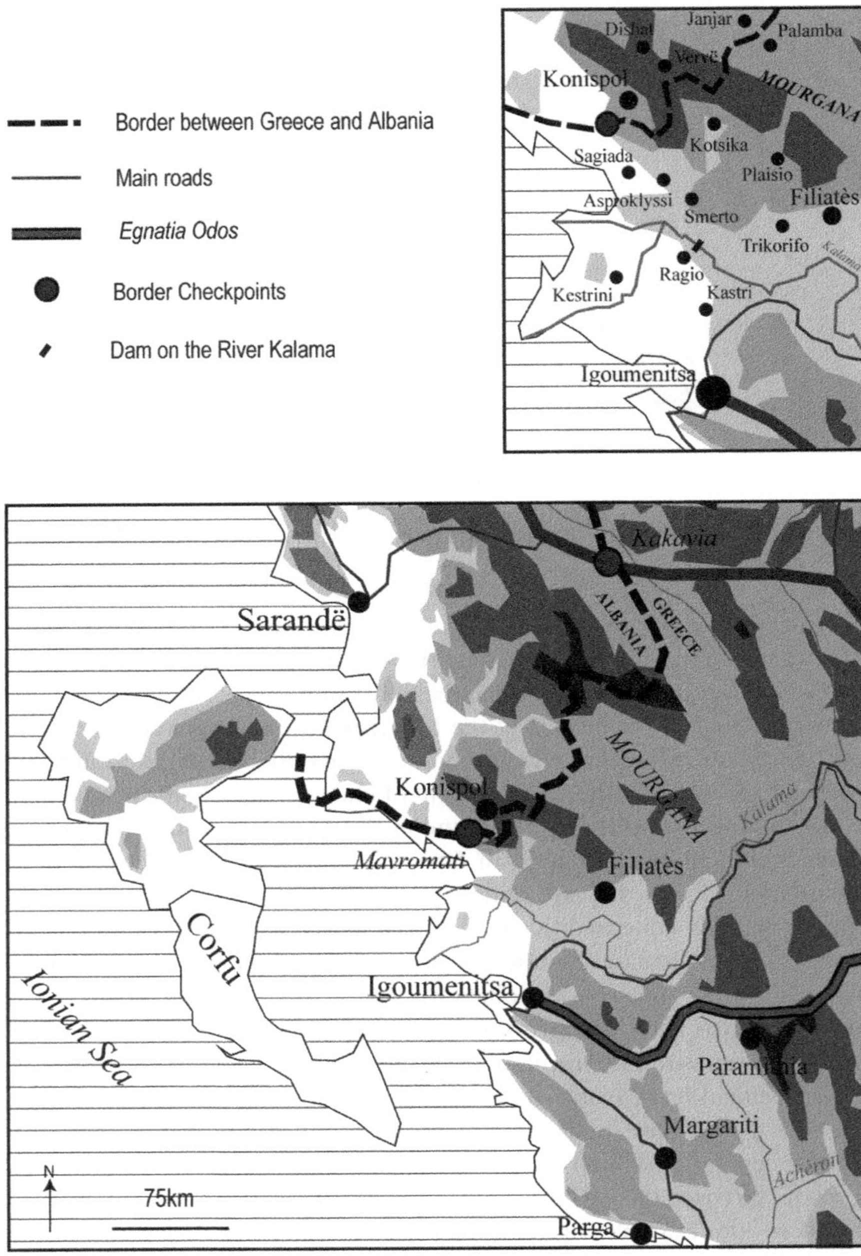

Figure 2.6 Study area in the north of Thesprotia: location of places cited in the text

villages of Dishat, Janjar and Vervë, where the strength of the resistance movement held the Germans at bay. After their return in the winter of 1943, they were confronted by the final vestiges of the war and the beginnings of the civil war. A 'visit' by partisans to forcibly recruit young men from the village in January 1948 forced the inhabitants to flee to the coast to seek refuge. However, the authorities sent them to the island of Corfu, from where they did not return until the very early 1950s (between 1952 and 1953) when they constructed the new village of Sagiada between the plain and the coast (Tsogas 2009). Through these different movements, the main elements governing such relocations, characteristic of these marginal situations, are readily apparent – both the violence that drove the people from their village of origin, and the state's intervention, seeking to prevent people from signing up or being forced to join the communist troops.

This concern to control through relocation can be found even more explicitly in the case of Asprokklisi, the neighbouring village to Sagiada. Here, many of the inhabitants, who had sometimes travelled from quite distant areas, were forced to settle shortly after the civil war, in order to limit the movements of groups that were still highly mobile up to the 1940s: for example, the *καλαντζήδες* (Kalantzidès*) of Mourgana (travelling tinsmiths), or the different groups of shepherds distinguished by their language (Greek-speaking Sarakatsani from Pindos and Vlachs from the neighbouring region of Pogon). These historical narratives concerned many regions of Greece in the same period and stemmed from the pro-active efforts of the authorities to encourage greater stability for the highland populations and to keep them away from the areas of conflict where they might provide assistance to the democratic army. This also demonstrated the intention of the authorities to nationalise border areas, and to ensure the stability of those populations perceived to be loyal to the Greek state. This latter quality did not, however, prevent the authorities from implementing a strict system of surveillance: for instance, as elsewhere on the Greek border, an exclusive buffer zone (*παραμεθόριες περιοχές*) was established which remained under special administration until the 1990s as a result of the area's close proximity to Albania. The relocations and regroupings of the populations in the area meant that the people went through different phases, from the precarious to the spontaneous, from the construction of permanent housing to the planned occupation of the surrounding space. The domestication of this new territory occurred mostly through a development project in which progress seemed to be the driving force. In Sagiada, those returning from Corfu in the early 1950s initially settled in thatched huts (*καλύβια*) on the beach, with no running water and surrounded by animals. The state then undertook the establishment of a settlement in these low-lying areas, with the construction of twelve houses made up of four two-roomed apartments, each on two floors, in which around fifty families would live, and which became the first neighbourhood in Sagiada, known as the 'kernal'. Following this, roads were built, water and electricity were supplied, and it was this, as well as the fear of insecurity that prevailed in the region, that persuaded the Sagiadinis to not return to the old village: 'What would we have done up there? It was here in the new village that we had the most comfort because the state had installed the electricity and water that were missing in the old village'. And this is truly what drove the ten families who had returned to live in the ruins of the old village to come back down to this new location.

Nevertheless, the lifestyle was quite spartan in the newly built and somewhat cramped apartments in the heart of the new village and in the surrounding areas; those who could not get an apartment continued living in huts until the 1960s. With the development of cash crops (first rice and then mandarin oranges) in the following decade, permanent houses were the order of the day. In the fertile plains surrounding the village, the state again instigated the expansion of the new village of Sagiada by constructing a dam on the Kalama River in 1962. This work enabled the fields of the plain to become more fertile and the agricultural land to be divided up among the inhabitants, through the drawing of lots according to the number of people in each family. The land was allocated both to the communities that had relocated to the new villages of Sagiada and Asprokklisi and to those who were present before the wars, such as sharecropping tenants from Kestrini, Smerto and Ragio. More generally, this type of project clearly affirms the benefits of modernisation through rationalisation. An office was opened to address the issues of irrigation and drainage (the TOAEB: *Τοπίκος Οργανισμός Εγγείων Βελτιώσεων*) crucial for management practices which imposed the economic development of the plain. The final act was to progressively open up the region through the development of a network of roads leading to the nearest towns. These coastal areas, which were once mainly linked to Corfu and from where seasonal agricultural workers mostly came, found themselves, as it were, once more attached not only to the continent but, in particular, to the whole of the national territory thanks to the installation of the dam, for the Kalama River had previously been a real obstacle.

However, local interpretations by the current residents of the area, when speaking of the transformations that occurred, are not about the great modernisation of the plain in the postwar period, but are more frequently based on the resolution of the sharp disagreements that had divided society between the two wars. The redistribution of land on the plain in the 1960s is often presented as the action which finally allowed the Greeks to recover the property they had lost during the Ottoman period, seized by Muslim groups – entirely Albanian-speaking – who were referred to locally as *Τούρκοι*, *Τσάμηδες*, *Αλβανοτσάμηδες* or *Τούρκοτσάμηδες* (Baltisiotis and Embirikos

2007). The Muslim population mostly lived in the villages of Smerto, Kotsika and Liopsi on the Kalama Plain, the majority of whose fertile land was owned by *Agas* ('landlords' in Turkish) and entrusted to their orthodox sharecroppers from Ragio (whose former name was Tchiflik meaning 'domain' in Turkish), Kestrini and Smerto. Thus, the villagers of Sagiada were either relegated to livestock farming and fishing, or were employed on a daily basis on the plain, in the fields or at the port. During the war, these Muslim landowners were accused of siding with the Italians and Germans in an attempt to regain the dominant position that they had started losing due to the annexation of the region to Greece in 1913 (Manta 2004; Margaritis 2005). Such positioning was fatal to them because, like all Muslims in this region of Thesprotia, they had been driven out by the nationalist Napoleon Zervas forces, or at least would have left after learning about the acts of violence committed against their co-religionists in the towns of Filiates and Paramithia (Meyer 2007; Péchoux 2002; Péchoux and Sivignon 1989). The area is therefore spoken of as having been re-conquered by Greekness after the Ottoman period and especially after the eviction of these Cham Muslims in 1945. Moreover, the way the relationships between the different groups are presented confirms this version of local history. Muslims are often identified as *Τούρκοι* (Turks) in terms of their religious practices which connected them to Ottoman rule; in a similar context, the Orthodox population (whatever their vernacular language) are usually called *Έλληνες* (Greeks). Hence, in the narratives of the inhabitants of both Sagiada and Asprokklisi, these Muslims always appeared to represent a bygone era, almost an anachronistic legacy of Ottoman rule, and whose disappearance went hand-in-hand with the emancipation of the Greeks and the release of the land from their menacing presence.

Table 2.3 Albanian-speaking groups in Epirus in the 1940 and 1951 Greek censuses

	Orthodox		Muslims		TOTAL
	No.	%	No.	%	No.
1940	32,712	65	16,890	25	49,632
1951	22,207	98	487	2	22,736

Source: National Statistical Service of Greece

Many sources attest to the blood shed throughout the region as a whole by the violence between communities, of which there were many victims, especially between 1942 and 1945. Publications in Greece by witnesses, activists, improvised historians and university academics attribute different orders of magnitude to these events when recounting them. All agree, however, on one and the same version of this historical narrative. Muslims in the region lined up behind the forces of occupation, even going as far as donning their uniform. They committed atrocities against the Christian population in preparation for the hoped-for annexation of the area of Çamëria/Τσαμουριά, the current Thesprotia, to Albania. Some authors even went so far as to draw up an exhaustive list of victims, as was the case in Giorgos Sarra's work (2001), *Μνημες της τραγικης Περιοδου 1936–1945*, which states that, in the Igoumenitsa diocese alone, more than 80 people were assassinated by the Chams during this period. His book provides the most detailed circumstances of these murders, derived from narratives collected in the field. Without going into such detail on this subject owing to the fragility of the sources, the historian Eleftheria Manta (2004: 137), using Italian and especially Greek diplomatic archival data, describes in her monograph the humiliations and uncertainties that presided over the lives of the people at that time and gives an unbiased account of the destruction and abuses that occurred during the period of occupation in Thesprotia.

However, these narratives of the past are today rendered more complex by the migration that has traversed the region since 1990. The existence of this original socio-historical background may indeed give it a particular dimension (Kretsi 2002). For instance, as noted for other borderland areas (Sintès 2008b), the Vlachs of Asprokklisi, settled on the plain by the authorities in the 1950s, were able to reunite, when the border re-opened in 1990, with relatives and friends who had remained in Albania after the war. These latter, on deciding to migrate to Greece, were quick to reactivate the family connection, which facilitated their migration (as explained above). But the originality here is the way in which migration or 'life at the border society' could also be shaped by the former coexistence of the different communities during the interwar period. This is how the traditional good relations between the Sagiadinis and the Konispoliotes took on a new footing from 1990 on. It is even said that, in the early days of this migration, when the Greek police tried to expel the illegal migrants, the people of Sagiada intervened, demanding that the migrants, who originated from Konispol, be left alone in the name of a sometimes uniquely proverbial friendship between the Sagiadinis and Konispoliotes dating back to the interwar period. Still today, in addition to the numerous agricultural workers who cross the border daily to work on the Greek side throughout the year, the winter period of intense work in the mandarin fields sees most people of working age arriving from Konispol. With the trust they have traditionally received, they cross the border and work for the day on the plain without any control or difficulty.

The oldest among the population bore witness to the close and mutually sustaining relationships which united the members of the different religious or linguistic communities situated today on each side of the border, even if the conflictual dimension of the relationship remained dominant in their minds due to the tensions of the previous period. It is true that, since 1990, the new relationships between the citizens of the two countries have mainly revolved around the migration of Albanians to Greece, as well as around leisure trips for Greeks going to Albania, such as the package tours organised by the municipal authorities for the KAPI (a care centre for the elderly or *Κέντρο Ανοιχτής Προστασίας Ηλικιωμένων*) of Sagiada in the 2000s and 2010s. The reasons for these links are varied: family relationships dating back to the period of intermarriages prior to 1945; cultural relationships between linguistic or religious communities; and memories of old neighbourhood relationships disrupted by the conflict. However, the new cross-border links are also the consequence of old interpersonal relationships. Thus, the older generation used to socialise across ethnic boundaries, as did, for example, this octogenarian woman from Sagiada who, when the border opened in 1990, met up again with her parents' Albanian Muslim shepherd, who had been driven from/had left the neighbouring village in 1944. They kept in touch and visited each other regularly, supporting each other through the trials of life, like the death of their spouse, up until the shepherd himself passed away in 2010.

> This kind octogenarian told me how she had so enjoyed going to Albania since 1990: 'You know, I had friends on the other side of the border, an old man of my age who died this year. We met when we were young. He was 16 and was my parents' shepherd. We have always been friends. He came from the "Turkish" village next to ours and my father took him on as a shepherd. He fled after the war, when the people of our village went to burn down his village. They took everything they could but I only took two hens.' When they found each other after 1990, she said to him, 'The two hens I took from you, my friend, will be replaced a hundredfold.' The first time, he came on horseback through the mountains. He found his friends again, even though he had not seen or contacted them since the 1940s. 'My husband took him to the store and gave him everything he could, everything that the horse could carry back to Albania. Since that time we saw each other constantly. He came to visit us and we went to Albania. His house consisted of two small rooms and a lounge with a fireplace. He had taken nothing from his former village in Greece when he fled. He was only a shepherd and had a very simple life. After 1990, we saw each other every Easter. Initially he would come over here, but later we

> had to meet up at the border as he did not have the papers he needed to cross into Greece. I always prepared some *κουλουράκια* (brioches), *γλυκά* (sweets) and lots of clothes for him at Easter, and he brought us a lamb. We used to call each other and meet up at the border crossing-point to pass on to his children clothes that our children no longer wore. He could no longer come here for lack of papers. In 2002, my husband died. My friend found out about it and came over. Anyway, he stayed all night long with his forehead resting on his friend, crying while softly speaking words in Albanian to him. He took part in all aspects of the funeral even though he was "Turkish". He went to the church and sat down with us at the meal that is prepared for the dead.' From then on until he died in 2010, they met at the border crossing-point twice a year: at Christmas and Easter. Once a border guard asked him: 'Do you want us to let you pass and take you to your old village so you can see your house again?'. He replied that he did not: 'The past is the past. I do not want to have a heart attack. Now only stones remain, nothing else (*πέτρες να μείνουν*)! Let me just see this lady. I ate bread in her house for several years and we "Turks" do not forget when we eat bread in another's house.'

The renewal of these links between the inhabitants contrasts somewhat with the reality of the formal relationships that have been developing since 1990, albeit with difficulty. Even though the two countries have joined forces within the framework of various cross-border programmes, especially the UE Instrument for Pre-Accession Assistance that incorporates the INTERREG and CARDS programmes on both sides of the border, it seems that the only relationships to have prospered on the Western side of the border were often established by the central services of the two capitals or, indeed, even by neighbouring Italy, as was confirmed by the Deputy Commissioner of Thesprotia during an interview conducted in July 2010:

> Many international relationships are established through relations with Italy, through INTERREG and ESPA. There are links with Albania through, for example, the construction of the road connecting Saranda to Konispol, which is extremely important for our region. But the only relationships that we have been able to develop locally with the Albanian authorities are mainly through the INTERREG programme that is being conducted with Italy, thanks to our close links to Brindisi and Bari in Puglia.

Even the only programme uniting the two countries, made public through the INTERREG website, links the municipalities of Saranda and Paleokastritsa

... on the island of Corfu, confirming how hard it is to maintain a peaceful relationship between the two authorities in this region, whose history is marked by the conflict of the recent past.

Landscape and places: relating the conflict or 'silencing the past'?

The social appropriation of space through the identification or the location of landmarks was studied in the regions still struggling with recent conflict, as, for instance, in the Balkans in Bosnia-Herzegovina and Kosovo during the 1990s and 2000s. These studies, conducted by researchers in social and cultural geography, showed how antagonistic territorialisation processes can produce a specific labelling of space. In particular, Bénédicte Tratnjek puts forward two somewhat meaningful processes in the case of Mitrovica in Kosovo: (1) the 'memoricide', which is the voluntary erasure of all the monuments and signs that recall the presence of the enemy in urban space, and (2) the construction of 'monuments of hatred', which are intended to retain the memory of an antagonistic past in the present (Tratnjek 2014). Without necessarily adhering to this no doubt too-radical terminology, it might be interesting to see how, in the context of a long-disputed but now peaceful border, this national hostility can be expressed and reproduced (but also transmitted and imposed) through an explicit display of landmarks designating the appropriation of places. During World War II, the villages in Thesprotia were barely spared the fighting that visibly raged from the Italian offensive of October 1940 until the end of the civil war in 1949.

Besides the ruined and abandoned villages found in the region, there are also many signs referring to the violent events that occurred in the 1940s. As elsewhere, the memorials honour the victims who 'died for the homeland' (*για την πατρίδα*) in Sagiada, or written in rather pompous 'pure Greek' (*υπέρ δε της πατρίδος*) in Kastri, or more simply for the 'those who fought in the war' (1940–1949) in the military section of the Filiates Cemetery. The description of the cause of death does not always have the same degree of accuracy. For example, a short explanation is inscribed on the monument in front of the church in old Sagiada for those who had died as 'victims of the German occupation' (*θύματα της Γερμανικής κατοχής*) and on the monument in memory of the hostages executed in the village of Palamba who had fallen victim 'to the communist army forces manipulated from abroad' (*εναντιων των ξενοκινητων ενοπλων κομμουνιστικων δυναμεών*). Nevertheless, in addition to these 'generic' memorials, or at least those conforming to the memorials that are generally found in all war-affected Greek spaces, more original monuments can be found in this region which can only be understood with a more precise knowledge of local history.

They were built at the scene of the crime – at crossroads or by the roadside – or in symbolic places such as the peribolos or outer wall of a church in Kestrini or in front of the state building where the victim served – for example, the old Igoumenitsa prefecture. These stelae were inscribed with the names of the dead, often their age and sometimes their nickname. The major peculiarity comes from the fact that these people are not presented as having been killed by the regular armies of the occupying powers (Italy and Germany), nor by the enemies of the civil war, but rather by hostile neighbours. These aggressors are clearly identified in more or less explicit terms on these monuments: they are often *Αλλόθρησκοι* (people of another religion, i.e. non-Christian, for the stelae often bear a cross) or *Αλβανοτσάμηδες* (Alvano-Tchams) or *Αλβανοί* (Albanians). Therefore, this terminology invariably identifies the murderers as Albanians Muslims, the so-called Chams, who lived in the region until 1945.

The memory of these crimes is ever-present in the minds of the different generations of villagers and they are still able to describe them without difficulty, and in great detail, often revealing the circumstances of the murders and the identity of the murderers. A learned local resident from Sagiada calmly explained: 'During the war, after the Italian offensive, but especially during the German occupation, the main leaders of the Muslim villages in the region, former landowners whose advantages had been threatened by the union with Greece in 1913, engaged in acts of revenge against the Christian populations'. Carried away by strong passions and bitterness, other testimonies recount horrific crimes – inexcusable in the eyes of those who tell them: 'My uncle was killed by gunshot while outside his house. His body was dragged by a horse around the village before being thrown into the Kalama River' (in Smerto) or 'Muslims raped a young girl in the village (Ragio) and then killed her'. And again, 'I lost my father during that period. It was a "Turc" named Hassan D* who came from the neighbouring village, and beat him and threw him into the river with his hands tied. His name is now inscribed on the monument in front of the church' (in Kestrini). These different testimonies reveal how this memory remains permanently etched in the minds of the people and, in the latter case, the to-ing and fro-ing that went on between the memorial stela and the permanence of this memory.

Compared to the more formal monuments erected in public places and in the cemeteries, commemorating the victims of various conflicts, these small stelae which mention the specific violence perpetrated by the Muslim Chams therefore recount their own local history. Firstly, they recall the ravaged memories of families affected by the killings, and some of these elements make them seem like private monuments: they show signs of closeness to the deceased, such as the names of the orphans left behind or

Figure 2.7 Monuments commemorating the victims of conflicts (1940–1949)
above The Palamba Monument in memory of the hostages executed in 1947
right The Military Cemetery of Filiates 1940–1949

even the mention of the nickname used in their lifetime. Sometimes the names of the stele's patrons are found on its base, clearly confirming the family origin behind the initiative. Such characteristics make them resemble the private chapels or small roadside memorials to commemorate the death of a person in a car accident. However, by their presence and the details they give on the murder, these monuments also seem destined to carry a message beyond the mere family circle of the victim. Undoubtedly, if private emotions are invested in these places, they also become a support for more collective memories that clearly refer to a sacrifice plunging into mourning the entire community, targeted by these acts in the name of religion or nationality. Hence, these stelae can also be seen as the material component of the oral testimonies mentioned above which, explicitly identifying the murderers (which official monuments only very rarely do), also reveal to the beholder a political message (in the broader sense of the term) about these past events.

At state level, in remembrance of the atrocities of a group closely associated with neighbouring Albania (for example the *Alvanotchamidès* or *Αλβανοτσάμηδες*), these monuments designate Albanians as enemies of the Greek Orthodox population and bear witness to the state of war between the two countries which was only partially lifted in 1987, and feeding the current rancour of past violence. On a regional level, they also explain the reasons for the disappearance of the Muslim populations from Thesprotia after the Second World War. The killers would certainly have feared retaliation, but they would also have had to answer to these numerous crimes, which is why they would have chosen to leave. Moreover, the murders that the Muslims from Thesprotia were found guilty of would now negate their entitlement to the land and oblige them to forego any claim to Thesprotia owing to their many crimes. This argument is found, for example, on the Radio Igoumenitsa blog in a note dated 21 June 2011 which details the names and number of victims of this violence, and which is unambiguously entitled: *Να γιάτι δεν έχουν δικαιόματα στην Θεσπρωτία οι Τσάμηδες* ('This is why the Chams have no rights in Thesprotia'). This opinion echoes that of the inhabitants of the places where the murders were identified: 'Now, they (the Chams) are back there in Albania and they cry that they want to come back here, but if they hadn't stolen and killed so much, they could have come back' (Sagiada), or 'It's better that the Muslims have gone, because religion always poses problems, as we saw in Cyprus' (Filiates). Thus, the murders committed by Muslims during the war period are therefore regularly used in opposition to the threat of an Albanian claim on the coastal regions of Epirus. More than the transmission of a tragic memory, the underlying message on these stelae is projected into the present (or indeed the future) to counter the supposedly hostile intentions of Greece's Albanian neighbours.

Figure 2.8 Memorials dedicated to the victims of intercommunity violence of the 1940s *clockwise from top left:* Kastri, Kestrini, Mavromati (border)

These small monuments are, somehow, the ramparts that are supposed to help to protect the region against them.

Such a hypothesis would be further enhanced by another persuasive factor. Effectively, if the war memorials in the villages and cemeteries all seem to have been built during the postwar period, those that commemorate the victims of violence perpetrated by the Chams are, in all evidence, much more recent. Some even bear the dates of their construction in the 1990s and 2000s, and this originality raises further questions about the function of such monuments, for the period in which they were built was marked by the strength of the migration flows described above. Moreover, owing to the relatively flat landscape, this coastal section of the border was greatly troubled by the Albanian migrants' clandestine crossings after 1990. The villages on the Kalama Plain were the first destination for these migrants, who then either made their road for the bus station at Igoumenitsa, from where they continued their journey to other cities in Greece, or stayed in the area for a short time and worked in the fields. Alongside these workers, there are also testimonies recounting the arrival of Cham descendants curious to see where their families originated from, or who wanted to use the information provided by their parents or grandparents in their quest to succeed in their migration project (directions for the best routes to take, names of eventual acquaintances who could accommodate them etc.). These visits to the ghost-villages of this border region even seem to have become, in recent decades, a striking feature. Greek inhabitants speak easily about the Chams' visits to find their ancestral home, even recounting the exchanges they had with them… but also express the anxiety that these visitors cause them.

> Christos is from the village of Sagiada. His parents and grandparents were born there, as were the previous generations. They even owned land, whereas people like him (Orthodox) usually worked for the wealthy Muslim owners, up until Greece's annexation of the region in 1913, and World War II, when they were evicted. Yet, in the early 1990s, two young 'Turkish-Chams' from Albania came across him while he was in his field and said to him: 'This field is ours.' 'I replied: 'You are mistaken, it has belonged to my family for several generations; to my father and my grandfather before him. The village at the top is yours, but not this field.' He continued:
>
> 'All this still shows a certain frame of mind … they think that everything here is theirs! Is it a big or a small problem? I do not know … it's a big problem in my opinion. And yet it's true that they had more assets than us here. But why did they have them? How did they get hold of them? It was not the result of their own work. They did

> not have them because they worked hard like us. We, who have been here for so many years, what are we going to say them? Come and take everything! Take the fields! Even if they were a minority here, they still had the best fields. This is not normal. They say they were driven out but it is also because they were afraid of what they had done to us. Of course, they could not have stayed because relations between us had significantly deteriorated during the war.'

So what better way to affirm the Greekness of this disputed region when faced by these visitors from Albania than by reminding them of the antagonism and conflict that took place here between the Greeks and the Albanians? One of these stelae has even been placed directly on the border between the two customs posts. It welcomes, so to speak, Albanian migrants at the moment of their entry into Greece, while reminding them of the sacrifices that the Greeks made to guard against Albanian irredentism. As regards the other stelae listed in Thesprotia, they all face towards Albania – to where the alleged killers had fled … but from where the migrants also come today.

Finally, there is one further theoretical hypothesis to consider: that the messages of such monuments are also directed towards the inhabitants of the places themselves, to remind them of their common belonging. It is true that a detailed description of the society of these border regions has already revealed the highly heterogeneous nature of the people settled there since the Second World War, and this diversity could also be identified as one of the factors presiding over the spatial markers evoked here. Moreover, until recently, the different groups – both indigenous and placed by the authorities after the war – established very closed and endogamous social entities where 'Each remained in their own group' (or '*ο καθένας στο σόι του*', as heard in Asprokklisi). These inhabitants (Aromanians, Arvanites, Gypsies, Grekis), even if all are Christian Orthodox and have no hesitation in associating themselves with Greek national identity, do not necessarily speak Modern Greek at home. These monuments reminding the inhabitants of the crimes committed in the past by Muslims enables them to distance themselves once and for all from the Albanians, while also strengthening the links that bind them as co-residents of the same place. Anyone thus reading the inscriptions on these monuments will be immediately aware of the strong character of the message conveyed, establishing in his mind the difference that separates him from the murderers and the ties that bind him to the victims. Hence, these stelae are involved in a dual movement of fixed identity assignment, by default national, whereas the reality in the region is that it is more unstable, particularly since, after the border was re-opened in 1990, and old relationships, as described above, were renewed, language and ethnic barriers have once again become an issue.

These commemorative memorials are, in themselves, markers of national territory, whose purpose is both to establish 'spaces of memory' (*lieux de mémoire*) and turn the whole of Thesprotia into a *région de mémoire*, a testament to all that its inhabitants had endured in their fight for Greekness. In addition, it seems that two other notable functions can be attributed to these monuments: both to show the Albanian migrants of the 1990s just how Greek the region is through the commemoration of the Greek dead, and to remind the locals of a tragic history that saw them as the victims of intolerable violence, thereby strengthening their sense of belonging to the Greek nation. These functions notwithstanding, these monuments also clearly offer an unequivocal perception of the history of the places in which they were built. Conversely, it is striking to note that, today, the localities of Thesprotia, reputed for once having been important centres for Muslim communities, no longer bear any traces or monuments recalling them. The 'memoricide' that Bénédicte Tratnjek mentioned is now barely visible on the stelae, which collectively designate them as murderers. The same goes for all the Cham villages – abandoned since the departure of their inhabitants in 1944–45 – which can be found on old maps and whose ruins are visible in the landscape, but which are, nevertheless, completely non-existent on road signs and more recent maps. For example, although the old Orthodox village of Sagiada is indicated by an improvised sign, the abandoned Muslim villages nearby are not. Other villages, while still inhabited, have been renamed using only Greek-sounding names. As the bookseller from the small town of Paramithia, located further south, willingly told me, if 'the victor writes the history', he will also obviously write the names of the places and select the events that he feels should be remembered. To find a different version of this narrative, it is necessary to cross the border into Albania. Just a few kilometres away, in the main square of the small Albanian town of Konispol, stands another monument, built in the 1990s. It has no name but bears only the inscription *Memoriali i kushtohet martirizimit te shqiptareve te çamerise prej gjenocidit te shovinizmit grek* (memorial dedicated to Albanian martyrs from Chamerie whose genocide was perpetrated by Greek chauvinism). Unlike the stelae described on the Greek side, this monument commemorates all anonymous victims – those of the 'Cham genocide', which is how it has officially been recognised by the Albanian state since 1994. Nonetheless, owing to its presence in the last Albanian town before the border, it also serves as a milestone, activating the representation of a space traversed by a front line. The decorations that flank it also tell stories of the victims. For instance, stylisation of a tradition feminine headdress, characteristic of the Chams and perched on top of the momument, or the depiction of a woman lying next to her children in bas-relief, retelling the stories of murdered women which regularly appear in the descriptions of the massacres of the Cham Muslim populations in 1944–45 (Kretsi 2007). This monument goes hand-in-hand with the introduction of a day of remembrance of the Cham cause which takes place every year in Albania on 27 June. It conveys a message which contradicts that which is visible throughout the neighbouring region on the Greek side of the border and leaves little doubt about the transmission of a still-disputed memory.

A never-ending fragmentation?

Yet within this way of presenting historical reality is hidden a great diversity of 'belonging', evident in the notable ambiguity that sometimes puts in an appearance in the definition of terms which people use to define themselves. For example, Lambros Baltsiotis and Leonidas Embirikos (2007) have shown how the label 'Cham' could, in this context, be highly significant, as it is used to designate sometimes quite diverse realities. In the same vein, the recent adoption of the label 'Arvanite' (rather than Cham) to indicate Albanian-speakers still living in Thesprotia today effectively neutralises the question of linguistic 'otherness', which then ceases to be a transnational issue and becomes one which is internal to contemporary Greece. The Albanian-speaking group in Thesprotia thus finds itself split into two, due to these distinctive labels. On one hand there are the 'Arvanites' (understood as Orthodox Albanian-speakers), who consider themselves to be of Greek national consciousness, as did the Arvanites of 'old Greece' illustrated in the preceding section; on the other are the 'Turco-Chams' or 'Alvano-Chams', understood to be Albanian Muslims historically linked to the building of the Albanian nation – is it not said that they were 'sent home' during the Second World War? Adopting this terminology also enables the Albanian-speaking Greek citizens still present in the region to clearly differentiate themselves from Albania by deactivating all links between a potential Albanian irredentism and their presence in Thesprotia.

In the field, this separation is reinforced once again by the radicalism of the narratives encapsulated on the memorials. For example, on the stela in Kestrini, a *'Αλλόθρησκος'*, (i.e. someone 'of another religion') is said to be responsible for the death of the person commemorated. The most explicit monument showing the identity of the killers is found in the village of Kastri, which cites the 'Turco-Cham assassins.' It is interesting to note that the two cases mentioned here, the two most explicit identity labelling of the murderers, were found in the villages where many Albanian-speakers still live, confirming that these monuments are part of a desire to distinguish between language difference and national affiliation. This 'exit strategy' was designed to differentiate between these Albanian-speaking Orthodox groups, who still reside in Thesprotia, and the 'Chams', understood here as Muslims hostile to Greekness. Yet we sometimes heard the term 'Cham' used in a more unexpected way which went far beyond the simple designation of the group of Albanian Muslims. In private, a Sagiadini (Greek-speaking Orthodox) might say that he was 'Chams' to indicate his regional affiliation... to Thesprotia, a name given recently to an area that everyone here also knows by its other name... 'Chamouria.' These different names, which are best not used in just any circumstance, appear to be accepted sometimes as endonyms by all the inhabitants of the region. This flexibility of place names and linguistic, religious and regional affiliations are of great interest, for they act as spatial markers, embedding paradoxical mechanisms within that highlight the discrepancies between the plural reality of a border society and the nation-state discourse on the country's past.

In the same way today, on different occasions, the inhabitants of the area have sometimes made their feelings heard, as when attempting to establish a person's legal right to own land on the plain which s/he was granted in the 1950s and 1960s. This is how the Sagiadinis are able to justify their former presence and perfect fidelity to the canons of Greekness – they are Orthodox Christians and genuine Greek-speakers, thereby designated by the other inhabitants as being totally *Greki*. The inhabitants of Smerto and Kestrini, descendants of local sharecroppers, sometimes formerly came from the nearby villages of Agios Vlasios or of Kastri, near Igoumenitsa, are known in the region for speaking an Albanian dialect known as *Arvanitika* or *Alvanika* (depending on the context, as we have already seen) while remaining Orthodox. Although this enables them to be introduced as *Hellinès* (i.e. Greeks), some of them are more often than not identified by their skin colour: *mavri* (black) or *guifti* (gypsies), thus giving them a rather revealing ethnonym for their supposed origins (Egypt, according to some). Moreover, the current inhabitants of Asprokklisi, on the ancient lands of the ghost-village of Liopsi, the ruins of which are visible from the road that leads to the border-crossing at Mavromati, are split into three distinct groups: the *Grekis*, who came from a village also called Asprokklissi in the Mourgana Mountains and who had been displaced during the civil war, the Vlachs, who were accustomed to spending winter on the lands they rented from the *Agas* of Liopsi, and the Sarakatsani, whose transhumant lands were located relatively far from coastal Thesprotia (Grevena and central Thessaly), but who the Greek government had decided to settle in the region. These issues of land redistribution, restructuration of farming areas and repopulation therefore made it possible to hold discussions with the different groups that made up the society in this border area. Nevertheless, other lines of fracture still traversed this society, albeit discreetly – such as those that were activated during the Civil War – even if my interviews often showed that these divisions could also adapt to existing lifestyle situations by opposing sedentarists and transhumants, mountain communities and those from the plains, etc ... oppositions that can today be heard... between supporters of the Olympiakos football team and those of Panathinaikos.

This detailed account once again illustrates how much life for the people in this small border area still remains fragmented into different groups whose historical constitution is rooted in memory. Despite more than fifty years of living together in these villages and the rapid growth in mixed marriages, the distinction remains. This situation was not helped by the Albanian migration flows which, since the 1990s, have no doubt served to accentuate these differences by reviving the issues of cross-border relationships and their conflicting memories. Indeed, despite the wide variety of narratives that are proposed, it is hard to deny that the positioning of the inhabitants on the Thesprotian ethnic chessboard generates different attitudes *vis-à-vis* the Albanian migrants. Some residents expressed a feeling of closeness to those Albanian migrants who descended from Chams who left the area after the war, indicating that one day, with the Greek economic crisis, it was not inconceivable that they, the current residents, would turn to these Albanians to help to them find work ... in Albania. Without being able to affirm that migration is the sole cause of the (re)fragmentation of local Thesprotian society, we can see that it can take on this role in relation to certain discourses or cross-border practices.

Yet, at the beginning of the 2010s, during my fieldwork, new geopolitical concerns seemed to hit the region. In effect, the fragmentary movement had also visibly affected Albanian society and, after several decades spent in Albania, the Chams' descendants started, once again, to make their voices heard on the other side of the border. The historical plight and the expelling of the Chams in 1944–45 were already perceived as an injustice in Albania, permanently marring relations between the two countries. According to some, the violence of the 1940s is even said to have wrenched a piece of 'Albanian land' from the country, and many are the activists who are today claiming that this Cham land of Chameria be 'returned' to the bosom of the motherland of Albania. These militants have even united within a political party, the PDIU (the Party for Justice, Integration and Unity), founded in 2011 and whose doctrines are today defended by the *Aleanca Kuq e Zi* (Red and Black Alliance), created by Kreshnik Spahiu in 2012. This latter called (among other things) for a referendum on the union of Kosovo and Albania, lobbying for an ethnic Albania that would stretch 'from Prishtina to Preveza'. The date officially recognised by the Albanian government – 27 June – as the anniversary of the 'genocide of the Chams', gave them the opportunity

Figure 2.9 Remembering Chameria in Albania
above 'Remember Chameria' (Tirana 2011)
below Konispol-Mavromati, 27 June 2011

to demonstrate in Tirana and other southern Albanian cities and to bring their vision of this chapter of Greek–Albanian history to the fore. In 2011, a march even took place near the Greek border and had to be stopped by the Albanian police as the activists headed for the border-crossing point of Mavromati. These stories of spoliation and reciprocal violence seem to have been partly revived by the migration of Albanian workers to Greece, which greatly affects this border region. Since the 2010s, the fear of seeing a new Albanian presence in the border regions of Greece also seems to be related to the strong political activity around this issue in Albania.

These different movements may, here and there, have influenced relations between the two states. Already in 2005, the President of the Greek Republic, Karolos Papoulias, had to abandon the idea of meeting his counterpart, Alfred Moisiu, in Saranda because of the hostile demonstrations by those demanding the reopening of the Cham dossier. More recently, the former Albanian Prime Minister Sali Berisha even declared, during the November 2012 centenary celebrations for the creation of Albania, that the country extended as far as Preveza, a town south of Igoumenitsa. This angered the Greek authorities, even though his office immediately rectified the statement by saying: 'The Prime Minister's words were intended to refer to the historical context of the Declaration of Independence. Today, Albania has no territorial claims whatsoever, whether in the neighbouring countries to the south, east or north'. Undoubtedly, within such a context, several factors must be examined: the migration that brought the Greeks and Albanians into contact again, and the economic crisis in Greece, which led to the return to Albania of many migrants, leaving them with a somewhat negative image of Greece. Finally, the role of movements that famously are a by-product of globalisation, like the primordialism mentioned at the beginning of this book, and which seem to favour, within social and political discourse, a return to a more radical ascription of identity that may stem from a sometimes contentious history.

* * *

So, it was within this new context that my investigations in the Thesprotian region were put on hold. The many questions I asked concerning my interviewees' cross-border experiences did not always leave them indifferent and some ended up avoiding me or refusing to respond to my requests. During my last survey in July and August 2011, two young men who, after having stopped my car on the side of a mountain road and politely asked me to spend the rest of the summer on the beach rather than to continue my visits to the border villages. My success was such that many strangers photographed me as soon as I arrived in public places. Judging that my presence should perhaps not interfere any longer in the very interesting processes in development for much longer, I considered it appropriate to thus suspend my study on the fragmentation of societies in the region for a while. To wait or to continue, that is the question.

Chapter 3

The Jewish community of Rhodes: a revitalised fragment of the Greek mosaic

The second study began on the island of Rhodes in 2006. Its objective was to study a different kind of mobility that affects the territories of Greece. Although featured in the media less prominently than international migration, this other form of mobility just as ably raises the issues which today link different global actors with the outlying Greek territories. We are talking here of the 'memory-based mobility' of the descendants of different communities (often minorities) – communities which have long since disappeared – a phenomenon also known as 'identity tourism' or even 'roots-tourism' (Legrand 2006). In this particular case, we are referring to the descendants of the Jewish population of Rhodes who come to the island in search of the places where their ancestors lived. Just as for Albanian migrants in other parts of Greece, the presence (albeit temporary) of this group in Rhodes provides an opportunity to consider the conditions in which this memory can be expressed – a memory that challenges the official version typically presented to tourists by, for example, tour guides and most of the museums to which they have access. As with some Albanian migrants, these visitors hold the key to an alternative version of the historical narrative of this place: their presence creates the possibility of revitalising dissonant elements of belonging or claiming their autochtony, which is, of course, one of the central tenets upon which the legitimacy of contemporary Greek society rests. The Dodecanese Archipelago to which Rhodes belongs is that much more susceptible to this type of examination because it was the last region to be amalgamated into the Greek national territory, because those who witnessed this unification are still living and because they could well become the heralds of these subversive frameworks of belonging, whilst quite legitimately presenting themselves as 'locals' or 'natives'.

In such a case we can see how a minority group, despite having disappeared almost entirely from the Greek context (and specifically, here, from the local one) can nevertheless, through relying heavily on its well-developed networking skills, still successfully and publicly express its vigorous spatial and temporal memory. Studying this phenomenon will enable us to examine the processes which today breathe new life into small groups – whether diasporic or transnational – who share a common identity, and which, above all, will enable them to continue with the transformation of places to which they still have a very strong emotional attachment, even if they rarely find themselves there. More generally, this example will finally allow us to illustrate the effects of globalisation on social spaces such as these, using the global 'production of locality' – an expression coined by Arjun Appadurai – which posits the contemporary interaction of widely diverse groups and logics of scale in one and the same place (Appadurai 1995).

Historic fragments of Aegean Andalusia

According to various sources, it appears that a Jewish community already populated the island of Rhodes even before King Ferdinand and Isabella the Catholic threw the Sephardic Jews out of Spain in 1492. Moïse Rahmani even goes back to King Herod's decision to give assistance to the city of Rhodes – as reported in Flavius Josèphe's *The War of the Jews* – as a means of establishing the existence of a Jewish community on the island during Antiquity (Rahmani 2000: 23). Nonetheless, it is possible that the Knights of the Order of St John discovered Jewish people on Rhodes when they arrived in 1309: when they built the city wall, in fact, they named the part of the wall that enclosed the eastern quarter of the fortress 'the Jewish wall'. From this period onwards, there was a community composed probably of Romaniote* Jews, in other words, of Greek-speaking Jews who lived in the zone of the current district of Evraïko. Later, it was two Italian travellers en route to the Holy Land (Meshullam de Volterra and Obadia de Bertinoro in, respectively, 1481 and 1488) who confirmed the presence of Jews on the island through their description of the town in their travel logs (Angel 1998). From the end of the fifteenth century, and despite an eviction edict drawn up in 1502 by Pierre d'Aubusson, the Grand Master of the Order of St John of Jerusalem, the profile of the community changed radically, as many Sephardic Jews from Spain arrived on the coast of Rhodes (Fintz-Menascé 1991: 8). They linked up not only with the Romaniots mentioned earlier but also with thousands of Jewish prisoners who were said to have been captured by the Knights of St John on the sea routes of the Mediterranean, as well as with the first Sephardics who arrived after the persecutions in Aragon in 1280 (Col. Rottiers, cited in Fintz-Menascé 1991: 157).

> When the Sephardim came to Rhodes after the Turkish conquest in 1523, they found a synagogue building already in existence (…). It had been built during the 1480s. Due either to an increased number of Jews or communal dissension, another congregation was formed by at least 1570. (…) The second congregation, Kahal Kadosh Shalom (Holy Congregation of Peace), built its own synagogue building no later than the end of 1577. In the courtyard of the synagogue, there still stands a water fountain, which was used to wash the hands of *cohanim* prior to their giving the priestly blessing. This fountain bears an inscription dated the month of Kislev, 5338 (1577). (Angel 1998: 114)

These settlements became even more numerous, however, after the Ottoman Conquest (1522) due to the status of *dhimmis* (a protective statute granted by Islam to faithful followers of the religions of the book) which was granted to the Jews in the Ottoman Empire. Throughout this long period, the Rodesli* community thrived in this way from the arrival of outside populations – as in 1523, when 150 of the richest families in Thessaloniki were exiled on Rhodes by order of the Sultan. The income of the community was then assured by concessions of sulphur and other products, thanks to the renting out of property that belonged to the community and, increasingly, from the sixteenth century onwards, through small businesses in crafts and the textile industry which livened up the workshops of the Jewish Quarter (Benbassa and Rodrigue 2002: 82). It is striking to note that, in the different texts emanating from the Rodesli community, the Ottoman Empire, which reigned over the island for 390 years, is often presented as a time of peace and tranquillity. This is also what the president of the community in 1933, Hizkia Franco, eloquently bore witness to in *La Boz de Orient*, a daily newspaper from Istanbul, when he had to describe to the Italians the authority that had preceded them:

> I believe I was following an obligation of my conscience when I affirmed that, generally speaking, the Turkish people, as well as the authorities, always treated the Jewish people with kindness. Their relations were always cordial. The Turk protected the Jew, considering him as someone with a deep attachment to the land. The proof is that the Jews and the Turks lived together inside the same fortress which surrounded the town, something which the Greeks were not permitted to do. (cited by Rahmani 2000: 30)

Throughout this period, and as the above text points out, the entire Jewish community settled in the present-day quarter of Evraïko, in the Eastern part of the old fortified medieval town. The authorities determined this location but this could also be interpreted in a favourable light in respect of the Jews, for the Greek population at that time was forbidden to be in this precinct of the town after sunset. At the end of the Ottoman period, the community even engaged in a meaningful process of social climbing, thanks to one important activity, in terms of school structure – the creation in 1899 of a school under the tutelage of the *Alliance Israelite Universelle* (UAI). This promoted the education of children and consequently embedded the practice of speaking French amongst the Jews on Rhodes. After the Treaty of Ouchy in 1912, which marked the end of the war between the Italians and the Ottoman Empire, the military occupation and annexation of the Dodecanese Archipelago by Italy gave the Jews a further opportunity to improve their lot and their influence (Pignataro 2011). The Italian government was counting on the support of the Jewish community of the Eastern Mediterranean in order to increase their influence in the region. From the earliest days, therefore, Italian replaced Turkish as the second language used in class by the Alliance, before all aspects of education were converted to Italian in 1925. This policy became apparent when the new authorities established a Rabbinical College in 1928. Thus it was that the Jewish community assured its wider reputation at this time, both in its immediate environment and in the area of its privileged relationships and matrimonial alliances: the communities of Asia Minor and Egypt. During this period, the island appeared completely focused on the Eastern Mediterranean basin, having very few relations with the Balkan Peninsula.

From the beginning of the twentieth century, however, the economic situation changed. If some if its members made a fortune and had the freedom to leave the old town and live in beautiful homes around the Italian-designed new port, others decided to try their luck by migrating. As usual, the young men left first, in search of new sources of income, intending to stay away only a short while. They maintained close relationships with their families and their place of birth, despite at times being separated by considerable distances. Little by little, these first migrants nevertheless ended up putting down roots, inciting often quite numerous family groups to follow in their wake. The United States, Africa and South America were the places in which they settled. In the US, New York was their first destination and, in 1912, they set up the *Agudat Achim* (i.e. the Rhodes 'League of Brothers'). The Rodesli also became established on the West Coast and in the south of the country. Family networks played a crucial role in determining these migrations.

We see this, for example, in the trajectory of one such person, Joseph Capeloto, who left Rhodes in 1907 at the age of 14 to join his brother-in-law in Seattle, via New York, and who, in 1909, was followed by his entire family (Hasson 1974). The reasons why these Rodesli were drawn to the New World in the first place are not well known. Moïse Rahmani cites the case of a certain Salomon Calvo who, by the end of the nineteenth century, was finally persuaded by a Greek fisherman from Rhodes who had settled in Seattle to join him and to remain there. But whatever name or history we give to these pioneers, further groups followed in sufficient numbers to Seattle for them to be able to establish, at the beginning of the twentieth century, their first institution (the *Kuppat Ozer Dalim* or social fund for the needy), with a view to helping other migrants from Rhodes to settle in the area. A little later, we find these Rodesli settlers in the towns along the West Coast, primarily those of Portland and Los Angeles (Hasson 1996). In this latter town, they united with the Jews from Thessaloniki, Alep and other lands of the Ottoman Empire to establish, in 1932, the congregation of *Tifereth Israel* and the first Sephardic synagogue in the town. In the first decade of the twentieth century, this same type of community developed in southern regions of the United States. This led in 1914 to the setting up of the congregation *Or VeShalom*, which is today still influential in the towns of Atlanta and Montgomery. Once again, these implantations were sustained by a stronger migratory flow from this region of the Mediterranean:

> As happened in Seattle, the first Sephardim from the Greek Peninsula to arrive in the South followed Greek Orthodox friends and townspeople to the 'America filled with gold.' They had heard stories from members of the Greek Orthodox community who had emigrated to the United States and returned to their home towns in the Ottoman Empire to visit their families. Cooperation and good relations between Rodesli and other Turkish Jewish and Greek Orthodox immigrants to the South continued throughout the twentieth century. (Kerem 1997: 374)

We can observe similar processes of dissemination of the Jewish community of Rhodes towards Africa, following hot on the trail of a certain Salomon Benatar, the first migrant to go ashore in Southern Africa. Having spent some time in Egypt, he arrived in Salisbury, Rhodesia, in 1885. The Benveniste and Alhadeff families wasted no time in following the Benatars and settling in Rhodesia with a view to setting up a business. They then established themselves in Elisabethville in the Belgian Congo (now Lubumbashi) as of its foundation in 1907. Their knowledge of the French language made it that much easier for them to develop contacts and, above all, legislation in the Belgian Congo was more open to the settlement of citizens from the Ottoman Empire than was that of the British crown. In 1930, the 60 or so families from Rhodes then living in Elisabethville founded the first Sephardic congregation of the colony, along with around 30 other families (Rosenthal 1963) and were instrumental in the foundation of one of the two synagogues in the town. They thus became one of the most significant Rhodian Jewish communities in the world, benefiting from the partial closure of the United States due to its quota policy (Benatar and Pimienta-Benatar 2000). During those same years, certain Rodesli also headed towards the Southern Cone of Latin America. Even if this was probably a migration by default of people wanting initially to go to the United States, there were soon enough of them to establish a community centre in 1914, once again with Jews from the Ottoman Empire, followed by, in 1923, a Sephardic Cultural Centre in the district of Colegiales in Buenos Aires. They christened it the Chalom Temple, after one of the synagogues in Rhodes. In time, this community spread out towards Montevideo and other surrounding towns.

Development of these far-off ramifications unfolded at a pace all the more sustained as the situation became difficult in Rhodes (Fintz-Menascé 1991: 205). Relations with the Italian government during the 1930s had become increasingly complex, due to the rapprochement between the fascist regime and Nazi Germany. The Italian racial laws of 1938 made things worse, as they obliged the Jews to open their shops on Saturdays, closed the Rabbinical College and excluded the children from school. Migrations increased in the wake of the first wave of migrants who had left for Africa, the United States or South America. Rodeslis also went to closer destinations where they had family connections, such as to Turkey and Egypt and, in some instances, to the British Mandate of Palestine. During this period, Juderia (i.e. the Jewish Quarter in Judeo-Spanish) emptied of a significant part of its population, and the number of Jews declined progressively from 5,000 to some 2,000 individuals. At the beginning of 1939, the island's Italian government even declared as *personae non gratae* those Jews who had become naturalised Italians after 1919 or those who had settled on the island after this date – coming mostly from the coasts of Asia Minor (Fintz-Menascé 1991: 272). These 'undesirables' thus made their way to Africa or America. By dint of this expulsion, they were in fact spared the tragic events that followed.

Effectively, after the Italian surrender, the island passed into German control. In July 1944, SS Officers came from Athens and ordered the deportation of all Jews living on the island. More than 1,600 people were deported to Poland. Fewer than 150–180 survived (Franco 1994; Picciotto-Fargion 1991). Some 42 Jews with Turkish citizenship were saved by the Turkish Consul in Rhodes, Selahettin Ulkman, who, in June 1990, was recognised as 'Righteous among the Nations.' This episode brought the story of the Jewish people living on the island to a close. Little by little, Christian Orthodox populations from surrounding villages or from some of the other islands of the Dodecanese moved from their district, fleeing the rigours of war and its aftermath. For many years, one sole survivor of the deportation lived with her husband in the old town of Rhodes. They were thus unique witnesses to the history of this community in the old quarter of Juderia.

Figure 3.1 The final remains of Jewish history on Rhodes: the Shalom Synagogue
right Tablet in memory of families deported in 1944
below Interior of the synagogue (August 2005)

A community of memory

Despite the disappearance of this Jewish presence from what appears to be its historical birthplace, the descendants of Jews from the island know how to maintain a strong sense of identity, based on an intense memory of their shared origins. They still define themselves as 'Rodesli' wherever they are in the world, demonstrating an undeniable solidarity and mutual recognition. This term Rodesli was defined by Renée Hirschon in her presentation of this group (Hirschon 2005: 925) as 'the Jewish inhabitants of the island of Rhodes and the original migrants, Rhodes (-origin) Jews, Sephardim. These are Sephardi Jews (Spanish-speaking) who settled on the Aegean island of Rhodes following their expulsion from Spain in 1492.' It is, in fact, the autonym currently used by the descendants of the Jews from Rhodes and it means 'Rhodian' in Turkish. In French, they call themselves, somewhat indifferently 'Rodesli' or 'Rhodiotes,' a name derived this time from the Greek. Today these individuals are dispersed across those regions to where their parents and grandparents migrated in the first half of the twentieth century, and in those places where their personal or collective journeys have since taken them. The example of Samuel and Esther, encountered in Rhodes in the summer of 2006, gives an eloquent insight into the relationships that unite them and the specific places which these people have established:

> Samuel and Esther were both born in the Congo about 60 years ago – Samuel's father worked in the textile industry and had gone there from Rhodes in the 1920s. He traded between Italy and Africa and married a girl from the Capellutto family whom he brought over from Rhodes in 1933. Samuel naturally took over his father's business in Elisabethville when he was old enough to work but, once Zaire proclaimed its independence in 1960, with the troubles and violent clashes that followed, he decided to leave for Argentina where his sister had married a distant cousin a few years earlier.
>
> After three years (and one marriage), he wanted to go back to Africa and settle there again but, by 1974, in the wake of the government's Zairianisation policy, he was once again forced to abandon his plans. Despite additional experience in Buenos Aires, he decided to resettle for good in South Africa – in Cape Town – where he found work alongside other Rodesli who had arrived before him. Some years later, in 1979, he was able to open his own company manufacturing sports bags. He had met Esther in the Congo, and she became his second wife, in Cape Town, few years later. She also had Rhodian parents. Esther's family were scattered in a similar way across the world (Brussels, Israel, Australia). Today, her children have all migrated to

> the United States because of the difficulty of finding work in South Africa. Her son in New York married 'one of our own: a Congolese woman from Cape Town, a true Rodesli!' Between themselves, Samuel and Esther increasingly speak in English but their 'first' language is French, which was the language their parents spoke. He is a Belgian citizen whereas she is Italian but they know very little about these two countries of which they are citizens.
>
> Since they retired, they have spent considerable time travelling, going to visit family. Almost every year, they travel to the United States, to Israel and Argentina ... and so, as they themselves admit: 'We are strangers now in Rhodes'.

Through this interview, Samuel and Esther seem worthy representatives of the descendants of the many Rodesli from the Congo, the majority of whom today live in South Africa or Brussels. The different places they mention are characterised by family relationships that neither distance nor time have diminished. Links with Rhodes are justified by effective discussion of the root causes of displacement, the reasons for maintaining contact with others, thus linking inherited memories with spatial practices. These different groups, although dispersed across the whole planet, form a network-space, a discontinuous territory with global dimensions that is frequented through mobility, to the point where some people see this 'natural' capacity for displacement as an essential aspect of their Rodesli identity. For example, this is what one young woman from Brussels said: 'My parents are used to being on the move. In their home in Brussels, they still haven't unpacked all the boxes that they brought from the Congo in the 1970s.'

This intermingling is created through the ties of friendship, cousinhood, family or marital connections, the maintenance of which is facilitated by the interweaving of these kinships which provide a strong sense of cohesiveness. Contact between the places is often in writing – to celebrate special occasions or family events. It is also maintained through visits whenever possible. These relationships are clearly strengthened through an awareness of a shared community of origin, and given backbone through an associational tradition, undoubtedly inherited in part from the philanthropic practices of Juderia. This 'community' has nonetheless remained fragmented into several distinct areas between which exchanges are less frequent: that of South Africa (to which we should add Belgium), the Americas and the diverse poles of the Mediterranean. Today this geography of the Rodesli community is affected by several new considerations. The first is the growing importance of Israel, which has attracted such considerable numbers of Rodesli that an association has been established, with its own newspaper. In addition, with the spread of the younger generation across a greater diversity of locations, and with marriage practices more likely to be exogamous, the Rodesli have suffered a further blow. This does not necessarily signal a weakening of their relationship with their family history, especially as crossing continents by plane and the existence of the Internet enable more frequent communication between people. The Internet, in particular, effectively ensures that these connections survive thanks to specialist websites and discussion groups dedicated to Rhodes and the Sephardic traditions of the island. Information technology and communication – for example through the creation of specialist websites and, recently, a discussion group on Facebook which has several hundred followers and a network on the family history research site Geni, which has a multitude of posts – have breathed new life into the kind of relationships that were previously nourished by more traditional methods such as newsletters or newspapers amongst the Sephardic communities to which the Rodesli Jews belonged (*'La Lettre sépharade'* or *'Los Muestros'*).

These relationships make it easier to maintain a narrative of memory in which the island of Rhodes plays the central part. A true paradise lost, in many of the interviews the island is presented as the origin of the community's roots, more so than Spain or the biblical land of Canaan – a metaphor adopted by Vittorio Alhadeff in the title of his autobiography *'Le Chêne de Rhodes'* (Alhadeff 1998). As a way of evoking the incredible gentleness of life within this community at that time, it was given the name 'Island of Roses' from which its current name derives in Greek. The exceptional nature of the area is highlighted: the climate, the colour of the Aegean Sea or of the sky, the wonderful produce grown there. Without questioning the historic reality of these narratives, concordant factors always depict life on Rhodes as idyllic. First of all, relationships within the community are always described as easy and brotherly: 'Everyone loves everyone else on Rhodes', a Holocaust survivor in Ashdod declared to me. Life during the Italian time, the numerous schools, the flourishing of some of the commercial or financial organisations and the opening of the Rabbinical College are the main sources of pride. The quality of life for the Jews in Rhodes was also maintained through the memory of a deep commitment to religious practice, to which the significant number of religious establishments bear witness: six synagogues, a Rabbinical College, several Yeshivots. The Jewish quarter of Rhodes was in fact nicknamed *Chica Yerushalaim* – Little Jerusalem – as a result of this strict religious practice. However religious the interviewee may be, respect for religious traditions such as the divine commandments seems to have been at the heart of their social life, and the Jews in Rhodes are remembered as very respectfull of its importance to family and community. In the eyes of the different witnesses or their descendants, and despite being one of the smaller communities in the Eastern Mediterranean, this group was still one of the most advanced in terms of religion or of community life. Adding to the group's inner calm, relations with the island's other religious communities, or at least with the Italians and the Turks, are also described as peaceful and respectful. The final testimony to this harmonious local life is always presented by fact that the *Sefer Torah* were saved from the hands of the Germans by being entrusted to the local Mufti, who hid them in the Mihrab of the Murat Reis Mosque until the end of the war.

The old town, enclosed by walls built by the Knights of the Order of St John, and more particularly Juderia, plays a significant role in this narrative. Amongst its emblematic spaces, the main square of the Jewish quarter or '*Kaï Ancha*' (the 'wide' street in Judezmo) is a place full of memories for the Rodeslis, a spatial cue for very real memories. Evoking the sweetness of life can quickly merge with the pain of remembrance and of a disappearance perceived as unjust and unjustifiable. The counterpoint of deportation reinforces the nostalgia for the good times that went before, which were brought to an end by an act of incredible barbarity. In most of the literature and in the evidence from that period, the happy setting of life on Rhodes for the Jews provokes the expression of mixed emotions for its heirs: nostalgia and sadness. This tendency was also evident in the opening minutes of a documentary, filmed in 1995 by Diana Perelsztejn, called '*Rhodes Nostalgie*.' The excerpt depicted former members of the community wandering throughout Juderia, searching for memories of their deported parents. The omnipresence of this event, the traumatic nature of the disappearance of some of the parental generation, makes the act of remembrance imperative, as if a debt is owed to the disappeared, whose memory is repeatedly evoked each time their origins are spoken of.

In all the countries where they settled, the descendants of the Jews from Rhodes seem to highlight this particular origin, initially linked to the definition of community, in the religious sense, and strongly territorialised. Generally speaking, the main groups of Rodesli descendants make up their own congregation where they represent an important share of the worshippers. Their temple, like those in Cape Town, Atlanta, Harare and Buenos Aires, might even have been christened 'The Kahal Shalom,' after the temple in Rhodes. In Cape Town, a photograph of the Synagogue in Rhodes, hung in the entrance hall, clearly testifies to their desire to demonstrate this parentage. The descendants of the Jews from Rhodes may also live in close proximity, as is still the case in Cape Town and Brussels (Sintès 2013). This geographical proximity derives initially from the establishment in the town of a community originating from the same two groups who migrated to the Belgian Congo and to Rhodesia at the beginning of the twentieth century, and who were subsequently displaced at the time of independence (Hirshon 2005; Sintès 2010c). This spatial concentration is sustainable depending on how it conforms to the socio-spatial reality of the settlements. In Los Angeles, the

Figure 3.2 Displaying parentage
above Memorial plaques (Cape Town)
below The name of the place of worship (Atlanta)

Sephardic Jews initially settled in the town centre. They left in the 1920s to set up a 'new Juderia', according to those who actually witnessed it, between Vernon Avenue and 56th Street, where they were able to build their own synagogue in 1934, attracting 300 people from Rhodes (Hasson 1996). Then, depending on their residential mobility, a temple was opened in 1966 in Ladera Heights (a district to the south-west of the town centre) before all the Sephardic congregations merged and a new place of worship was adopted in Westhood in 1993, once again as a result of the growth of residential locations on the outskirts, a classic tendency in this town. In Ashdod, the only town in Israel where a dozen families originally from Rhodes lived together for several decades, this co-location was in fact short-lived, and the next generation, integrated into Israeli society, left the town or the neighbourhood.

In Cape Town, when talking about the neighbourhood where they live (Seapoint), some still explicitly compare it with the Juderia of Rhodes, not because of the number of Jewish communities who live there (Shain and Mendelsohn 2008: 182), but because it is where the greatest majority of Rodesli descendants are to be found. Even today, they usually declare that they attempt to prolong the relationships which their ancestors had on Rhodes. Family links between people are also said to recall the time of Juderia, backing up memories and influencing their close connections – reinforced by the narrowing of these family links whereby practically everyone is related to everyone else. In Buenos Aires, a fifty-year-old man speaks of 'the great Chalom family' as a way of describing this interlinking of relatives among the Jewish Rodesli descendants – descendants who founded the temple and the Sephardic cultural centre Chalom in 1929 in Colegiales, where the majority lived at that time. A business man from Brussels, having traded with Rodesli entrepreneurs in the Belgian Congo, sums up this connection in this visual description: 'Even if, sometimes, they played dirty in business between them, they cultivated the art of calling a truce, playing at being siblings.' Locally, it would be impossible not to invoke the intense social relationships favoured by the neighbourhood or which generations have maintained from afar. In this respect, the oldest in the community have an impressive knowledge of family history that allows them to situate many people in family trees, occasionally across great spatial and temporal distances.

Geographical proximity, or close ties, imply the existence of communal practices which establish the identity of the group and in which memories of Rhodes still sometimes blossom. This is also evident in the special features adopted (even claimed) by certain religious traditions (*minhag* in Hebrew): 'Throughout the world, Rodeslis celebrate in the same way.' In the synagogue, this lies in the introduction of Ladino* into the liturgy, especially for Roch Hachana and Yom Kippur. Although kept separate from a strictly Orthodox religious observance, these linguistic practices were also the source of negotiations with other groups in their new countries of settlement when it came to sharing a space for prayer. Within the family, the *Haggadah* of the *Pessa'h seder* is read in Ladino but, more generally, it is the whole set of family traditions that is intended to recall Rhodes, the '*baño de novia*' being the most frequently evoked – a bath given to the bride on the eve of her wedding by the women of the community. These traditions are brought together through a host of sayings (*dichos*) which, here as elsewhere, are classic vectors for the transmission of community values. They lay down rules to follow and prohibitions which must not be transgressed. Culinary know-how is another element which reinforces this shared sense of belonging: among the specialities, *richikos* (biscuits), *patelikos* (meat pastries) and *yaprak* (vine leaves) share top spot. These specialities are linked to religious festivals or with other social events in the community, where these special dishes are served at shared meals. They are even sometimes the occasion for more distinguished gatherings – confirming such traditions – such as those organised in the Congo in 1956 for the WIZO ball, or in Cape Town for the Sephardic Food Fair, which took place in the room adjacent to the synagogue on 1 August 1993. In Los Angeles, every year in August, the Rodesli descendants meet for a picnic on the island of Santa Catalina, 25 miles from the coast, 'a distance, which coincidentally, is the same as that which separates the island of Rhodes from Turkey.' They meet to rekindle their shared island origins over dishes reminiscent of Rhodes. This ritual is explained in the following way by one of the regular participants: 'When you are born on an island with water all around you, you cannot help but love the ocean. The sea calls to us' (Hasson 1996: 392).

These diverse moments are an opportunity for group identity to take the stage, when social practice becomes normative discourse (Goffman 1974). They also posit the field of reference, and can be understood through observation of everyday spatial practices (Di Meo 1996), which are derived here mainly from a set of subjective and representational relations which the Rodesli maintain with places. Communities from Brussels or Cape Town, for example, have completely taken over certain spaces: thus 'parliament,' a pillbox on the beach overlooking the sea in Cape Town, where the elders from the Congo used to meet for a chat, or the bars in the Louise gallery, on Avenue Louise at the gateway to Ixelles. In Cape Town today, it is the bars on the ground floor of a shopping mall, that some descendants of the Rhodian Jews have nicknamed '*Kai Ancha*', which have become the meeting place for the oldest among them. In Seattle in 2010, the congregation of Ezra Bessaroth even went so far as to reproduce some emblematic monuments of the *Kai Ancha* on Rhodes on the patio of their community building: the monument in tribute to the memory of the deported, a replica of the fountain located at the heart of Juderia and a rosette made out of *sheshos* (or *sheshikos*) – pebbles placed upright – a traditional road surface used in the old town, which all of the descendants of Rhodes know to be typical of the island. Rhodes is also gestured to in a material sense by the Sephardic area of the Jewish Cemetery in Cape Town: directly mentioned in the epitaphs on headstones, or more symbolically through the presence of olive trees. As claimed elsewhere (Collignon and Staszak 2003; Segaud 2007), this connection can also be found in private homes, where elements of the decoration are directly reminiscent of Rhodes. These take the form of family photos and paintings of the island or, more discretely, a finely wrought spoon-holder (a *cucharera* in Judezmo) – reminders of the tradition of Ottoman hospitality still in use in homes in Ashdod or Cape Town – or even the *sheshos* used by one Argentinian, the son of a Rodesli, to pave the courtyard of his holiday home in Punta del Este in Uruguay. In the most intimate circles, family memories are based on the great many photographs which serve to illustrate the narratives of our interviewees.

From these observations carried out even at such a distance from the island itself, the descendants of the island's Jewish community show how well they fit Stephane Dufoix's (2003) definition of a diaspora group, however small: a group of people who share the memory of their historical birthplace and, at the same time, keep up the close relationships they have with each other, even across occasionally significant distances. In their daily life, many objects and practices are used which, perennially reminding them of Rhodes, seemingly allow the continuation, by hysteresis, of those attributes of the group who descend from this diaspora. Relationships between generations are the key factor in this never-ending *travail de mémoire*: the oldest are keen to pass on to the younger generation the reality of life in the places where they or their parents lived – 'They filled our heads with Rhodes,' tenderly confirms one Congo-born descendant, while showing the biographical work she has dedicated to her father.

Juderia rediscovered

For these individuals, however, Rhodes is not just the setting for a family or community myth. Since the end of the war, some Rodesli have regularly made their way across the kilometres which separate them from the capital of the Dodecanese. The first return visits were made by the survivors of the Holocaust in the years following their liberation from the concentration camps. Generally, these reunions with Rhodes brought back memories of great suffering and emotion, due not only to the atrocities that they had undergone during the war but also to the situation which they found in Rhodes on their return. Everything about this neighbourhood that was so familiar reminded them both of their earlier happy and carefree life there, and of the memory of those relatives lost in the camps. This Juderia where they had grown up was now simply 'peopled by ghosts' as so many of them testified. Houses occupied by Greek refugees from other islands or surrounding villages, famine – all pushed them to once again leave this place, where a future was unimaginable. Unlike the observations made by Béa Lewkowicz in Thessaloniki, where some survivors have resettled long-term (Lewkowicz 2000), these initial return visits had no tomorrow in Rhodes and, with the exception of the Soulam and Soriano families, no Jew originally from the island remained there after the war.

It is hard to have a clear picture of the precise arrival of Rodesli descendants on the island in the decades that followed. It seems, however, that the drop in the cost of air transport – and the ensuing democratisation of long-distance travel – is the cause of the increasing volume of visits that we see during the 1960s. From then on, there is much greater variety in the types of people who travel. People's motivations also change: no one comes to Rhodes with the idea of resettling there or recovering their property. Parents of the deported of the same generation come for a holiday to wander through the streets of their childhood, to reconnect with the ambiance of the old town – in a word, to 'feel their roots.' The first trip thus always stirs up the same sense of suffering for them as it did for those who survived the concentration camps. Yet somehow, despite this difficulty, returning to the island seems to be something of a moral obligation; so much so that we find the following lines in the autobiographical narrative of Nisso Pelossof (2007: 9):

> Even if my attachment for this region of Picardy which has so welcomed me is deep, the nostalgia I feel for my roots, my homeland – the island of Rhodes – this nostalgia seems to get stronger as the years go by… the future for me increasingly seems to hold a return to Rhodes. It is inescapable.

This pilgrimage belongs, implicitly, to the victims of deportation as well as to previous generations. Now it also concerns younger people who go to Rhodes to discover the birthplace of a parent and especially 'to discover their origins, the land of their ancestors.' Occasionally they decide to celebrate the special events of family life there (a *bar-mitsva* or wedding) or the main festivals of the liturgical calendar (*Roch Hachana* or *Yom Kippur*). In 2005 and 2006, 120 people from Zimbabwe and 200 from Dallas went to a wedding; in June 2007, more than 100 people from the United States went to celebrate a *bar-mitsva*. Those younger people who can afford it might go on honeymoon there or as a family, with their children or parents. For them, the visit is principally a kind of spiritual quest or a search for identity, a sort of journey destined to resolve some of the tension created by the nostalgic narrative to which they

Figure 3.3 Groups of Rodeslis on a trip down memory lane
above In Rhodes (2007)
below In Modiin (Israel) from an album

have been subjected since childhood. 'We all love Rhodes, even if we have never lived there,' said one 50-year-old woman from Brussels who has spent practically every summer in Rhodes since the 1980s and whose daughter now does the same. More prosaically, however, for everyone concerned, the trip is indisputably an opportunity for a holiday in the Mediterranean sun. The destination is no longer exclusively Rhodes. Stopping off on the island is often part of a longer itinerary which includes a number of destinations, particularly Israel and Europe. The interviews reveal frequent references to the tourist aspect of the visit to Rhodes: the quality of the hotels and beaches, the discovery of Greek cuisine and the hospitality of the locals are often mentioned as significant reasons for its success. The effectiveness of the trip in emotional terms also appears in several testimonies, with no doubts about the pilgrim's sincerity. 'I was so upset when I came to Rhodes for the first time that I couldn't get off the plane,' said the child of a deportee. Or 'We were on a cruise and we docked in Rhodes. We met one of the other passengers in the synagogue. We realised that we were related. We fell into each others' arms sobbing.'

The journey can also be an opportunity for people to amass new objects which all serve as reminders – photos, of course, of places of special significance that might be likened to holiday shots, and sometimes other, more original things which remind them that Rhodes is unlike any other destination. Thus one visitor wrote the entire synopsis of a film when he had never done anything like this before – the simple fact of being in Rhodes seemed to have enabled him to compose a technically perfect text, 'as though it were not me who was writing.' Another visitor wrote poems *in situ* in Judezmo. In these two examples, their creations are inspired by the place itself. These almost magical situations, brought about, it seems, by the journey, implicitly make the connection with the departed. More anecdotally, the phrase 'Ladino comes more naturally to me when I am in Rhodes,' is often heard, as if the simple fact of being there could give those individuals greater linguistic abilities. For these different reasons, the Rodesli descendants are indeed all participants in what we might call 'genealogical tourism,' as has been observed elsewhere, for example for the Jews from the Maghreb (Dakhama 2005) or Germany (Coles 2003), Irish descendants from the US (Legrand 2006) or even members of the Lebanese diaspora (Butler 2003). As such, they demonstrate certain characteristics and their behaviour *in situ* is indisputably different to that of the many other tourists who come to Rhodes on holiday and for whom the place does not have the same personal associations, whether for them or for their parents.

Despite the diversity of the people encountered on the island during my survey, it is obvious that the descendants of the Rodesli generally behave in their own particular manner when in Rhodes, even though they are also there on holiday. In this respect, they have 'hybrid holidays for hybrid people,' as Coles (2003: 337) suggests, as they can be taken neither as tourists nor as indiginous people, like the others. Whatever an individual's age or origins, the stated objective of the Rodesli visitor to the island wherein lies his or her heritage is always to see, to ascertain, to know: it is the 'experiential' aspect, as Coles (2003: 329) highlights in respect to a similar kind of visitor to other locations. In the course of their short stay (generally less than a week), the descendants of the Jews from Rhodes go without fail to the old town and to the Juderia district, even if they choose to sleep there only occasionally, often preferring the comfortable hotels near the beach instead of the modest inns of the old town. The last remaining synagogue on the island, the Kahal Kadosh Shalom is the symbolic destination for the sojourn, along with other signs in the old town that recall the ancient presence of a Jewish community. In addition to this edifice, other signs of this memory are indeed present but it is always a delicate business trying to locate them, as they are not valued to any degree by the Greek authorities, who prefer the Byzantinian heritage or traces of the reign of the Order of St John. Consequently, but also as a result of increasing visits by the youngest generations, a new actor is starting to play a part in this Rodesli roots tourism – a *passeur de mémoire* or 'carrier of memories' (Ciarcia 2011), someone who is often encountered unexpectedly and who guides the descendants, their parents or their friends through the narrow streets of the old town. The first of these, the Soulam and Soriano families mentioned above, were permanent residents, the last evidence of a Sephardic presence on the island. They are mentioned in nearly every single narrative from the 1960s to the 1990s. Since their disappearance, however, this role has passed to those returnees who bear witness through their regular visits to Rhodes. The visitors who meet them remember them as a significant moment of their stay. Effectively, these 'carriers' enable others to make the connection between the past and the present, giving them useful insights into the landscape of Juderia beneath the old town of today, now overrun with tavernas and tourist shops. Under their watchful eye, a real initiation takes place which enables outsiders to discover more about the places and the lives of the community of their ancestors. These guides, however, can also be casual visitors – Rodesli descendants well versed in their family history, who decide to share their knowledge of a place that sometimes they, too, are discovering for the first time. Furthermore this informal role is transferable and, once the various bit of information have been gleaned from other 'carriers of memory', it is not unusual to see a *repeat visitor* 'give a guided tour' for their friends. If someone more knowledgeable appears, the visitor will, however, give way to him or her. Certain individuals, particularly those who were born and raised there, are very proud of this knowledge, as they 'feel duty-bound to show what has been.' This pride can sometimes become competitive: 'Some say they know but they don't really. In fact, I am the only one who really knows what it was like. I am the memory of Rhodes,' explains one of them.

The Jewish past in action

On Rhodes today, the old Jewish quarter, situated in the easternmost area of the old fortified town, partly owes its appearance to the history of this group. This zone, always known as Evraïko by the residents (or Ovriaki, more traditionally, in Greece), appears to have been abandoned and left to crumble many years ago. This brings to mind other neighbourhoods which Jewish communities have left behind in other Mediterranean countries – such as the Moroccan *mellahs* where, for many years, desertion of the neighbourhood prevented the maintenance and development of these spaces, and led to their spontaneous occupation by groups of poor people, often fleeing from rural areas. This is why, in Rhodes, the present-day inhabitants of the old Jewish quarter are some of the poorest in the town: they were often refugees who came immediately after the war from the surrounding islands and countrysides where famine was rife (Skevofylakas 1988). Thus the old Jewish quarter in Rhodes still bears the scars of deportation and the departure *en masse* of the community, despite classification of the entire fortified town by the national authorities in 1959 and by UNESCO in 1988. These characteristics distinguish it from the other neighbourhoods of the old town, especially in the summer, where they are the site of intense tourist activity. In the immediate postwar period, the scant Jewish presence in this quarter only increased very slowly. Even the settlement of a few famillies, particularly Romaniots originally from the continent, under the auspices of the central Jewish authorities of Greece, together with care lavished on the rare survivors, was not enough to rebuild a truly autonomous community. This situation changed radically from the 1990s and 2000s, with the evident expansion of the expression of a Jewish heritage in this part of the old town as their descendants began to visit more frequently, as described above. At the same time, the emergence of a thriving tourism on the island also affected the Jewish quarter. The Shalom synagogue became more and more popular with visitors, especially foreigners, despite its unsuitability in terms of this change of use. In line with these diverse developments, some individuals decided to promote the Jewish heritage and equip the synagogue with greater facilities to make it more accessible. This is the case for a third-generation descendant from the United States who lives in Los Angeles and is already very active in the safeguarding of this heritage in California. He designed a project which would give tourists greater insight into the Jewish history of the region. Several years later, this initiative resulted in the opening of a museum designed to communicate the history of the Jews from Rhodes to visitors. On the project's website, the explanation he gives for his motivation clearly demonstrates his concern to reach out to as many people as possible.

> I was inspired to visit the island of Rhodes in 1975 by stories told to me by my grandparents. Its special charm and history fascinated me. Several years later, in 1995, I went back to Rhodes with my family for my children to learn of our family heritage. It was during that trip that I noticed the need of advancing the public awareness and appreciation of its unique history unfortunately devastated by the Holocaust (…).
>
> Today, the island of Rhodes is one of the most popularly visited vacation places in the Mediterranean Sea with vacationers coming from all countries of the world, utilizing international charter air flights as well as cruise ships. These visitors walk the streets of 'La Juderia' lacking knowledge of its Jewish history many of whom visited the sole remaining synagogue, the Kahal Shalom. Unfortunately, there was nothing at the Kahal Shalom to inform its visitors of its unique history. Although most of the remnants of Jewish life are absent as a result of the Holocaust, this Museum is an important first step of more expansive efforts in preserving the unique history of the Jews of Rhodes.
>
> In 1997, I created two institutions to fulfill this goal. First, I established the Rhodes Jewish Museum, which exhibits photographic materials and other artifacts, and secondly I set up the Rhodes Jewish Historical Foundation, which is a non-profit organization to be used as a vehicle for furthering this goal. In October 1997, I created this web site in order to be an information source for people interested in the history of the Jews of Rhodes as well as those planning to travel to Rhodes. (…). I hope the web site will be an enjoyable learning experience for all viewers (www. rhodesjewishmuseum.org).

In recent decades, this North American is not the only person to have supported such a movement in Rhodes. Several years later, the local Jewish authorities became more active due to the fact that a powerful family of entrepreneurs, originally from Rhodes, took over the leadership. The main motivation for these different community players seemed to be the desire to do justice to previous generations. They wanted to rekindle the Jewish presence of the past in the same places and streets of that part of the old town. In this way, the synagogue became the main vehicle for a new visibility. The Kahal Kadosh Shalom on Rhodes effectively found itself at the centre of the transformations which had taken place over recent decades and became the beating heart of Jewish heritage on Rhodes. It was the last active synagogue, the other five in the old town either no longer belonging to the community or having been destroyed in the war. Although initially people's efforts went into the upkeep of the cemetary – witness the commemorative plaques recording donations (in 1953 and 1971, and then, in 1997, a mission to save the tombstones) – the focus from 2000 on was the renovation of the Shalom synagogue.

According to various documents, the condition of the synagogue had greatly deteriorated since the end of the war. The damage caused by the lack of maintenance had put the building at risk. A restoration project for funding was submitted to several international institutions, both public and private, for the repainting and stabilisation of the structure and the restoration of the interior stone flooring. These improvements resulted in the building's classification in 2000 by the World Monuments Fund (an NGO supported by private investment) as one of the '100 most endangered sites in the world.' This grant, together with one other from the European Union in 2004, paid for the complete refurbishment of the building, including the roof, and for its connection to the town's drainage network, in collaboration with the municipal restoration office. Alongside these major donations, there have also been many small private patrons who have paid for the redecoration of the inside of the synagogue and the replacement of the furniture, which dated back to the postwar period and was very basic (plastic chairs; a pulpit enclosed by a balustrade as the only *tivah*). A new *tivah* was donated by a family from Belgium in the 1960s whilst the benches that could be seen in photos taken in the '50s were replaced by new and much more comfortable chairs in the summer of 2006. The air conditioning was eventually installed in 2010. These new facilities were necessary due to the influx of visitors, as testified in 2002 by the president of the Jewish community of Rhodes, speaking into the microphone of an Israeli documentary-maker at the inauguration of a monument in memory of the deported: 'It's the first time in 58 years that the synagogue has been full. There were not enough chairs for everyone to sit on.' Donations are often made in memory of parents who had died, sometimes during deportation. Whether the *tivah* or the marble plaque at the entrance to the synagogue listing the surnames of the deported, these gifts, as is the custom, are all inscribed with the name of the donor and a dedication: '*A la mémoire de mon père, ma mère, mon frère et ma soeur et de son mari, tous deux déportés*' in French ('In memory of my father, my mother, my brother and my sister and her husband, both deported'), thus 'honouring their parents' or 'in memory of their parents', acknowledging that the gift is given in the name of a relationship with the place, because the parents' origins are here, whereas the donors now often live very far away. The end of the 2000s saw an acceleration in the renovation work and in the transformations around the synagogue, in particular with the opening in 2007 of a museum in an adjoining building, dedicated to presenting this community to the wider public. There is a permanent exhibition here of artefacts collected from around the world, accompanied by written explanations of the significant moments in the history of the Jews on Rhodes. Now there is a veritable heritage complex surrounding these first spaces, for a library was opened in 2008 and, in 2009, the community offices were moved so that they could be in the same building (they were in another part of the old town before). In the space of a few years, as a result of all of this work, the Shalom synagogue has changed from a little-known place of family pilgrimage to a complex, multi-purpose heritage facility, a genuine resource centre for both heritage-related and tourist activities across the whole of the old town of Rhodes.

The installation of these facilities demontrates the processes involved in coordinating patchy recollections with a view to providing information about this community. What is more, the material provided by personal narratives (biographies, films, collections of recipies, stories and proverbs etc.) also finds its home in the synagogue's premises, where a noticeboard displays these different works. Some of them have even become heritage media, 'merchandising' even, for the community, and are now on sale in the gift shop attached to the community office. More generally, each year since 2005, the quantity of posters and explanatory material shown to the public has multiplied within these walls, resulting in the communication of it to visitors. Compared to the larger space in the surrounding neighbourhood, these installations also diffuse a narrative of appropriation which gives meaning (back) to those lost places in Jewish memory. Thus, since 2007, a satellite picture of the entire fortified town is on display inside the museum. It is based on an image imported free of charge from a satellite imagery website, to which have been added those places which are relevant to the history of the Jewish community. Situated in the last room in the museum, this panel clearly encourages visitors to walk around the lanes of the old town in order to rediscover these places and, in so doing, play their part in keeping these memories alive. Since 2010 and the opening of the community offices, a small map of the neighbourhood has also been displayed in the patio area of the synagogue. This *Tour Map of the Jewish Quarter* outlines the route and links the places that have significance for the Jewish community – *Present Landmarks of the Jewish Community*. This map is also available online from the website of the museum's founder and author of the map, along with the information booklet for the area, which the community sells (Hasson 2012). This last item has taken the work of reappropriating the quarter a step further, as it offers, on the same webpage, maps established by the last living witnesses bearing the names of former occupants of the houses and indications as to the Jewish shops in the surrounding streets.

Figure 3.4 The Shalom Synagogue and its facilities
left Access ramp (2012)
below left Gift shop (2010)
right Donation box and prospectuses (2010)
below Museum (2007)

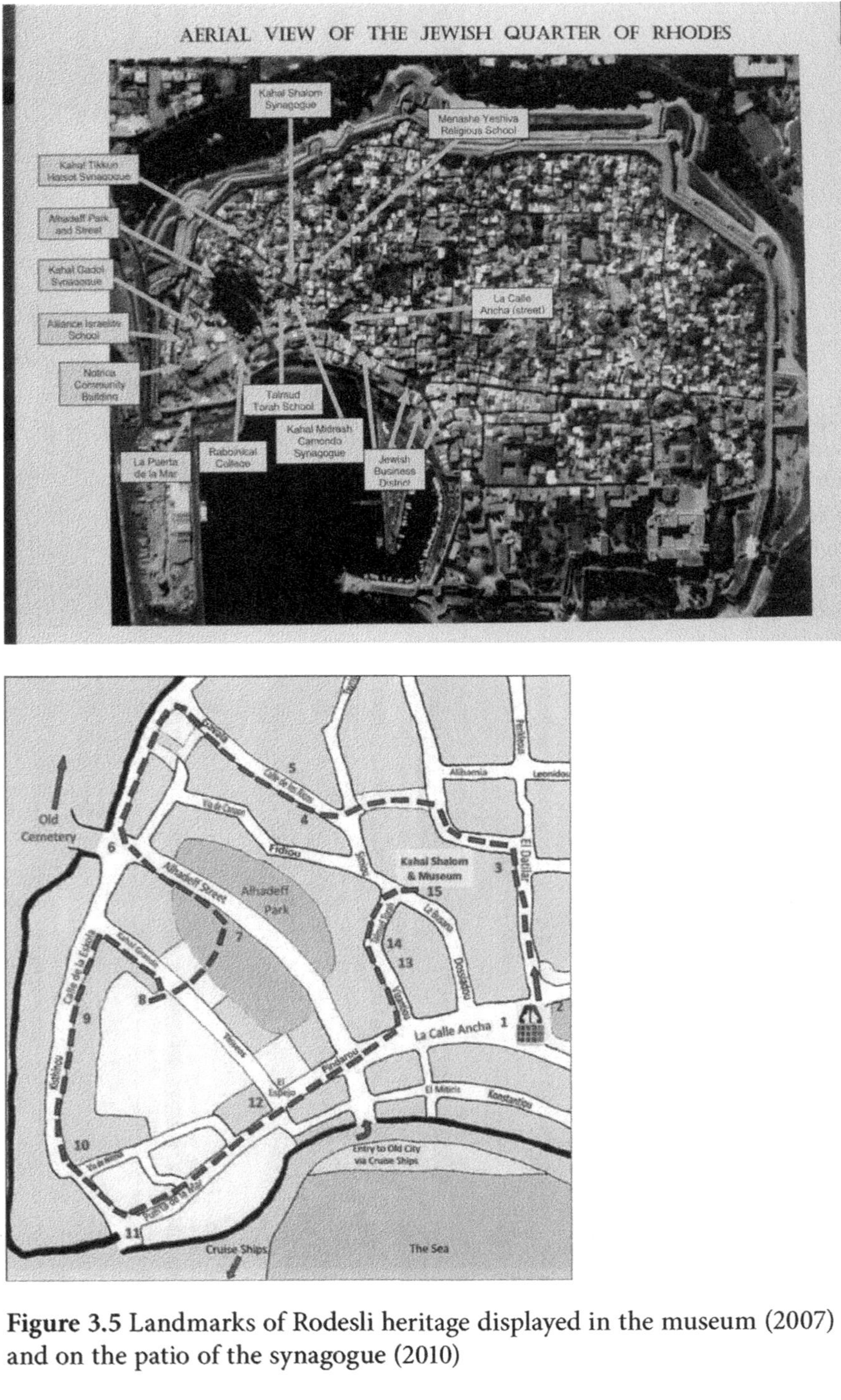

Figure 3.5 Landmarks of Rodesli heritage displayed in the museum (2007) and on the patio of the synagogue (2010)

Apart from the synagogue itself, visits from relatives and descendants of the former Jewish inhabitants have led to the physical reappropriation of certain spaces in the old town, at least for a very brief period each year. These particular visitors are effectively seeking in the streets of Juderia elements which prove the presence of Jews in Rhodes in ancient times. It is interesting to note that these practices are increasingly surrounded by facilities or manifestations of remembrance which give a spatio-temporal organisation to these visits. From 2009 onwards, these neighbourhood walking tours were even organised by the community for those tourists who wanted them. Such a trend is clearly part of a process of institutionalisation and of normalisation of narratives of memory.

The traces of this Jewish past now form a kind of circuit through the old town which marks out the identity of the former Juderia. This circuit is followed by visitors keen to find tangible signs of the reality of the Jewish past, a practice which initiates a process of territorialisation that initially undergoes a symbolic appropriation (or, for some, a reappropriation) through frequentation of these places. The different signs discovered there are nonetheless quite varied and particularly fragmentary. They give little factual evidence as to what life in the quarter might have been like when the Jews lived there. Today they can even be difficult to identify amongst the jumble of signs produced by the tourist industry inside the medieval town. Except the synagogue, the most clearly visible signs of the local Jewish history are the inscriptions on the outside walls of some houses in the streets of the old town. The most easily distinguishable, written in Hebrew, in Italian and in Judeo-Spanish, cite the donations made by individuals to the community. These gifts date back to 1915 and 1935 and are connected to the strong migratory outflow that widely embraced the Jews in the town at that time. Another inscription, entirely in Hebrew this time, is visible in a small dark lane just above the entrance to an abandoned house near the old Talmudic school. This discrete epigram, clearly older than those mentioned above, gives the date at which the house was built: 'On the 8th day of the month of Nissam, in the year 5527 (1767) after the creation of the world.' Another sign on an old fountain overlooking a little-used street near the eastern wall of the fortress bears the inscription, in French: '*Alliance israélite universelle, fondation de Mme la Baronne de Rothschild – 1904*' ('Universal Jewish Alliance – Baronness Edmond de Rothschild – 1904'), then just below in Italian: '*Al generale Giovanni Ameglio, La communita israelita riconoscente*' ('To General Giovanni Ameglio, with the gratitude of the Jewish community – 1913'). This fountain confirms the multilingualism of the community, as noted elsewhere. We also note the community's closeness with the Italian authorities (with the mention of the first govenor of the Dodecanese), which enabled them to be granted a privileged status in Rhodes (Bocquet 2004), as well as the educational role of the Universal Jewish Alliance. The only signs in Greek (even if their link to Judaism is not openly visible) naturally date from after the war and the island's unification with Greece. There is one on the building of a boys' school, the former property of an eminent member of the Jewish community, and today rented by the municipality of Rhodes. It still carries the name of its previous owner, written right at the top of the facade, on a plaque that is difficult to read from the street: '*Ίδρυμα Ιώσηφ Νότρικα,*' (Joseph Notrica Foundation). The name of a nearby street, indicated by the usual blue panel, is also noteworthy: '*Όδος Αλχάδεφ Σολωμόν,*' (Salomon Alhadeff Street), the name of a prominent and rich member of the community whose children, in 1946, donated to the municipality of Rhodes the large garden which crosses the road in question. Beyond this first collection, which includes the most tangible signs of this former presence, there are other, much more discrete, traces that are visible to those in the know. On the floor of the entrance to certain houses, provided the door is left open, we can see a mosaic of pebbles, typical of the cobbled streets of the old town, which gives the year, in the Hebrew calendar, in which it was built, or the floor was relaid. The best-informed visitors can finally discover the ever more discrete remains of remarkable old community buildings such as the former '*Kahal Gadol*' (Great Synagogue), in ruins since the allied bombing in 1944, the old Rabbinical College, the former synagogue '*De Los Rikos,*' (of the rich), which appears to have been abandoned, or even the old Talmudic school – a house which has become completely anonymous and whose location is never clear to visitors.

In a once-a-year but otherwise momentous event, the Jewish community of Rhodes, in collaboration with the municipal authorities and the Jewish Museum of Athens, have instituted an annual day of commemoration for the victims of the Holocaust around the 23 July, the date of the deportation of Jews from Rhodes by the Germans to the Haïdari camp near Athens, in transit to Poland. If, elsewhere in the world, the memory of the victims of the Holocaust is celebrated on 27 January (the date of the liberation of Auschwitz), here the choice was made for practical reasons, as Rhodes is completely deserted in the winter. It seemed more appropriate to organise the event in the summer, when the greatest number of people, both tourists and residents, can participate, and when the island is at its most attractive for Rodesli the world over.

This ceremony is an occasion for many people to come to the island from all parts of the diaspora. The events which surround it give rise to a veritable pilgrimage or organised journey that is as good as any professional excursion on account of the packed programme of group activities it offers (dinners, visits, concerts), together with coaches and guides laid on by the organisers where necessary. The event was set up in 2002, and the first occasion included

Figure 3.6 Commemoration in memory of the deported (2008)

the inauguration of a monument – a hexagonal column which describes the fate of those deported from Rhodes and Cos in six different languages – in the central square in Juderia, the '*Kai Ancha*,' renamed the *Πλατεία Εβραίων Μαρτύρων* 'Square of the Jewish Martyrs' in 1946. The actual day of the commemoration begins with a religious ceremony in the Shalom Synagogue followed by official speeches. It brings together several dozen descendants of the Jews from Rhodes, as well as several survivors of the Holocaust. This first ceremony is followed by a laying of wreaths at the commemorative monument. These two moments have a discrete interfaith quality, as representatives of other faiths attend, even if they do not speak. It is also an official act of the Greek Republic, as the involvement of the authorites, together with the attendance of the municipal band which plays the Greek national anthem at the closure of the ceremony, demonstrates. From this point of view, however, there is still something somewhat unfocused about the occasion that gives it the quality of a private event at which visitors feel part of a common and specific group, even when they are in the public space. Since 2007, the participants have sung the *Hatikvah* on several occasions after the laying of wreaths, and the incomprehension of passers-by or residents living close was palpable.

Through its presence, the monument has transformed this spot into a *lieu de mémoire* (place of remembrance). It is clearly visible and now indisputably contributes to the identity of the space: it is regularly photographed by tourists, and appropriated by residents who arrange to meet up there or sit in the square that surrounds it. But the harm that appears to have been done to it since its construction – for example, its general deterioration (the letters on the inscriptions were frequently vandalised), or graffiti written large on the ground in front of the monument (such as 'Palestine' in November 2009, and 'Sabra, Chatila, Gaza, Lebanon: Israel's best student of Nazis,' in July 2006, a few days after the commemoration ceremony for the deported) – is interpreted by visiting Jews as clear evidence of a common visceral rejection of any public demonstration of minority identity in public spaces on Rhodes or of the anti-semitic feeling that is likely to be relatively widespread here. This rejection merely reinforces an agonistic perception of the process of making Jewish heritage more visible in the quarter, in the eyes of those who feel that this is where this memory legitimately belongs. This double-edged experience of acceptance and rejection also shows itself in the discourse of the municipal authorities and the Greek prefecture. It is true that such an event cannot happen without there being some issues regarding the functioning of the old town and society on Rhodes more generally.

The grindings of memory

Watching this event take place on six occasions between 2006 and 2014 enabled me to understand why certain tensions exist, both within and beyond the group, tensions which reveal the issues involved in reactivating this Jewish heritage on Rhodes. Firstly, the place where the event is held has sometimes been at the heart of the polemic. Some of the Rodesli who regularly visit the old town talk of the problems they have had in making clearly visible in the central square of the old Jewish quarter the plaque bearing the name 'Square of Hebrew Martyrs'. They say that it was only after Greece joined the EEC at the beginning of the 1980s that they were satisfied that the plaque was displayed in such a way that everyone could see it (despite it being officially named by decision of the municipal council in Rhodes on 1 October 1946). What is more, if Greek officials attend the ceremony on Remembrance Day, their presence may be commented on by certain participants. The unofficial line is that they have to be there by law, that they are required by law to honour the memory of victims of the Holocaust once a year. A degree of tension or misunderstanding can be felt in the speeches made by some officials. In his speech in 2006, the Dodecanese Prefect wanted to use the event to publicly denonounce Israeli military intervention in

Lebanon and recalled the right of the Palestinians to have their own state. He used the ceremony, inappropriately, to reinforce the current confusion in people's minds about Judaism and Zionism, as it could be seen again, notably, during the commemorative events of the summer of 2014 in the form of thinly veiled references to the conflict in Gaza.

However, apart from these references to the near-eastern geopolitical context, there must surely be other issues that make it a somewhat delicate matter to recall a Jewish presence on Rhodes through this symbolic occupation, however temporary, of both space and memory. Would they enable us to properly understand the context in which the revitalisation of this heritage is taking place? It is important to recognise that, if the many signs of the former presence of the Jewish community in the eastern part of the fortress are taken as proof, the fact that today (almost) all the houses are occupied by Christian Greek residents raises the issue of the transmission of property assets to the heirs of the families who either fled the island between the wars or who were deported in 1944. Just mentioning the Jewish past in Evraïko can engender a kind of ill-feeling amongst today's residents. Oftentimes, the issue is avoided and there are few who want to talk about it openly. Yet today, there is not a single Jew from Rhodes, or a descendant, who goes to the island without looking for signs of their house or their parents' or ancestors' property, armed with the necessary information to help them find it. The house is, in effect, a genuine embodiment of the connection to place and equally to the preceding generations, often long dead, which makes the visit so painful. Family history can still be discovered within the confines of a building: 'When I saw the house, I saw the steps up to the front door and I recalled the stories that he told me about these steps where he had played, where he fell, where he waited for his Dad to come home from work etc.' Nonetheless, when the memory is lost, visitors need to have recourse to a witness, a 'carrier of memory' who is *in situ* or who can be called by telephone, and who will not hesitate to guide the visitor to 'his or her' house (Sintès 2010d). This type of practice gives rise to interactions with the current residents of Juderia, or even with the municipal authorities, and the experience may be why visitors do not feel welcome. Some even feel a degree of hostility towards the Greeks, who they accuse of not having protected them from the Germans and of having ransacked their houses once they had been abandoned. More generally there is the almost unanimous feeling: 'When we arrive on Rhodes, they look at us quite suspiciously.'

The sense of dispossession, born from the disappearance of all traces of Jewish presence, thus rebounds on the residents of the old town and likewise the authorities, accused of denial and of repressing the past history of the quarter. This sense of disenfranchisement is based on the fact that those features that made the houses Jewish ones have been stripped away.

The *Mezuzah* that was typically nailed to the doorpost is no longer there. Visitors look for and scrutinise this object, fundamental to the Jewish home, or the marks that it might have left on the door. Thus, in an Israeli documentary depicting the visit of Jews originally from Rhodes, resident in Ashdod, we saw in some shots how the visitors ran their hands over the reinforcements that were carved in stone on the arched doorways of the houses in Juderia, no doubt where the *Mezuzah* would have been, remembering the ritual gesture made whenever crossing the threshold into the house. Some South-African descendants, having visited their parents' house, found the little box underneath the paintwork and took it with them, without a moment's hesitation. Some visitors suspect that there are goods concealed in these old houses – treasures that Jewish families could reclaim from the present occupants. Stories of lucky finds abound in the old town, such as one family who were meant to have found gold in the house and the father said that it should be returned to the former Jewish owners. Often, though, the occupants are accused of hiding objects and valuables that the deported left behind. This fantasy of imagined riches has created a climate of mutual mistrust between the present occupants and some of the descendants of the former inhabitants. One resident from Cape Town talks about her first visit to Rhodes in this way:

> The first time she went with her husband to Rhodes, they tried to find the things her parents had hidden in the house before they were deported by the Germans. Arriving at the house, the occupants refused to open the door, so they were not even able to go inside. They said to the occupants that there was one particular thing that they wanted to take and they wondered whether perhaps they might have found it in the house. It was a piece of family jewellery, a locket in which her mother used to put photographs. They waited for 20 minutes outside. The door opened and they were handed the locket without a word being uttered.

Even more than these valuable items, however, it seems that it is ownership of the houses themselves which the descendants question on their return. This issue, more than others, causes embarrassment throughout the quarter: 'It's as if these people know that, morally speaking, their very presence inside those four walls is questionable,' says one of these visitors when talking about the current inhabitants of Juderia. Most of the descendants, however, often distance themselves from this issue. Nonetheless, some do remark that 'It's easy to benefit from the past history of a people without making any kind of contribution in return…' and that, without wishing to cause trouble, the issue of the ownership of the houses is not always clear for all of them. It is almost rare for someone to go further and say: 'Those houses are ours! Not theirs!' This question was, nevertheless, looked into by the Greek state in previous decades. Thus, after a conservative law on the seizure of goods was passed just after the war, several decisions were made which were supposed to have regulated matters. The first, taken in 1955, brought a wave of restitutions but people have said that there was also quite a bit of abuse of the law. As some interviewees declared, people apparently took goods that did not belong to them in order to sell them on at a profit. It is possible that these individuals acted in good faith but were tricked by interested third parties or simply misinformed. After several litigious cases, the Greek state tried to bring some kind of order to the process of restitution in the early 1960s, demanding additional pieces of evidence, which were often difficult for the claimant to gather. In the majority of cases, however, matters seem to have been resolved legally. Almost all the properties that were not reclaimed now belong to the public authorities and are managed by the town's archaeological services, who rent them legally to the occupants through a written contract. In spite of these restitutions, however, it is extremely rare for any descendants of the Jews from Rhodes to live in the old town or even to own a house there. The complexity of the procedures that were established in the 1960s seems to have put them off.... To legally own a house in these so-called strategic border areas, a person would have to be a Greek citizen or co-own a property with a Greek, which naturally makes things more complicated. Having put matters in the hands of local solicitors, some testify to having never received much money, due to the numerous expenses they had had. The difficulty of managing this kind of modest and often dilapidated property from afar led the majority of people to let them go; at the time the island had not yet become the popular holiday resort that it is now and the value of the houses in that part of the old town was low. Some simply did not want the bother and did not even initiate proceedings. This did not stop them from keeping an eye on their former family homes, however, to which they still feel sentimentally attached. They often know the person who lives there. Whatever the frequency of their visits, they are always recognised: 'Ah yes, I know you, you're the one from Brussels: come, I will open the house for you.' There are many examples, however, which demonstrate just how the status of these properties can become complicated for each and every one of them.

> We meet Ilan on the terrace of a restaurant he likes to frequent in the old town of Rhodes. He was born in Israel and it was his parents who set up home here. His father left Rhodes in 1937. Ilan owns his grandfather's house in the old town. His father came back to Rhodes for the first time in the 1960s. In the 1950s, he had begun proceedings to take back his property, after seeing a Greek government advert

asking the owners of houses to make themselves known, before their homes were appropriated. So he came from Israel in 1965 to take back his house… but there were complications.

In the beginning, the military dictatorship annulled the decision to return the house to him. Then, some years later, the tenant tried to take it off him. Ilan's father had gone through the whole process…. but he had forgotten to write his name in the land register and so the house appeared to belong to the municipality as one of many abandonned houses. The tenant, realising the situation, tried to acquire the vacant property, as was her right. At first she was successful and Ilan's family had to go to the court of appeal in Athens. They spent 15 years in court. Nine years ago, it was all finally resolved. As far as Ilan is aware, he is the only one to have found his family home in Juderia and to live in it. Ever since, he comes back every year and is restoring the house bit by bit. He has borrowed 100,000 € in order to do this. The house was in a terrible state initially. There was damp everywhere. It is not rational but sentimental. He cannot leave it. He has sunk thousands and thousands of dollars in the house but, even if he had to spend three times that amount, he would. His grandfather and grandmother lived there. They built it with their own hands.

Another descendant also seems to have had enormous difficulty in establishing his rights to his family's former property. 'My parents began proceedings in 1962. The court allowed them to take back their assets in 1964 but this decision was contested by the state and we had to appeal'. In the meantime, the Junta that had taken power in Athens annulled all these decisions 'sometimes for good reason, imprisoning rogue solicitors who were carrying out suspicious transactions in the old town in the name of the descendants of the Jews'.

Since then, for some of his houses, there have been three rulings in his favour but in 2000 the state wanted to take them back as they were old houses in ruins that had been bringing in rent and taxes since 1964, which gave the state rights. Once the restitution had taken place, he sold two of the houses at rock bottom prices in an attempt to solve the problem. It has to be said that the situation is not an easy one: he is unable to get a bank loan, for example, to renovate the houses as he does not have all the necessary papers. His friends in Rhodes often say to him 'Why don't you sell to someone from here who would know what to do' and, when he insists, they say ' It will be long and complicated.' But he refuses to give up and says: 'It's not a question of money. It has already cost us a lot but, every year I saw my father get so worked up over this whenever he came here. I can't just give up. It's hard to admit that what the Nazis started still isn't over. How can

> we put this and the deportation behind us if we cannot conclude the matter of the assets?' How can a democratic country not return to me something which I did not choose to leave behind? This issue just adds salt to the wound of deportation. Why can something which belonged to my grandfather not now revert to me? Does the Greece of today want to finish off the work of the Nazis?'

The notion that the Jews might return to the old town is not a realistic one. Apart from the Shalom synagogue, only three houses until very recently had *Mezuzot*. With the exception of Ilan's, the other houses were either linked to the revitalisation movement begun after the war, or belong to the community. A future Jewish presence is only entertained by a few dreamers, like this former Greek migrant to the Congo, who returned to Rhodes and now states that he would like to bring the Jews back to Rhodes.... for his own ends, as he possesses 50,000 square metres of land at the foot of Mount Philerimos where he would like to build fifty-odd houses and sell them to the descendants of the Jewish community. Rhodes has thus remined essentially a place of memory. The descendants have their lives elsewhere, as one of them confessed from his apartment in the north of Tel Aviv: 'We are always moved when we see where they lived…the synagogue, the cemetary…but in the end…now, we have our own country.'

Without stronger connections with the local society, it is hard to imagine how the 'revitalisation of Jewish heritage' on Rhodes might endure further than the next generation, as those from this community who were born and brought up on Rhodes are already dying out. It is still possible, though, that the authorities might endorse this kind of tourism, which is so different from that which disfigures the coastline. It seems, however, that the powers that be are more interested in engaging with groups whose identity conforms more closely to the Greek national one. This is particularly true of the tourism of Greeks from the diaspora (Thanopoulos and Walle 1988) which, as far as the Dodecanese Archipelago is concerned, has been promoted for several years now by the organisation 'Dodecanesian Dream.' In contrast with events for the Jewish community, the public authorities, like the municipality of Rhodes and the intercommunal body of the Dodecanese Archipelago, have actively participated in the commemorative events for this group right from the first international day of the Dodecanese diaspora held in Rhodes in August 2008. On this day of remembrance, no activity recalls the multiconfessional history of the island, instead implying that religious barriers, inherited from the Ottoman past and the greek nation building, have been irredemably extended to the structure of a diaspora which had, nonetheless, been in existence for several generations throughout the world. When compared with studies carried out elsewhere – as in the case of the Catalan town of Gerona, where local elites claimed a link with previously hidden Jewish tradition – the difference seems significant. Through this comparison, we can clearly understand how this particular type of tourism, which involves a connection with places based on a sense of belonging, 'does not rely on stakes linked to international competition for attracting tourists but brings into play, from an ideological perspective, representations of nationhood, history and the role of the different groups who participated in the past in the cultural construction of the nation' (Lévy and Olazabal 2003: 65). This comes to explain the extremely exogenous dimension of the mobilisation described in the case of the Jewish community of Rhodes, a characteristic which questions its sustainability in the medium term.

Towards a successful heritage status: tourism as an ally?

The history of the Jewish community of Rhodes may well, however, act as a positive factor for the future, enabling it to develop its own style of tourism on the island. In this respect, its revival and maintenance at the heart of the old town could offer several advantages for its inhabitants to share. First of all, it is the *raison d'être* behind a specific type of tourism. From a financial perspective there are non-negligible benefits to having the Rodesli children there in terms of the town's activities. Frequent observations of the visits to the Shalom synagogue during the summer and the reading of the entries in the guestbook provide clues as to the feasability of this special type of tourism and how many tourists are actually interested in these things. It is no surprise that visitors to the synagogue are largely neighbouring Israelis who 'pop in', and those who come on organised tours. These Israelis are much more numerous than the North American tourists who come largely from the United States even if flows of the former are not particulary large when compared with those of other countries. In 2005, only 71,000 Israeli tourists were registered in Rhodes. There are some distinguishing features, however, that deserve a mention. Most of the Israelis who travel to Greece come to the island of Rhodes because it is nearby geographically and therefore an inexpensive place to have a holiday – and because they could not afford a holiday in countries neighbouring their own. In fact, 54 per cent of the 133,000 Israelis who came to Greece in 2005 did so via Rhodes. Furthermore, their means of transport is also unique, as they travel by boat (70,000) as opposed to flying (24,000). They make up only 2 per cent of the one million tourists who land at Diagoras airport each year but a much greater percentage of the 90,000 people who arrive on Rhodes by boat. Even if the response of the Rodesli is somewhat mitigated towards these tourists, whom they accuse of 'being consumers', lacking consideration for the prestigious history of their community, it cannot be denied that, during the summer, when the Israeli cruisers stop over on the island, their efforts to restore the island's heritage gain attention, to the point where these tourists have become an important element in the weekly activities of those members of the community who are involved in the tours of the synagogue and the neighbourhood. The impact of this tourism on the running of the port gives it another, more general, function for it supports the economic activity of this part of the old town.

In more general terms, the reappearance of the Rodesli heritage in the old town of Rhodes can also be understood as one consequence of the evolving development of the relationship between tourism and culture, or between tourism and the rehabilitation of historical heritage, as seen in other parts of the world. In fact, something much greater could be playing a part in this rediscovery of the heritage of the Jewish community of Rhodes, that of the image that Greek society has of itself or offers to others. The significance of this image is all the more fundamental because the Dodecanese Archipelago is one of the main tourist destinations around the Aegean Sea, with more than 20 per cent of overnight hotel stays in the country each year. Even if the island is known more for its beaches and holiday complexes than for its cultural tourism, it is quite obvious that the old town of Rhodes is a high-spot for the latter in the summer due to the exceptional patrimonial framework it offers. It is also a place with a high concentration of gift shops for tourists. In terms of display, the old town is presented almost exclusively as a site of Greek antiquity, or related to the town's medieval history and the era of the knights which constitutes its architectural heritage and, more recently, a place shaped by its Ottoman past, which brings an oriental feel to the landscape.

If we talk of the zone classified by UNESCO for its architecture, we see that it is presented as a medieval town enclosed by a ring of fortifications from different periods. This ancient city-state is the only neighbourhood in the town to offer so many traces of the rich and complex history of the island which define the countryside. The general shape of the site dates back to the medieval period, in particular to the rule of the Knights of the Order of St John of Jerusalem, who built a citadel (the Palace of the Grand Master) on top of an ancient Byzantine fortification (Luttrell 2006: 63), and a fortified urban settlement which has since been the monumental heart of the town (Kollias 2001). Ottoman rule, which began there in 1523, brought only minor transformations to the urban fabric but it did leave its mark on the Rhodian landscape through the construction of monumental new buildings: mosques (of which the most important was the great Soliman mosque, built in the 16th century), an *imaret* (caravanserai), a *hammam*, a *merdersa*, a library and the famous clock tower, typical of so many Ottoman towns of the nineteenth century. But this period is also often presented as a time of disengagement and

Figure 3.7 The old town of Rhodes: an urban landscape marked by its history

significant destruction, linked to catastrophies such as the explosion of the power magasine in 1856 (originally the Agios Giannis tou Kollakiou church), which devastated the surrounding buildings for 300 metres, or the earthquake in 1863 that destroyed the huge Naillac Tower which dominated the port (Kollias 2001). From 1912 onwards, Italian rule, by contrast, appeared to be a first step in the administration and conservation of the old town's heritage, through the creation of an office for the conservation of archaeological relics and of the ethnographic and archaeological museum of Rhodes, as well as a raft of renovation or conservation projects, as one part of the town was even legally protected under Italian law (Kollias 2001). But above all the Italians undertook rebuilding work and even genuine reconstructions – particularly after the fascists seized power – of which the most emblematic involved the Palace of the Grand Master and the Hospital of the Knights, which Mussolini wanted to make into a summer residence for King Victor-Emmanuel III.

After the Second World War and the unification of Rhodes with the modern Greek state, the new authorities wanted, firstly, to render the old town functional again, clearing it of the ruins from bombardments it had experienced. At this time, the town saw the settlement of many refugees, who brought agricultural crop and livestock activities into the heart of the medieval town, especially in the moat. Adapting the old town to this way of life for its new population was the priority for the authorities up until the 1950s–1960s, with the drawing-up of a grand traffic plan in 1954 and then the construction of drains in 1955. However, in parallel, concerns about preservation, in response to specific aims to develop tourism, came to light with the establishment of protection laws. As of 1947, the general Dodecanese authorities forbade any construction on the empty bombsites, before the old town was declared a 'protected area' in 1960. In 1980, the 'complete contingency plan' was drawn up; in 1985, an 'office for the conservation and rehabilitation of the old town of Rhodes' was set up (Kollias 2001). This was a fundamental step because, for the first time, it united the efforts of the different institutional agencies such as the Ephorate of Byzantine and post-Byzantine antiquities, the Ministry of Culture and the Municipality of Rhodes. It embodied in Rhodes the new preoccupation with the preservation of the architectural heritage that Greece had agreed to when it signed the Grenada Agreements in 1984 (Manoussou-Ntella and Ntellas 2007).

These efforts were rewarded in 1988 with the classification of the old town as a UNESCO world heritage site. This and earlier decisions confirmed that, in Rhodes, a new cultural and administrative elite – often trained abroad – was taking a different stance and was concerned to take measures towards conservation in the country. From this point on, the zone was protected through a regulatory framework destined to preserve the built environment and, in 1987, a new urban master plan was put together. Throughout this period, restorations, which should perhaps more accurately be called reconstructions or reallocations, were taking place at every scale. The most significant was achieved in the summer of 2000 with the opening of the archaeological promenade in the moat at the foot of the ramparts which, up until then, had been used for the production and sale of fruit and vegetables, and for parking. The main problems, at least as far as the municipal authorities were concerned, involved equipment (the underground sewage systems and electricity networks were in need of modernisation), the circulation of traffic, and conflicts over the use of space by commercial projects, habitation or tourism. For tourism has, indeed, become one of the principal activities of the old town. The island is itself an important tourist destination in the Eastern Mediterranean and the old town of Rhodes attracts 1,250,000 tourists every year. The larger-scale restoration projects now prioritise the needs of the tourist industry, such as, for example, the St Catherine's Hospice project, which won the Europa Nostra prize in 1997 and which structured the building as if it were an open-air museum, rather than considering itself as part of the economic fabric of the urban centre or improving the living conditions for residents.

However, we can also question whether these restorations really represent the town's historical reality and its multi-denominational past. From this perspective, could it not be said that the various restoration projects enable us to see this as a narrative that is based on a biased point of view? In fact, given this particular history, this restoration of cultural heritage, as presented to the public, seems to bear the hallmarks of a desire to appropriate for Hellenism a space that has long been fought over. Indeed, the alternative versions of the history of these places are barely visible, if we only consider the acts of restoration and patrimonialisation undertaken by the authorities. Muslim heritage is a case in point; it has been barely visible in restoration policies for the old town until 2014, even if it leaves its indisputable trace upon the skyline. There is still a Muslim community on Rhodes, however, whose situation in Greece is very particular, as the great majority of Muslims in this country were subjected to the population exchange that took place in 1923 with Turkey. Yet in Rhodes, administrated by Italy at this time, this exchange did not take place. This community therefore survived to this day and counts nearly 2,000 individuals. The occasionally imposing mosques in the old town, however, seem to belong to a forgotten way of life rather than a living practice since, with the exception of one or two – such as the Ibrahim Pacha mosque – they are all closed down. Closer examination actually reveals, however, that Muslims in Rhodes owned a significant share of the cultural edifices of the old town, the reasons for which we need, once again, to search out in the particular history of this archipelago and its tardy unification with the Greek state. Contrary to events in the rest of the country, the Muslim religious authority (or *Vakouf*) was acknowledged and therefore kept on Rhodes by the Greek government, where it had legal possession of religious buildings in the name of its community of believers, whilst elsewhere in Greece (with the exception of Thrace), these buildings had been nationalised during the 1920s and made into public spaces. On Rhodes it was as much a case of monumental grand mosques as of other smaller ones, often old Orthodox Byzantine churches reallocated in the Ottoman era. It was only in 1982 that some of these assets were handed over to the Ephorate of Byzantine and post-Byzantine antiquities (Konuk 2008). The result of this transfer was the renovation of the last buildings…and their reconsecration as Orthodox churches. Nowadays they are presented to the public as such by means of small plaques fixed to the façade, which carry the original name of the church next to its opening hours.

This process of revaluing and display has thus indirectly helped to render 'invisible' some of the history of these buildings. Thus the overriding narrative is that intended for tourists, sometimes despite the appearance of these small buildings, some of which still have their minarets. The situation of the largest mosques is quite different. They were renovated in the 1980s and 1990s (Bouskari 2009) but fell into disuse and were even closed to the public almost as soon as the works had been completed. The association of devout Muslims demanded in vain to be able to use them at the very least for the most important festivals of the religious calendar, as the only mosque in use had become too small to accommodate everyone on feast days: the number of Muslims had, in fact, increased due to the migration of workers to the island since 1990. The devout also demanded to be able to use the prestigious Soliman Mosque which, since its renovation, has remained firmly closed both to them and to the tourists, despite its obvious good condition.

The way in which the Muslim heritage has been treated begs the question: Could the fact that the Jewish heritage runs contrary to the Greek national narrative have equally led to a deadlock over the possibilities for urban, touristic or patrimonial planning in the relevant part of the old town? In the same way as for the traces of Islam, public efforts to develop Juderia still often completely disregard its Jewish past. The above-mentioned restoration of St Catherine's Hospice overlooks the fact that, for many years, the building housed the town's Rabbinical College, the influence of which was widespread across the Eastern Mediterranean. Close by, the remains of a Paleo-Christian basilica were considered worth protecting, whilst the ruins of the former great synagogue were abandoned, and removed from the tourist trail. Whether it be synagogues, Jewish assets or Muslim cultural sites, we can find the reasons for this state of affairs in the way in which the Greek nation was built, typical of all nation-building in the post-Ottoman era (Drettas 2003). Having permanently created confusion between concepts of religion and those of nationhood, this latter conflated all minority religious groups with all ethnic or national minorities (Clogg 2002). A further aggravating factor is that the geopolitical and strategic importance of Rhodes seems to have even further complicated the public expression of those groups whose distinguishing features were different to the canons of Greek identity. These abandoned architectural elements conform to the given definition of a *patrimoine sol* ('land heritage') in which the majority group in a particular place does not feel part of the heritage of the group which created it (Gravari-Barbas 1997). On Rhodes, however, this hiatus between architectural heritage and the national majority narrative does not (or no longer seems to) lead to the disappearance of that heritage, due to a new movement amongst certain individuals in the old town to symbolically appropriate these sites. In fact, since the beginning of the 2000s, there seems to be a connection between the growth of tourism and the returning visibility of alternative Jewish and Muslim heritage: even if the beaches on Rhodes are more attractive, we have to recognise that the numerous gift shops in the old town are proof of its attraction for tourists. As regards advertising, the professionals know their job very well, and the 'Charms of the Orient' are readily visible in the different products that are available in the equally 'oriental' old town: finely wrought-iron objects, rugs, *hammam*, Turkish Delight and ceramics – a good many of them imported from neighbouring Turkey. In this context, religious diversity might be one element able to give its 'Ottoman patina' back to the old town, in which both Muslim residents and Jewish visitors would be the perfect accompaniment. It is, in fact, tourism which the association of devout Muslims uses in their arguments for the re-opening for worship of their largest mosques: cultural and religious diversity are put forward not only as an integral part of the cultural richness of Rhodes but also of the island's attractiveness to tourists, as illustrated by the following interview extract from one of its members outside the Ibrahim Pacha Mosque:

> The great Soliman Mosque, for example, was renovated thanks to funds from UNESCO, so it can now be used. At the moment, we have the use of only one mosque for prayer. In normal times, that is enough but, with *Bayram* next week, there will be so many people that they will be praying outside the mosque. In our view, making this building available again would be good for everyone. It would make a significant contribution to our country (Greece), and would greatly enrich its culture.
>
> If that were the case, there would be no problem about this monument having visitors. In summer, we do not always have the manpower to keep the Ibrahim Pacha Mosque that we manage open all the time, but when we have, we will. It is already open five times a day for prayer and all day on Fridays. We know that tourists are interested in visiting it. Even the residents want to come. Fifty people come in and take photos every day when it is open. For us it is no bother as long as they are respectful.
>
> We would like to use the big Soliman Mosque as a mosque and for tourists to be able to come and visit it too. UNESCO renovated it some five or six years ago. Why is it still closed? Did UNESCO renovate it just to keep it closed?

We could say the same about the Jewish heritage, for this, too, has been preserved and given value by the unique energy of the original commemorative tourism which has kept its memory alive. Just as for the Muslim heritage, the revaluing of such a patrimony could become part of what draws tourists to the town. This seems even more self -evident when we note that the central focus for tourism in the old town has shifted to the Jewish quarter, due to the significant number of tourist cruise ships now docking in this part of the port. Could the development and improvements that the quarter needs be beyond this interlacing of ideological issues, which are dependent on the definition of nationhood and legal questions regarding the ownership of the

Figure 3.8 Different ways of marking space in Rhodes' old town
right Official signposts to places of interest
below left Panel put up by the Jewish community
below right Café frontage evoking its oriental ambiance

assets of those who were deported? Some of the research results have given rise to possible responses to these questions. In fact, even if Jewish heritage is not mentioned on official signs and noticeboards put up by the authorities, its promoters do occasionally use the vocabulary employed in the signage system for tourists. This need to conform demonstrates the manner in which the normal presentation of information and the dynamics of tourism can also be used as a lever to promote this minority heritage in the old town. So it was that, in 2006, the Jewish community replaced the old sign indicating the way to the synagogue with a sign in English which reads 'Synagogue and Jewish museum,' reproduced in the usual colours and layout of signs put up by the authorities to indicate an historical building. The same is true for the display panels that are now outside the entrance to the Shalom Synagogue. In the same way, close to the Panagia Gate – an opening in the medieval wall between the Jewish quarter and the port – another sign provides a detailed description of the route to the synagogue, with the aid of a stylised street map leading to it. In addition to using the official colours, this panel, placed at the main entrance leading from the arrival point for cruise-ship passengers to the old town, confirms that certain aspects of Jewish heritage have been redeveloped for their tourist value. One final point, the use of Greek on this last panel is an additional indication that it now conforms to the official rules of expression prevailing here.

The Greek language also appears in some of the community's more recent projects, such as the name of the sponsor on the monument in the Square of the Jewish Martyrs, which has been recently replaced, or on the panels hung in the museum which tell the story of the community and which, up until 2007, were only written in English. As a result of these changes in signage, as well as of the different places where they have been fixed, we can safely say that these public expressions are an excellent indication of how essential these minor negotiations are when it comes to affirming a heritage which differs from the dominant historical discourse of the country.

Counter-memory and local feeling

Finally, in order to ensure its longevity, the Jewish heritage in Rhodes could even find an unlikely ally in the current residents of the quarter, although at first it seemed that events commemorating the Jewish past might be viewed with anxiety by these residents, as if the reappearance of unwelcome descendants could threaten their presence in the houses they live in, sometimes illegally. On the one hand, as discussed earlier in this chapter, these initial hypotheses can be corroborated by some of the experiences reported by Jewish families seeking to revisit their ancestors' homes. On the other hand, however, the present inhabitants of Juderia no doubt have other priorities. These individuals are the poorest in the old town as the neighbourhood, due to the delays caused by the legal imbroglio over Jewish assets, has not yet become as gentrified as some of the other districts, which have witnessed the settlement of 'neo-residents,' some of them foreigners. These inhabitants are also victims of the bad reputation suffered by the *paliopolitès* (inhabitants of the old town). For some time now a space of declining social status, the quarter has always been considered as a sort of ghetto, rife with rampant drug use, alcoholism and prostitution... A real town within a town. The low rents imposed by the authorities, and even the spontaneous installation of occupants who sometimes do not pay anything, also help to explain the poor state of the houses. Some people are very open about this, such as this man in his fifties living near the synagogue:

> The authorities are ripping us off, forcing us to pay rent that is meant for the maintenance of our houses. They made our illiterate parents sign contracts obliging them to pay rent in exchange for the authorities maintaining the buildings. In actual fact they haven't maintained these places and have let them go to rack and ruin. They want us to leave but we are staying. They have no right to force us out. One of the main articles of the Greek constitution prohibits the state

> from making anyone homeless who does not have the means to pay for accommodation and we, in the old town, are very poor indeed. The Greek state settled us here because the old town was empty and the island was demographically weak. They needed workers – four generations have lived here! Our parents and grandparents, ourselves and our children!'
>
> He tells us that, when he moved into his house, he first of all had to dispose of thirty lorry-loads of rubble and that, according to him, he has since spent at least 60,000 euros of his own money doing it up… 'Having paid for all of that, I don't need to pay rent. I am the one who is looking after Rhodes' valuable heritage.'

In November 2009, one of the town's barristers confirmed that legal issues between local authority landlords and residents were indeed often the cause of conflict over the houses in the old town. She was soon to defend a case in which the house used to belong to Jews but had since become the property of the state. It was occupied initially by a family of refugees from Kalimnos who simply took it over free of charge. In the 1970s, the state published a list of properties that would henceforth be rented to those who were living in them, and this house was one of them. From then on, the inhabitants had to pay a low rent, 'low, but rent even so,' and the state discharged itself of responsibility for maintenance and passed this to the tenants. But the present occupier does not have the means to pay the maintenance costs and is asking the state to help. To renovate this house, he would have to pay for an architect and apply for planning permission from the archaeological services due to the listed status of the entire old town, both very expensive actions. It is true that her client did not really understand what was written in his contract but some of the clauses are clearly unrealistic, given his level of income. This is why she is planning to make a case for an unfair contract, given the circumstances. She does not hold out much hope, however, as 'if this sets a precedent, then the state will have problems throughout the old town.' One of the employees of the archaeological service confirms how difficult relationships are with the inhabitants of the quarter. The process of renovation is straightforward but relatively expensive due to the buildings' heritage status. For the most complicated work, a request with a complete project proposal must be submitted, particularly if the building does not belong to the occupant but to the local authorities. If the work is straightforward and the tenant can pay, the work is given the green light but, in the opposite case, the building has to be left as it is. However, those living in the houses are poor and do not have the means to carry out the necessary renovations. In the long term, this situation could also raise questions about safety.

In such a context, the revitalisation of Jewish heritage is thus only one of many parameters for these inhabitants. However, the complexity of their situation helps to explain their sometimes rather strong reactions and the suspicion that surrounds the return of the former Jewish owners or their descendants. More generally, a lack of understanding of their own situation makes them very wary. Some are even convinced that the rent collected by the archaeological services is given to the Jewish community authorities, which is not the case at all. The ongoing revitalisation in this quarter at the heart of the old town also supports their tendency to see themselves as different in the town. Some even consider themselves to be the rightful heirs to this Jewish heritage from a spiritual point of view, as the authorities seem to be interested only in money (Sintès 2011b). A series of interviews conducted with the residents led to a somewhat nuanced version of how people feel about Jewish heritage in their quarter. The interviews all covered the same topics: firstly, the harshness of their family history, the length of time they have been there (since just after the war) and the tough living conditions (poverty, famine) always seem to justify their presence in these parts. Some even say that they were 'born there', pointing out one room or another in the house in which they live. Above all, they often seem to link their presence to the continuity of the Jewish community, as if they are the only ones who can ensure the preservation of the quarter, given the neglect by the authorities who, according to them, are only interested in lining their pockets with the rents they charge or with international subsidies, and not in the historical, cultural and even spiritual value of Juderia itself. This kind of discourse accords them a fresh legitimacy that dovetails somewhat with the way in which Jewish heritage is typically undervalued. The words of Mr V., a resident living a few feet away from the synagogue, are suitably eloquent:

> Mr V. has worked hard to renovate the house, and he is still working on it. When he arrived, there was rubbish everywhere. He cleared it all up, wearing gloves: 'There were rats as big as this! When I first came here, it was raining inside. How can they ask me to pay rent when I am already taking care of the maintenance?'
>
> He has restored it to its pre-war condition. The things he has collected all date from the nineteeth century. He wants it to look like a Jewish household 'from before,' (a new *kippah* is visible on the sideboard in the hall). 'The house belonged to the Menasce family and, when their descendant came back to visit, she told me that it was incredible, that it was just like their mother had left it when they moved to Africa.' (Further down the street) 'Look, this is where I was born. Just opposite the Shalom temple. You know, the first thing I saw in my life was a synagogue.'

> (On the authorities) 'I wrote a heap of letters to get the authorities to take better care of the house. They did nothing. One room collapsed this year. The day something falls down and kills a tourist, well they won't be able to say that I didn't warn them!'

This narrative involving connection, and material as much as spiritual preservation, can be found here and there amongst the rare actors of gentrification – other residents. One such person is an Italian woman, the owner of a guest house, who sees herself as 'the reincarnation of a Rhodian Jew.' And another Italian woman whose focus on Jewish heritage is quite extreme, despite the fact that her history as a militant communist is hardly in keeping with the piety she displays during services in the synagogue. And finally this hotelier, who sees an opportunity in this normalisation of Jewish memory, and who talks of buying the neighbouring house from the local authorities so that themed guest rooms, such as 'a room that is typical of the Jews on Rhodes' can be offered. This kind of appropriation through a narrative of Jewish heritage in the quarter, seems to echo the creation in 2009 of an association of residents of the old town, whose aim was two-fold: to defend the well-being of the residents, confronted by the spread of noisy night clubs in the medieval enclave and, more generally, to promote a more responsible kind of tourism, something they feel the authorities are incapable of doing. This movement stems from the residents' desire to appropriate the quarter, and who never talk of cultural heritage or the value of tourism as being threats to their way of life. Instead, in the name of good management or ethical practice, they denounce the guidelines given to them by the authorities.

* * *

The changes that are taking place in the old town of Rhodes thus do so in a singular manner. Where we might expect to find an unequivocal dispute between groups with conflicting narratives making legitimate claims on the same places, we find instead a shared sense of belonging to this inhabited and appropriated neighbourhood, despite there being no real connection between them. The discourse that is evolving picks up the theme of threat to a valuable heritage, due to the management imposed by the state. In one sense, the process that has been going on for several decades in the old town of Rhodes has been one of bringing administrative order to human and social situations that are strongly stratified, often inextricably so. From this perspective, the houses in Juderia have found themselves at the heart of processes which bring to mind those which concern the identification of people in the region, as depicted in this volume. For a long time, however, the prevailing logic has been that of the nation-state, structurally reticent about the presence in these peripheral regions of Greece of minority groups who are suspected of being disloyal to the state. It seems, however, that both the current conditions for the mobility of individuals – which allow groups to mobilise in larger numbers and to be better connected even if they are spread across the entire planet – and the interventions of supranational insitutions keen on the preservation of architectural heritage and the commemoration of lost communities, might have the power to alter the situation. The Jewish presence here, like the memories of links between Greeks and Albanians invoked in the previous chapter, is now reflected in line with processes observed in other parts of the world. In effect, it seems that these scattered memories of fringe groups are finding new channels of communication even in those places which, up to now, they had difficulty accessing. Through these groups, a new pluralist history is being written in which the (different) past(s) meet(s) the present. This past introduces new (rediscovered?) complexities which will enable the inhabitants to redefine their position together with their narratives of belonging.

Chapter 4

Mobilities, heritage and the construction of border territories

Research carried out in the different fields presented above leads us to question the origins of a common misconception about the Balkan countries. Where this region is concerned, both the academic and the political world generally portray an image of a society grounded in small, bounded areas, where local belonging strongly influences how groups are defined (Prévélakis 1994). This leads in turn to a rather limited understanding of the locality, inhabited by the *ντόπιοι* (*dopii*, or 'locals' – the popular Greek term). The transformations of the last few decades, which I have seen in many different parts of this region, make one wonder just how this society, supposedly anchored in tiny spaces, is today confronted with, reacts to or interacts with, the increased mobility of actors who become, at one and the same time, both 'locals' and 'strangers', 'tourists' or 'inhabitants', 'returnees' or even 'ghosts from the past' (Givre and Sintès 2013). These various terms highlight the multiple upheavals which, over time, and still today, affect the various case studies chosen specifically for their marginal or peripheral location, where the relationships with places can seem problematic, conflictual and even traumatic, as we have already seen for Rhodes and for the Epirus region of Thesprotia. In these remote regions, nevertheless, current processes suggest new forms of appropriation of space, involving numerous interactions between society and the places, justified by twenty-first-century lifestyles but which also take into account (or make do with) the territory's turbulent past, as shown so clearly by the frequent promotion of its heritage or, more generally, of its past.

Such processes, linked to migratory movements or other geographical mobilities, are good indicators enabling us to foresee how spatial mobilities shed new light on social relations with places, which appear less like fixed entities and more like situated, contextualised and, occasionally, performed experiences. This is particularly true when one realises the capacity of some mobile actors to create 'new links to old places' for themselves (Givre and Sintès 2013), as the Rodeslis or the Albanian migrants have shown us in previous chapters. In the following sections, observations carried out in Thesprotia will again be used, initially, to demonstrate the different trends which, today, characterise these rural Greek peripheral spaces, but which are also emblematic of wider dynamics. Thus, living in this border region, like most of those where the bulk of this research is carried out, takes on, yet again, a paradigmatic dimension, this time concerning the evolution of grounding processes or mobility. These are generally related to a history of conquest and of use of space, but are particularly associated in this border context with the permanent negotiation of a sense of locality. However, today the situation in the area is widely changing: a border barrier (here a real military border) – leading to the isolation of these marginal areas – now coexists alongside (one could even say 'is replaced by') a 'border as filter' (or membrane), which becomes more permeable and reveals processes of opening as much as of closure, of passage and of retention, even a frontier whose edges thicken, where liminality can even, henceforth, become a real resource. This implies a rethinking of usage of space and traditional neighbourhoods.

Study of the rearrangements of the ways in which such spaces are inhabited has, for some years now, focused part of my attention on different research fields. Surveys in the area along the Albano-Greek border or on the island of Rhodes, like that with Guy Thuillier (Sintès and Thuillier 2009) on the island of Tinos, had already provided some background information about the new relations between increasingly mobile social actors and the divers and distant places they frequent. Since 2010, new research in the border territories between Greece, Albania and the Republic of Macedonia is providing me with some original food for thought. Although not seen from the perspective of migration or diaspora studies, starting point for my earlier research in Greece, this latter study is concerned with new forms of territoriality, particularly linked to the increasing promotion of cultural heritage. Through examination of what these processes involve in terms of the appropriation of space, this new work builds on earlier thoughts on the relations between social communities and places, now covering more directly communities' usage and perceptions of the past. The part of this chapter which treats this issue and, more particularly, which covers the localities of Nymfaio, Malovishte and Krushevo, is the result of collective fieldwork carried out in 2011–2012 with the geographer Jean Gardin, from the University of Paris 1, and the anthropologist Olivier Givre of the University of Lyon 2, as well as with Guillaume Javourez, doctoral candidate in geography at the reseach laboratories TELEMME of Aix-Marseille University. Pages 99 to 110 partially reproduce a number of already published texts (Balkabas, in press; Givre and Sintès 2015) and/or drawn up with the researchers mentioned earlier (Givre and Sintès 2013).

Return to Thesprotia

Several people encountered in the town of Filiates during fieldwork in Thesprotia in 2010 and 2011 had come to the region for the summer holiday period. Without necessarily being part of any associational structure, these part-time residents all had one common characteristic: when questioned *in situ*, they all invariably spoke of their love for the region, which they visit every summer. Some come originally from the area and speak of the 'blood ties' which bind them to these places or which are part of their personal history there. For the children of emigrants who left the mountains of Mourgana for Belgium or Germany, the region reminds them of their childhood in the 1960s or 1970s. Those who have 'returned' to Greece are now very typically settled in the main Greek cities of Athens or Thessaloniki, and only rarely in small towns in the region such as Igoumenitsa and Filiates. Their attachment to the villages of their ancestors is intimately linked to the memory of their now-departed grandparents, who left the family house to be a place of family reunion. One such returnee, a woman in her forties whose family originates from a village in Mourgana, spoke very nostalgically of the attachment she feels to her village:

> Here, the eldest child in the family always remained in the village for several years after the rest of the family had emigrated. I was born in Belgium, and was brought to the village when I was seven months old. I stayed here with my grandmother for more than two years. When my parents came to get me, I didn't even recognise my mother. I hid. I did not want to be taken back to Belgium. Because of this, I have experienced the most amazing things, like going to fetch water from the well. We cooked by lighting a fire and all that. I've seen some beautiful things. How cheese is made, how goats are milked…

Whether the ancestral home is repaired, abandoned, the source of dispute or of reconciliation, it feeds the imagination and the discourse of those who come back to it. The village festival provides regular support for these returns. Thus, in Athens, where she lives, our respondent is a member of the village community group (*αδελφότητα*) and devotes much time to the organisation of the patronal festival (*πανηγύρι*). As this falls in the very middle of winter, it is not celebrated on the actual day:

> No-one would be able to come … so we put the festival off until the time when people from the USA and elsewhere are here. We usually hold it in the summer, in the village. We fix the date according to the availability of the clarinetist we invite, who is also from the village.

She comes to the village each year with her family. The year we met, they had gone for two weeks. Her grandmother had died a few years earlier and she did not get along well with her parents, which is, in a way, why she had decided to take this association work on – to have a 'good excuse' for going back there. In Athens, the members of the group meet up every three months at the home of a cousin.

> We make calenders and organise two meetings and a lottery to raise money and then we go out and eat all together. [She also looks after the association's website]: I even had a Facebook group on Thesprotia and that's how I got to know all these people. The group was such a success that they voted me on to the board without me even having to apply. They contacted me after the vote to let me know about it.

The above example typifies a way of life common amongst these groups of 'natives', spread throughout the four corners of the country, if not abroad, and organised in associations of which the activities are not merely limited to the celebration of these groups' common origins, but which embrace certain modes of cultural renewal of the locality (Panopoulos 2005). As Panayotis Panopoulos demonstrates, a meaningful reorientation is emerging of the role of these associations, aimed initially at promoting the social integration of their fellow citizens in their new area of settlement – almost as if, after the initial stages of emigration, often synonymous with being torn from their place of birth and childhood, migrants' efforts were henceforth focused, through these associations, on processes of return to their roots. This, in turn, was beneficial to the region of origin thanks to the new economic status gained through migration. This reorientation is even more explicit for children and grandchildren, born in cities and countries to which their parents had emigrated, who had never lived in these ancestral homelands, but who promote the quality of these sites through their investment in the associations. (Re)building links to place of origin, principally through participation in festive occasions or ritual renewal, itself produces new cultural effects which become, in turn, a positive force for change. This is true, for example, in the case of the association balls for 'natives' described by Panopoulos: whether or not they try to incorporate elements of folklore, the dances bring to the village the practices, attitudes, conceptions and forms of action which cohere much more between themselves than with local cultural practices (Panopoulos 2005: 251). Every return must be negotiated and must take place in the village without overlooking the renewed link with it… Our first meeting in Filiates places us firmly on this path. Futher west, not far from Mourgana and the town of Filiates, the little village of Plaisio offers another configuration whereby permanent residents and visitors live side by side during the summer. Late afternoon, sitting outside a *καφενείο* on the village square, the 'president' once responsible for the *Κοινότητα* (*kinotita**) and representative of the municipal council sets the scene:

> The village has lost much of its population in recent years, but it has always been there. It used to be called Paravrisos, then Plesivitsa… and today Plaisio. Before the war there were 2,000 residents, with a school and a college (*σχολαρχείο*). In the past, it was known for its leatherwork but, since the war, this activity has disappeared and the residents have almost all migrated. The Germans burned down 85 per cent of the village in 1943, and it is from that moment on that the majority of the population left. Since then, there has been a dramatic and continual decline in numbers. People moved to Filiates, Igoumenitsa and, especially, Athens. In the village, electricity was only installed in 1956–58 and it's the former President of the Republic (Constantin Tsatsos, president between 1975 and 1980), himself originally from the region, who arranged for the road to be tarmacked. Today, most of the residents are elderly retirees. The main products are the 28,000 hectolitres of olive oil produced on the 36,000 acres of the community.

And yet, on this afternoon at the beginning of August 2009, there are several cars parked around the village square and quite a few youngsters playing football:

> Yes, it's true, there are many youngsters, but it is the holidays and they are visitors who do not live here all year round but whose parents were originally from the village. There is no work here. What would you have them do? They come for Christmas, and particularly for Easter and 15 August. We are like one big family. There are cafés in the square where we all meet up. (One of the villagers who joins our table confirms this. He raises cattle all year round and boasted of the quality of his animals]: It's organic! And they are the best, local breeds. [However, he does not sell his meat in a shop. He sells to families who, originally from the village, come regularly to visit the place. He calls them the 'Athenians']. They say to me: 'I'm leaving Friday; could

> you put 20 or 30 kilos to one side so that I can take them with me?' Sometimes, they even take the whole animal, that is to say 80 kilos!

The president spoke of the political implications of this type of link:

> We have many *Ετεροδημότες* (people recorded in the census as from the village but living elsewhere, especially in Athens): something like 700. The resident population of the village is 88, not including the Albanians. There are 20-odd Albanians. They live in families and all come from Southern Albania, from the Saranda region, and even, in fact, from the villages closest to the border. The number of inhabitants is crucial as the amount of funding we receive from the Ministry of the Interior is proportionate to the size of the population. The mayor can keep the whole budget if he wishes or only keep 20–30 per cent and share the rest out *pro rata* among the inhabitants of each *kinotita*.

The current context is none too favourable in his eyes:

> In Filiates, there are 19 municipal councillors and there will be 23 after the adoption of the Kallikrati Reform. Of the eight demes, or municipalities, in Thesprotia, only three will remain. In this process of concentration, the municipality of Filiates will annex the municipality of Sagiadas. In the last land reform of 1997 (known as Kapodistria), there was one elected councillor for each *kinotita* of fewer than 300 inhabitants, three for each *kinotita* with more than 300. Now we don't know what will happen. Things will be decided on the basis of the next census (i.e. in 2011). But the counting procedures exclude *Ετεροδημότες* and the population of our regions is going to drop considerably.

This failure to include people who wish to be 'counted' as being resident in their village or town of origin is confirmed by a census official who worked in the municipality of Filiates in 2011:

> The census procedures have been very different this year as they took place over 15 days whereas, last time, it was all done in a single day. People could no longer come to their village to be counted, as they did up until 2001: they didn't have the time'. He thinks that the population will fall from 10,000 in 2001 to just 7,000 or 6,000. 'No more! The municipality has what is an essentially economic problem with this drop in census returns. The state is likely to shut down all services, which will be run centrally from Igoumenitsa. Throughout Greece, for example, the 283 tax offices will be reduced to no more than 75.

It is true that, on this issue, examination of the census data from 2001 in Greece provides some eloquent clues. The general results did indeed depict the heart of the country as a true 'empty Greece', with the depopulation of certain outlying and mountainous areas of continental Greece. The mountains in the north, the Rhodope, most of the Pindus mountainous range, its eastern and western flanks (where Thesprotia is situated), the Vermion, many of the ranges of Phthiotis and Parnassus, the mountainous regions at the heart of the Peloponnese, and the southern slopes of Crete all essentially make up a low-density Greece where depopulation occurred from 1991 to 2001. However, based on this observation, it proved very useful to question such a depopulation thanks to the distinction made in the census between two statistical population categories: the 'resident' population (*μόνιμος πληθυσμός*) and the 'actual' or *de facto* population (*πραγματικός πληθυσμός*). This shows that, in the regions of this 'empty Greece', mountainous and inhospitable over the last forty years in terms of permanent residence, the number of 'actuals' compared to 'residents' was continually and significantly higher (a ratio of 1.4 'actuals' to 1 'resident'). Thus, taking into account only the 'actuals' could lead us to suppose that, in these regions, we are seeing a veritable demographic turnaround. The population of regions such as Evrytania, for instance, situated deep in the mountains, would appear to be on the increase, which would run contrary to the change in the number of 'residents' of this region, which instead indicates a tendency to follow an implacable abandon of the area. When we thus map the ratio between actual population and resident population at the level of the municipalities, we see that it is those very rural and inhospitable regions which show the greatest distortion. This 'empty backbone' of the country seemed to fill up, during the few days of the census, with people who did not live there but who went there just for the census enumeration on Sunday 18 March 2001. Nevertheless, the scale of the gap between the two populations is not insignificant and deserves interpretation. Returning to 'the village' for the census (before 2001, when enumeration methods facilitated this) in the same way that people return there for Easter, for the elections or for a family occasion, appears to be a common phenomenon in the country. Thanks to statistics, it is possible to track this phenomenon and to also show how, compared to the reduced number of inhabitants ('empty Greece'), these spaces are, nevertheless, integrated into a set of relations and circulation of people who make them more than mere abandoned spaces.

The roots of this territorial mobility, which is mainly in the direction of the mountains or the islands, can be found in the history of these regions, marked as they are by ancient mobilities, nomadism and transhumance, followed by mobilities at other scales and, finally, at least partially, by the out-migration flows of the 1950s to 1970s. These mobilities are, thus, representations of the

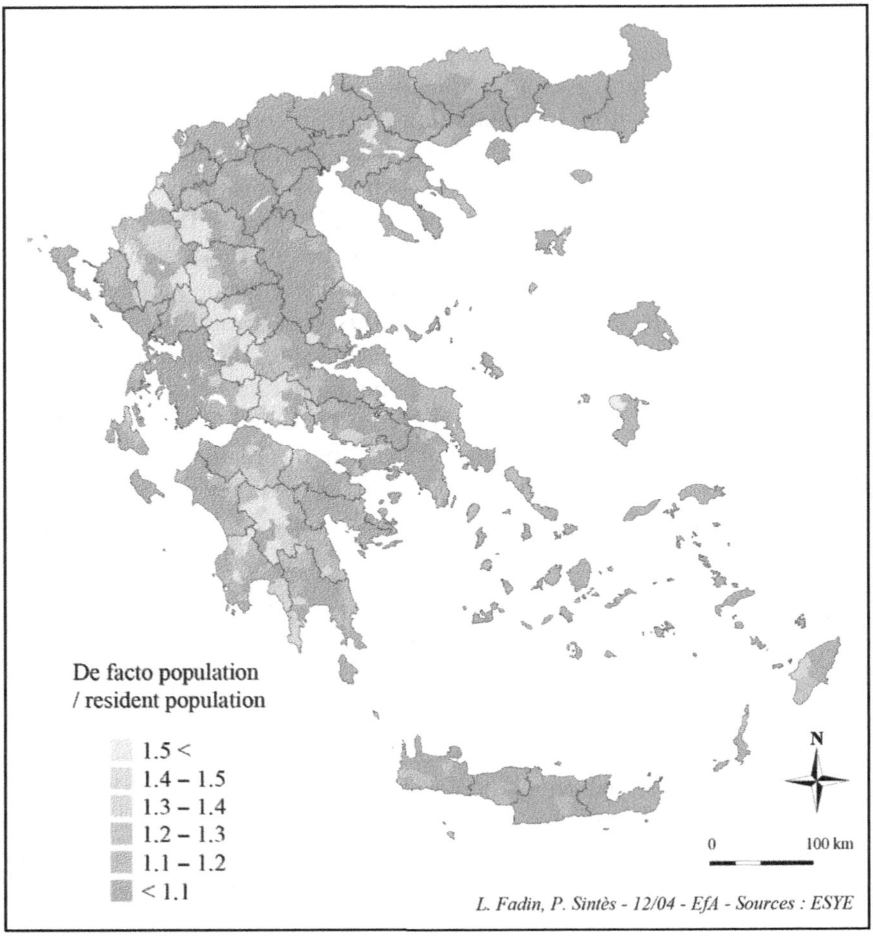

Figure 4.1 The residence of Greek nationals enumerated in the 2001 census
Source: Sintès (2010a)

local in terms of 'roots', leading to forms of reinvestment in 'my homeland' (*Πατρίδα μου*, as the song goes), for example in the euergetism which I describe below, and stemming from a profound attachment to the 'village', to a person's roots. The return of migrants from abroad in the 1980s, their resettlement, the most often, in towns and cities, together with the opening up of the whole Greek territory (Damianakos 1996, 2001; Sivignon 2001), has served to reinforce this attachment to the village of origin through regular visits without, however, resulting in a repopulation of the place.

Despite a certain rebalancing which has taken place since the 1980s, and the new forms of population dispersal in Greece in the 1990s, the outcome of the spatial dynamics of the Greek population over the last 50 or so years is unequivocal. The current distribution is profoundly marked by a half-century of concentration in the more dynamic zones of the territory – the towns and cities and the coastal spaces. In spite of a slowing down of certain tendencies which had dominated up to now, these coastal districts are today those where there is the greatest concentration of people, and the larger urban areas remain the anchor points of the dense territorial networks. Notwithstanding general dissatisfaction with city-centre living, the prefectures of Athens and Thessaloniki were still home to around 40 per cent of Greeks in 2001, and only a few less in 2011. However, study of the different census categories would seem to indicate that there is still, today, a level of complementarity between those spaces which have seen considerable depopulation and the most active towns and cities, to the point where some city-dwellers, up until 2011, were still trying to be counted as 'genuine' inhabitants of their region of origin. These commonalities lead us to think that the different regions of the country are all, in fact, rather more integrated elements in a complex whole than a mere centre/periphery binary opposition, and that these hidden vestigial links counterbalance the polarising effects of the widespread urbanisation of the Greek territory.

Reminiscences of 'home' … elsewhere

But do the regular visitors, who go to these outlying villages, still have a genuine attachment to these places through family ties or personal histories? Are these links between places really unequivocal, with the separation of the 'desired' place of origin from the place where they live being purely for economic or professional reasons? Over the same period, observations carried out in coastal localities in Thesprotia, like that of Sagiada, have revealed much more complex trajectories in which the resident population is slightly more dispersed throughout an ever-greater number of places. People living in cities like Athens or Ioannina regularly spend the summer months there. The reasons they advance to explain their choice are sometimes surprising in the way that they justify it through elements of their personal history – and also what they perceive to be their cultural heritage. This is the case, for example, for Christos, in his sixties, whom I met in front of his mobile home, under the arbour in his vegetable garden in Sagiada. Christos was born in 1948, at the end of the civil war, in a mountain village above the town of Filiates. Soon after his birth, the family moved to Filiates, and he was forced to leave his village. After three years in Filiates, the family returned to the village. The same scenario held true for many others who had fled the village and taken refuge in Filiates. Christos' grandparents had bought a house in the village. They were tinkers who repaired saucepans, and travelled as far as Thessaloniki, and even the islands, offering their services. Everyone in the village did this type of work. In 1953, when Christos finished at the village school, there was still a sizable population in the village as there were 45 pupils in the school. It was his teacher who encouraged him to pursue his studies but this was not easy as his parents had little money. He therefore went to college in Paramithia and slept in the church boarding-house.

> But we *συμπατριώτες* (fellow villagers) kept ourselves to ourselves. Before, the valley of the Kalama River was a real border. A person was from one side or the other. That made a difference. Even here, there are differences between the villages in the higher part of the Filiates region and those from below. They sing different songs, and speak with different accents. Those of us from villages in upper Filiates sang polyphonic songs, the others didn't.

In 1966, aged 17, and following the death of his father, Christos finished school. That same year he sat the entrance exam for university and accepted a place at the new University of Ioannina, in the School of Philosophy. He was in receipt of a grant and was very well looked after by the state. In 1972 he graduated and went to do his military service in the army for a year only, as he was the family breadwinner. He returned in 1974 and settled in Filiates, where he taught in the secondary school. He was a passionate and committed teacher both because he loved his pupils and because he was a patriot and *τοπικιστής* (localist) and wanted the best for his pupils – 'I watched them grow up'. His mother remained in the house in the village. He himself has never severed his ties to the village; he is a passionate hunter and hunts wild boar from September to February at least three times per week. He married and remained in Filiates. In 1992, he and his wife moved to Stuttgart, where they stayed until 1997, teaching German Greeks. On moving back to Greece in 1997, they settled in Ioannina, where they had bought a piece of land six years earlier. They built a house on the plot, and still live there. Why Ioannina? 'So that the children could go to good schools'. From 1998, he wanted to learn about archæology and enrolled at the University of Ioannina, where he studied the history of the region. In Filiates, Christos owns an old house which is completely shut up; one of these old Filiates houses which his family bought after the war. The house is empty.

> We used to rent it out up until 1990 but then we did not want to rent it to Albanian migrants as they are always troublesome tenants. So the house remains as is; no-one lives there.

Since they live in Ioannina, the family has never been further than 65–70 kilometres from his mother's village. They were 32 kms away when in Filiates. In the village, only 20, mostly elderly, residents remain. His five brothers live in Athens, except for one who is in Igoumenitsa, and his sister in Boston. Many inhabitants migrated out of the village, mostly to South Africa. His grandfather had a grocer's shop in the village which was open until around 1985–1990 but is closed now. In 1950, his father had built a first floor above the shop, with four bedrooms. It is now a big house but his mother lives there on her own, which is not easy for her. In the last two months they have taken on a Greek Albanian lady to look after her. Christos visits her every fortnight, and they also go at Easter and Christmas. In 2001, they went to the village to be enumerated in the census; himself, his two children and his wife. However, in 2011 they were required to be registered in the place where they actually lived.

His mother's village is very beautiful, surrounded by forests, and clean, fresh air. At its most populated, there were 150 inhabitants. Away from the village there are two *αδελφότητες* (residents' associations), one in Athens which is still going strong and the other in Larissa. In the house, they have only carried out minor repairs.

> We've done nothing to this house, nor to the one in Filiates because, you know, we are seven children … so … who does the house belong to? That is the question. We have each gone our own way … and we don't really know what will happen when it comes to our inheritance of it.

He is keen to maintain it to keep a link with his village, rather than let it fall to ruins. But, now that Christos and his wife have retired, they spend most of their time in Sagiada, on the coast.

> We bought this field in 1983. It belonged to a native of Sagiada who had moved to Corfu and did not wish to return. It was a field of 12 acres which belonged to three brothers.

Why there? For Christos, the place has never been far. It was on the coast. He saw it as being quite close to Filiates. He has always maintained links with the place, where he feels at home:

> For me, who loved both trees and the sea … it was the ideal spot. In the field there was an old house where the children used to go to play basketball and volleyball in the 1950s, and a sort of cultural centre.

Christos and his family cleared the land and set up their mobile home there, complete with arbour. He planted trees and they go there every year. They have a lot of friends there now.

Christos' narrative reveals the multiplicity of places around which he has build his life-course, both in Greece and abroad. For now, the proximity of the various places helps him to explain some of the choices he has made, even if he is now in a region which seemed to him to be culturally quite different to his native village in the mountain, in fact not that far away. But today he declares that he feels completely at home in Sagiada, in the strongest sense of the term. He is documenting the history of the place, through his enthusiastic participation in events organised by the commune, where he mixes with residents whom he calls his fellow villagers (*συμπατριώτες*). More generally it is the territory of Epirus, as much as that of Thesprotia, with which he feels the strongest identification, and it is this which enables him to create a discourse on the space where he feels he belongs. As invoked by Christos, the buildings are physically affected by these transformations in the life-styles and the greater mobility of their inhabitants. It is the case, for example, for this house in the village of Sagiada, which has changed exponentially according to the family history of those who live in it. The three stages of its construction correspond to those which defined the rythmn of life in the household. The first two rooms had been built for the parents, when they settled in the village after the war. The self-built extension was intended to house the children but is today completely overflowing with the couple's belongings now that the children have left the village for nearby Igoumenitsa and Athens. The garage, a later addition, was turned into a bedsit, where the grandmother could spend her last years, closer to those on whom she was totally dependent. At present the grandchildren stay there during the holidays, as these young adolescents prefer to be independent … and to escape in some small measure from grandparental control.

Others, who live and work in Athens but who are natives of other regions in Greece, have also bought houses in Sagiada. They justify this choice of such a peripheral region as Thesprotia as the desire to make a more radical break from their daily lives… while renewing ties to what they perceive to be their 'true selves': 'The first time I came to Sagiada I realised that I belonged here', said one of them by way of explanation. But for them, as for Christos, respecting and adopting the traditional village way of life facilitates their full integration into places initially foreign to them. This type of resident invariably explains his or her presence there by invoking tradition and the 'spirit of the place'. Nevertheless, these people also leave their mark on the place and, in their turn, adapt village customs and even the style of house they live in to suit them. For example, in Sagiada, the summer residents seem to set great store by their peace and quiet. They are somewhat appalled by the

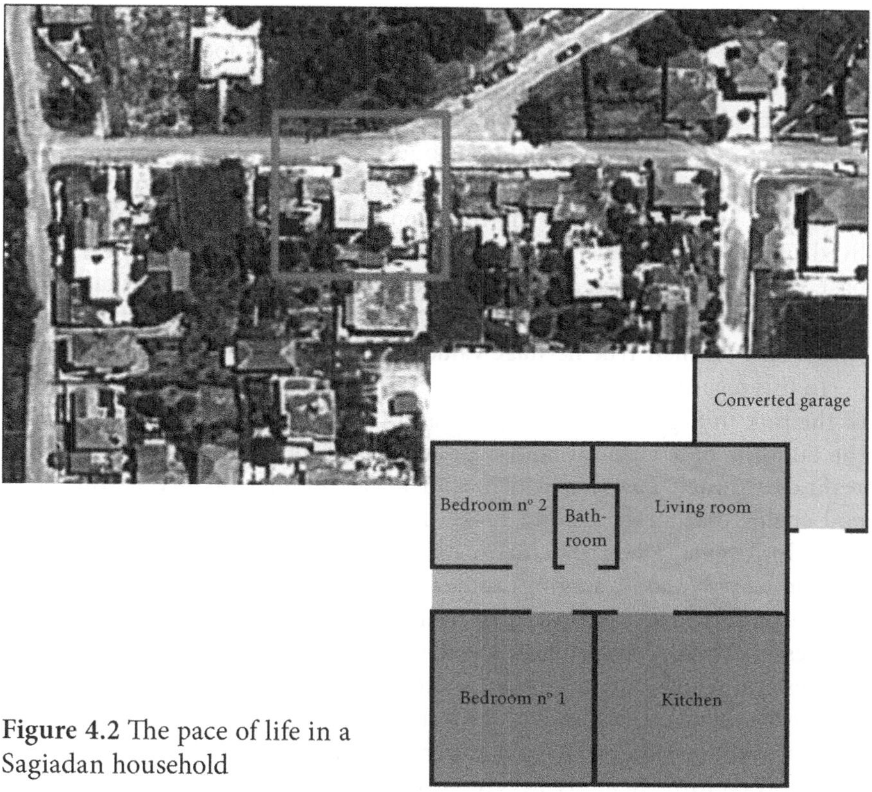

Figure 4.2 The pace of life in a Sagiadan household

young, who make such a noise at night outside the bars alongside the small port, drinking and throwing themselves in the water 'as though they were in Mykonos'. They gently make fun of the permanent residents of the village for being gruff, unsociable hermits, even while sharing their summer moments… In the dead season, 'life goes on elswhere', as demonstrated by the ironic tone in which this summer resident invokes a permanent villager. 'In winter, friend Sakis stays in the village. He even wears a fur coat indoors as it is very, very cold here! It is very humid because of the proximity of the sea'.

These situations refer to a process which can be used to describe many other rural spaces in Europe which, due to the growth of mobility and the increase in urban pressures, are experiencing what Bernard Kayser qualified, for France, as '*la renaissance des campagnes*' (Kayser 2004). In Greece, these multiple 'returns to a rural world' which is itself undergoing profound change are well described by Elini-Christina Sotiropoulou when she writes about the mountain villages of the Pindus, near Ioannina (Bossuet and Sotiropoulou 2007; Sotiropoulou 2007). There is a need, here, to underline certain tendencies through the prism of discourses about place and custom, how actors explain or justify their way of living in these places, with, often, the structure or performance of a discourse resolutely focused on tradition and heritage and, discretely but deeply, affected here by the proximity of the international border with Albania. Reference to the history and the tradition of this space effectively provides eloquent support for the socio-spatial dynamics invoked above, insofar as it enables a (re)new(ed) narrative of the locality to be established. If the tradition and patrimonial quality of these lived spaces are not new, the trend today is to firmly anchor society in the past. In a general context, we must nevertheless appreciate that heritage is not simply 'monuments which are lived in' (Fabre and Iuso 2011), but daily spaces which take on their true heritage value (Givre 2008).

In this regard, two particular events seem symptomatic of the reformation of the link in Sagiada between place and tradition. They both contribute to the building of a 'cultural landscape' which meets today's expectations and realities through customs which lend a patrimonial quality to the place and enable discourses around roots. The first event takes place every year in early August, when the *Πολυφωνικό Καραβάνι* (a travelling festival of traditional polyphonic singing) comes to a halt amid the ruins of the ancient village of Sagiada, bringing in its wake artists, the media and the public to these normally particularly silent spaces. According to the founder of this festival which, for more than a decade, has wound its way through the Balkan Peninsula, the idea is to link the different places through this vocal activity and to (re)create, from Southern Italy to Bulgaria, one huge network of shared culture. Here, as we saw in Rhodes with the revitalisation of the Jewish heritage, this cultural activity is well placed on the 'global hierarchy of value' already discussed towards the beginning of the volume (Herzfeld 2004), as it is generally accepted in the contemporary world and is internationally recognised. Polyphonic song is effectively presented in a way which brings to mind the intangible cultural heritage promoted by UNESCO. The 2010 festival reproduced, in Sagiada, elements already performed at other stages of the group's trajectory that year. Nevertheless, the originality of the representation there remained the absence of amplification, which was presented as a source of manifest pride by the organisers, as though the sound within these old stones and the old ruined houses which surrounded the scene were the most suitable frame in which to respect and reproduce traditions. Apart from this technical detail, however, the event was also an opportunity to confirm the capacity of certain actors in the mobilisation of this heritage (local intellectuals as well as political authorities) and to confirm the authenticity of the place through this sort of *de facto* endorsement.

More important by its size than by its local reach, the *πανηγύρι* of old Sagiada is the only event of this nature in the region which takes place within the ruins of an abandoned village. This *πανηγύρι* takes on all the

Figure 4.3 Sagiada: where place and polyphony rhyme…

more a mantle of reconstruction linking a lost community to the present day in that it is held each year on 26 July (Agia Paraskevi Day), anniversary of the day when German soldiers set fire to the village. The *πανηγύρι* begins with a religious service in the disused church, in memory of those who perished in the disaster. This is followed by a festival, with music and food, which is largely intergenerational, and in which it is customary to behave

Figure 4.4 Playing the community: the patronal festival of old Sagiada (2011)

in a way that promotes traditional values such as honour and family, all the while sharing the *kefi*, this 'unbridled, relaxed pleasure' (Herzfeld 1997: 89–90), as is expected on this type of occasion. Relations between the group and the surrounding territory are played out via implicitely shared values performed through commemoration, religious communion, hospitality and neighbourliness. During the *πανηγύρι*, these relations are clearly harmonious but also on this occasion strongly essentialised, even though a closer look at the participants would highlight, once again, the heterogeneity between the permanent inhabitants of the village (somewhat older) and their descendants, generally occasional visitors (whether coming to see their parents or having a house there) who often live and work in nearby towns, and the newcomers and second-home owners, to whom it is often pointed out that they are not really 'from here'.

For these 'newcomers', it is respect for the old traditions and the authentic and inspirational character of the place which moves them to attend, and to justify this: 'This is where the true traditions of Greece are to be found' said one. Finally, the presence of migrants from Albania who live and work there either permanently or seasonally highlights the diversity of those 'from here' who make up the population of contemporary Sagiada. Through these various elements, we can see that the locality is not composed uniquely of those who live nearby but is founded more on a form of communion of supposed common, shared values. However, one cannot help but notice the ephemeral nature of this communion, adapted for a society where ways of belonging seem, in the long run, quite fluid.

'New rural communities' and changing lifestyles

New ways of living of native or foreign urbanites of relatively long standing in the village, local population dynamics which speak of the historic and traditional qualities of life in the place, the transformation of family houses in anticipation of a 'return to' or 'a remaining in' the village, and also the possibility to welcome 'tourists' or 'visitors' etc., in all these new dimensions, the dynamics described above allow an entry (or a re-entry) into a sought-after locality, and the production of a consensual discourse on the latter. Henceforth these relations and performances act as a sort of 'mirror' which can be held up or shown to others … involving a *savoir-vivre*, cultural norms and values recognised locally as much as they are sought out elsewhere, other than the place where one usually lives but in which one can not feel completely at home (or where one at least feels differently). The promotion of this particular way of living is witness to profound territorial transformations. Alongside transient festive events, domestic space constitutes one of the principal sites of these transformations. As Olivier Givre shows for Bulgarian villages, the classic example of the transformation of the farm into the villa is the visible sign of this social, demographic and economic evolution in the countryside, and also a first step towards the invasion, which often follows, of public spaces by these new ways of living (Givre and Sintès 2013). These new 'ruralities', through the use that they make of the place and, in particular, through places invested with new qualities attributed by this same cultural, touristic, recreational and also speculative use, are seen to be important vectors of change, in particular by the provision of economic opportunities, themselves factors in new disparities (Bossuet and Sotiropoulou 2007; Givre 2008).

However, in such a context, how do we equate 'being here' with 'being from here'? Does inhabiting a place always signify spatial stability, when daily life is increasingly influenced by mobility, change, even uncertainty, and especially here and now by the Greek economic crisis? Visiting one's house in the village and regularly spending money to fix and modify it, thus begs the question of what 'being at home' actually means. These ways of living are proving to be intrinsically linked with mobility and circulation: 'People are increasingly having to live with a more portable notion of home' (Miller 2001: 9). From travelling back and forth, to outright migration, most spatial, and also social, mobility requires multiple conceptions of inhabited space. Experiencing movement nowadays implies the capacity to change places and homes, to move between houses, living a *polytopic* (i.e. multilocal) lifestyle (Stock 2006) and to link together different spaces and social worlds. In Sagiada, relations with village space are woven (or re-woven) around some quite remarkable discourses, which are working to bind together within the heart of the village an increasingly heterogenous body of actors. The descendants of those who emigrated abroad or migrated to the cities are today linked to the villages by a thousand and one types of mobility: second homes, holiday visits, weekend visits, attendance at festive events in the village, etc., which go much further than simple membership in a generations-old villagers' association. Stressing these practices highlights the appearance of a new type of resident in recent decades, one who settles there and also takes up the mantra of returning to one's roots, to a more tranquil and outdoor life, closer to tradition, even though their 'objective roots' may not lie in this region. These merits, much lauded by new residents, will, of course, be those merits which go against the 'ills of our society' – but which also make up a heritage, a body of values and traditions to be preserved, and to this end some resort to intense activity, as has also been seen in other contexts.

'Good patrimonial practices' in Macedonia

As well as these transformations in the ways of living, these peripheral regions are also experiencing new dynamics involving institutional actors. These dynamics are worth highlighting as they are also concerned with the protection of heritage and tradition which echoes those described above for Thesprotia. Here we are talking of transborder cooperation, a course of action much favoured by the European Union, and which is based on recurring themes such as 'peacekeeping', development or political and economic transition in these regions, normally considered to be fraught with a number of antagonisms which have resurfaced since the fall of the Iron Curtain (see Chapter 1). In the Balkan countries, where we find contrasting situations concerning European integration, these forms of cooperation are seen as a useful tool with which to implement peaceful transborder relations and 'good practices', designed to promote both the eventual EU membership of candidate countries and regional stability. This transfer of what is essentially an EU development model, though mitigated by weak results and the inefficiency of some of these projects, demonstrates the multiple ways in which these institutional frameworks can help to (re)define the local scale over and above international border disputes. Thus, observation of these dynamics enables the introduction of an enlarged conception of the border which involved different places situated in close proximity. The latter seems, effectively, to have gone from being a dividing line in confrontations between political, historical and even 'cultural' enemies, to being a thicker space, a 'border-territory' or 'borderland' which can also be a space defined by these projects, a space in which social and institutional bodies are acting. Although recently drawn national borders are often still confrontational, many cross-border practices are likely both to (re)surface in favour of these cooperative projects which lend value to the vision of shared territorial space, where new neighbourhoods can be constructed ... and also to revive ancient cross-border/transnational discourses and practices in the same way that the migratory movements examined in Chapter 2 did. Both cultural and natural heritage often play a role in the recognition of a certain communality over and above nation-state constructions, as they can be sources *par excellence* of shared cultural artefacts or practices in spaces recently divided by a border; spaces which for many centuries were part of the same imperial entity. This historical background is thus seen as a suitable environment for nurturing a more global transformation of the border region through a dialogue between cultures, the evolution of which may become 'a resource (...) henceforth seen less as a brake on and more as a lever for economic development' (Amilhat-Szary and Fourny 2006).

Institutionally, this type of project today takes place at the heart of the Institution for Pre-Accession Assistance, which more generally governs many of the relations between Greece and its northern neighbouring countries. In recent years, European policy towards Eastern Europe and the Western Balkans, both areas which are expected eventually to acceed to membership of the EU, has taken place within the framework of stabilisation and association processes set up to support these countries in the run-up to their full integration. Following signature of the Stabilisation and Association Agreements, the candidate or potential candidate states would be led to adopt a certain number of measures thanks to EU technical and financial assistance. Thus it is that the CARDS and PHARE pre-accession instruments were set up in the region, via which the first cross-border cooperations were undertaken. In 2007, these different programmes were merged within the Instrument for Pre-Accession Assistance or IPA. Actions carried out within this new framework had the explicit objective of preparing the candidate countries and institutions in the management of European Structural Funds and thus EU cohesion policy. Inspired by current INTERREG programmes in EU member-states, cross-border cooperation would appear to be the second of the five elements which make up this new instrument (Blondel *et al.* 2013). The opportunity given to states to put these cooperative programmes in place has opened up new sources of finance for local actors, on condition that they coordinate their activities within eligible border spaces and that they adhere to the terms set by European legislation. Transformation of regional spaces around the global theme of 'Europeanisation', understood as an incentive to change brought about by (prospective) EU integration, thus encourages the emergeance of these new project territories (i.e. derived from a project implementation area). Within this framework, EU funding is conditional on a certain number of criteria, which themselves presuppose the primary employment of rhetorical notions such as 'peacekeeping', 'cooperation' or 'political and economic transition'. Both local development and cross-border cooperation are perceived as driving forces for a more global transformation of the regions targeted by these projects, as can be observed in other European regions, where they are considered 'a functional resource with which relegated peripheral spaces can be (re)valorised. (…) the border appears if not as a locus of cooperation, at least as a support enabling the link to be made' (Amilhat-Szary and Fourny 2006). Thus, varied (though interlinked) contexts for the implementation and financing of this type of project in local heritage sites were considered, notably in Northern Greece (such as the village of Nymfaio, in Western Macedonia, Greece, which will be presented below), and then in the south of the Republic of Macedonia (the village of Malovishte and the town of Krushevo). These studies, the results of some of which have already been or are being published (Balkabas, in press; Givre and Sintès 2015), have enabled analysis of the links between local contexts, networks of actors, and institutional frameworks, through the financial, material, political and symbolic resources made available by EU development programmes.

Nymfaio: tourism as a sole perspective?

The first of these examples is the little village of Nymfaio, set within a landscape in which many operations of this type are visible. With the towns of Florina to the north, Ptolemaïda to the east and Kastoria to the west, and perched on a mountainside at an altitude of 1,300 metres, Nymfaio is accessed via a winding road which quickly opens up a view of the Pelagonian Plain. Once in the village, the contrast with localities down on the plain is quite startling: Aetos, 600 metres below Nymfaio, or Xino Nero or Amyndeo in the distance, both offer the spectacle of market towns where the smells and sounds of beasts and agricultural machinery pervade the air. Whereas, in the summer, the scorching temperatures down in this agricultural basin keep the streets empty during much of the day, Nymfaio is a haven of calm and freshness. Over and above the usual road signs indicating the way to the village, the visitor is welcomed by a whole panoply of signs vaunting the special features of the place. Half way up, after the first notices indicating the hotels in the village (as can be seen in almost all tourist sites in Greece), noticeboards provide information on the local flora and fauna, highlighting the environmental quality of the area. Arriving at the panorama overlooking the Ptolemaïda Basin, the visitor finds him- or herself in a 'beech forest habitat', following 'the traces of the otter, the wolf and the bear', as indicated on the many posters showing the logos of actors and funding bodies: The Association for the Preservation of the Brown Bear (Arkturos), the (former) municipality of Aetos (which became part of the municipality of Amyndeo following the last administrative reform plan Kallikratis), and the European Union through the LEADER and INTERREG programmes. A further sign of this opening up of the area to tourists, the footpath between Nymfaio and Agrapidia (a stretch of the E4 European long-distance path), directions for which are visible here and there, is one facet of protection of the environmental heritage of the region.

There is a vast car park just outside the entrance to the village, where all except the inhabitants and those staying there are obliged to leave their cars, as in many other tourist sites in Greece – a meeting point complete with maps of the network of hiking trails and a map of the 'Macedonian Wine Trail', on which Nymfaio is one stage. From the outset, Nymfaio shows itself to be an exceptional cultural and environmental space and a well

Figure 4.5 The village of Nymfaio: a haven of tranquility

thought-out and organised tourist site. This first impression is confirmed by the numerous signs of tourist development in the village itself, especially the noticeboards indicating local facilities, boarding houses and hotels, naming places, or paying tribute to different benefactors. The houses, with their zinc roofing – unusual for a region more used to roofs of heavy limestone slabs – are massive, without balconies and often encircled with gardens edged in small or large walls. The village is, of course, also a place of residence, often elegant and always neat and tidy, with its well-tended lawns and colourful flowerbeds. Some houses even appear to be very luxurious, with swimming pools, private chapels and several outbuildings enclosed out of sight and protected by a video surveillance system. Two such properties at the entrance to the village, brightly floodlit for a good bit of the night, are even linked by a little private footbridge over the main road. Other than a shepherd from another commune and horses belonging to some of the permanent residents, there is no sign of any agricultural activity in this little model village, well tended by inhabitants who are not lacking financially and who care deeply about the environment.

Late afternoon on the 20 July 2011 (St Elie's Day), thirty people, led by the Orthodox priest Yanni, good-humouredly climb the hill which leads out of

Nymfaio to the Prophytis Ilias Chapel. Most are in their fifties and sixties, sometimes accompanied by their young adult or teenage childen. They are all resident for at least part of the year in the village, where they possess either an old house or a new-build. They all know one another through having generally arrived at the same time in the 1980s or 1990s, although they were not all originally from the village and came from many different regions. Aetos, Xino Nero, Amyndeo and Ptolemaïda (towns and villages in the Ptolemaïda Basin), together with Thessaloniki and Edessa, are their main places of residence. So why did they choose this place to have a house? The peace and quiet, the wildlife, the good weather and the wonderful walks round about. And in the winter the children can go there to go skiing in the nearby resorts. In their eyes the village offers all the benefits of a secondary home, a new and occasional link with an area chosen for its quality of life and recent revitalisation:

> There are only fifty permanent residents but many more of us in summer. In winter it is mainly tourists: it is the best tourist season in Nymfaio.

The winter activities are the main resource for some of residents of the village who, sometimes at the cost of major work, have modified their homes in order to offer bed-and-breakfast to tourists passing through, even transforming them sometimes into actual boarding-houses, with several bedrooms and bathrooms, television etc…

Once at the chapel, the small group says Mass and freshens up before enjoying cakes brought up from the 'best baker in Ptolemaïda'. From the top of the hill, the view opens onto the Ptolemaïda Basin: Kozani to the south, Florina and the border with the Republic of Macedonia to the north. The panorama needs a little presenting: Xino Nero, Amyndeo and Aetos harbour the *ντόπιοι* ('natives' or 'locals' i.e. Slavic-speakers in this region), whereas in Lehovo we found Albanian-speaking Arvanites …

> … brought in by the Turks during the Ottoman Empire. They still speak an Albanian dialect but are of Greek national persuasion. Until recently these groups only ever inter-married amongst themselves. Even the Pontic Greeks who came from the Black Sea to Meliti or the Micrasiatics from Asia Minor. The Vlachs from around here also married only amongst themselves in order to preserve their community, however cosmopolitan they were. But today, this is all old hat, as in the rest of Europe.

On the other side of the hill is Nymfaio with its grey zinc rooftops, from amongst which emerge large buildings like the La Moara hotel, whose three storeys overlook the entire village space. In the centre, another imposing building also draws the eye:

> Nikios School, the school from the good old days! It is closed now and the five youngsters in the village (all Albanian) have to descend to the plain to go to school. (We learn that) Nikios was an important businessman who bequeathed this school to his native village. Everyone in the village was a trader and they all spoke Aromanian. They worked in gold and silver. In winter they went to Egypt, to Vienna, to Istanbul, and in the summer they returned to the village. If you go into the school you will see photos of the grandchildren of this Nikios. They currently manage the tobacco and drinks trade in Sweden, where they live. Many other families of powerful businesspeople are originally from here: they are responsible for much of the development in the village today. The most famous is Yannis Boutaris, who introduced the Arkturos Association: that's when tourism began here in the 1990s.

These accounts bear witness to initial impressions of this little village (413 inhabitants registered in the 2001 census, of whom around fifty were permanent residents), which appears both as a space of historic interest and heritage, as a tourist destination, as a select mountain resort, and even as an upper-class *gated community*. What changes have taken place since the photo taken in 1895 which adorns the front of the grocer's shop in the centre of the village! From systematic observation one becomes aware of the complexity of the powerful movement which has highlighted the value of its cultural heritage. The village space is marked throughout by signs of this revitalisation: commemorative plaques, tributes to donors (on fountains, chapels and buildings), noticeboards with information about UE programmes, explanatory notes about this part of the village or that house, and photos of ancient Neveska (the old name for Nymfaio). The success of this process visibly owes much to both the institutional sphere (state recognition and the intervention of the different public bodies are widely acknowledged) and to the family circle, with family homes (*πατρικά σπίτια*) being handed down to the next generations, who renovate or transform them. The preservation of heritage is also seen to be related to community spirit, with the village openly declaring itself as an Aromanian settlement and using Vlach names. Aside from frequent use of the old name of Neveska, old houses transformed into guesthouses have been rechristened with characteristically Aromanian names: 'La Galba', 'La Moara', 'La Moudé', etc. As for the natural heritage, appreciation of it takes many forms: from the discourse of the retired residents already referred to above, who vaunt the purity of the air and the peace and quiet of the environment to, more concretely, the cultivation of a deer park or the creation in 2005 of an artificial

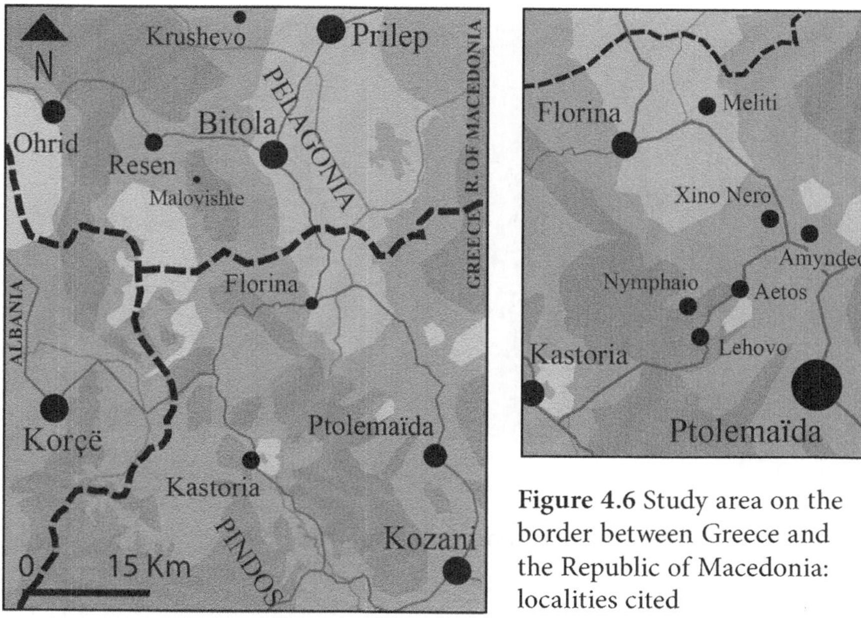

Figure 4.6 Study area on the border between Greece and the Republic of Macedonia: localities cited

lake nearby, both of which were designed to be an outdoor activity centre and a natural habitat for local fauna. The strong presence of the Arkturos Association (see below) also indicates the central position held by the village in networks of environmental protection.

Used both for fund-raising and as an example of a successful *mise en tourisme* (MIT 2000) (i.e. the physical transformation of the place into a tourist destination), this natural and cultural landscape is clearly associated with a narrative of the past evident in the many writings of an influential local author. In his writings we learn that the village of Nymfaio, built in 1385, would have first been known as a 'Vlach village' or, more precisely, as an 'autonomous borough inhabited by a Latin-speaking Greek bourgeoisie (the Vlachs)' (Mertzoz 2004: 2), who were gold- and silversmiths, and furriers. During its long history, the village benefitted from the proximity of Kastoria and of the urban centre of Thessaloniki – which were of considerable importance under the Ottoman Empire – and of many other boroughs and towns on the Balkan peninsula. The activities of these rich businessmen thus linked the village to the great cities of the Ottoman and Hapsburg Empires and of Western Europe. The prosperity of Nymfaio can be seen in its architectural collection of fortified bourgeois houses 'adorned with rich decorations and furnished in European fashion allied with local tradition' and in the urban infrastructure of the village (roads, sanitation, lighting) 'of which foreign visitors spoke with admiration' (Mertzos 2004: 2). The area

Figure 4.7 A village space brimming with information

which, in its time, has counted some 3,000 inhabitants, was strongly affected by the troubles which touched the region at the beginning of the twentieth century. The rapid decline which started in the 1930s seemed relentless, and 'by the end of the 1980s Nymfaio was completed deserted – those houses which had not yet collapsed completely disintegrated, abandonned, the roads were covered in weeds, and the remaining 45 or so inhabitants, mostly the elderly, simply waited for the end' (Mertzos 2004: 3). Designated by the Greek state in 1978 as a 'traditional settlement and a well-preserved historic site', the village knew a revival through the return to the area of 'old childhood friends', firstly for weekends, then more regularly. It was, in truth, the presenting of a list, during the municipal election of 1994, entitled 'New Perspective', led by the journalist Nikolaos Mertzos, himself originally from the commune and author of the proposals cited above, which was seen as the driving force behind this revitalisation, based on a 'gentle development which benefitted from all the possibilities offered by EU programmes and from the love of these former residents for their village of origin'.

This dynamic builds upon an 'impressive cultural heritage and an exceptionally beautiful unspoilt landscape' which has earned Nymfaio's place in the network of 'traditional Greek communities'. The aim is to create jobs for young people, notably in tourism, while 'differing from Greek development models employed thus far'. The project requires the commune to participate in its own reconversion through the 'improvement of its finances' and exploitation of its forest treasures. The commune 'has thus been able to raise the funds necessary to ensure its participation in European programmes (40 per cent of the budget of each project)' (Mertzos 2004: 4). This new era is invoked as a sort of experiment, in which engineers and architects, public electricity and telecommunications companies, universities, and national media all participate enthusiastically. Furthermore, 'three great benefactors, of whom one is not even originally from Nymfaio, have made generous contributions, as have many donors'. Amongst these 'Euergetes' making available their social, economic and often political capital, Yannis Boutaris, an influential wine-grower whose company is based in Thessaloniki, set up in the village in 1995 a model wildlife sanctuary for brown bears, as part of the Arkturos Foundation (Gardin 2012). The list of achievements speaks for itself, both in the realm of village infrastructure as in the restauration of its built heritage, its cultural activities or its environmental projects. Another prerequisite was 'social cohesion and close cooperation, the rejuvenation of local fêtes and traditional festivals' and 'the exclusion of all political rivals and of any identification with a political party'. The inventory is also much appreciated: 'ten hotels, seven restaurants, three coffee-bars, three shops selling tradition artifacts, a market, fifty thousand visitors annually and the creation of sixty-five jobs' (Mertzos 2004: 4).

In considering the relation between this discourse on the past and economic reorientation, the case of Nymfaio shows an impressive process of selection of valuable cultural characteristics, potentially economically promising, but always compatible with a broader discourse involving historical and political legitimacy. This compliance with the past, constructed according to a narrative on the place, aims to justify its general 'eligibility', to use the terminology of calls for application.

The very control of this narrative about the village gives an impression of conformity, particularly from a national point of view, where, for example, the particular Vlach heritage merges with a consensual 'Greekness', contrasting in particular with more acerbic regional issues: claims by the Slavic populations on the plain, as well as poor diplomatic relations with the neighbouring Republic of Macedonia; even less severe conflicts over the different uses of the space may have also been silenced – tourist recreation and secondary residences rarely being compatible (Givre and Sintès 2015). Does the neutral(ised) public space in the village reflect the ability of economic development to overcome tensions and conflicts, to settle potential disputes which are legion? Heritage is, in any case, a shared resource for those actors who have, in this way, been able to promote Nymfaio at many levels.

Creating order, starting projects

The 'rebirth' of Nymfaio is, thus, a well-thought-out scheme, involving a combination of bodies, programmes and networks around a double perspective: (1) the importance of the heritage–development nexus in the promotion of new ways to revitalise the village; (2) the recognition of local values in setting up various projects on architectural renovation and environmental schemes. These initiatives are all arranged around the construction of a 'model' of which the narrative presented above is witness. But this 'rebirth' of Nymfaio also stems from the willingness of a few powerful actors to work with direct donations to finance public works (roads, spaces, street lighting etc.) as well as the renovation of buildings such as the church of Agios Nikolaos or houses which have been transformed into guesthouses. This growth phase in touristic development coincides also with the three mandates as head of the local council from 1995–2006 of journalist Nikolaos Mertzos, whom we met earlier in this text. His social networks with the media are seen as one of the main drivers of the promotion of the village: 'If it snowed in Nymfaio, the television headlined "It is snowing in Nymfaio!"; if it rained in Nymfaio, the television also broadcast the fact', mocked a woman from the village. On a more serious note, however, other residents involved in the actual management of the village described the actions of the former *πρόεδρος* (president) as having enabled 'the development of sustainable tourism within small spaces, and especially rural tourism. The aim was to encourage people to come and enjoy the place without spoiling the original and traditional character of it.' The actions of these benefactors have not only funded the entire the project, but have also redesigned the space to give it its current look: 'Private investors have given so much. They have given money directly to the village. Thanks to this, we have been able to set up a communication network and a water distribution system, the car park and the ring road round the village. At the time the council had two snow ploughs and two fire engines to protect the woods. With our own funds (communal woodlands, shops and council taxes) we could never have managed it…'

Following on from these different initiatives, a strategic plan for tourism development worth 250,000 euros was put in place by the local council for the renovation of the area's cultural heritage. The work, which took place during the 1990s and 2000s, also received support from the EU programmes whose noticeboards are still dotted around the village. Between 2000 and 2006, funding from the European Regional Development Fund (ERDF) to the tune of 420,000 euros was allocated to the preservation of forest wildlife around Nymfaio. Plans for the renovation of Nymfaio's hotels went through the LEADER programme, while the Museum of Ethnography which opened in 2000 and the artificial lake situated above the village were realised thanks

Figure 4.8 Setting up the signage: Nymfaio and its noticeboards

to private donations, topped up yet again with support from different public programmes. As a source of new financing, the high level of activity in Nymfaio at a European scale is also behind the notoriety of the village, confirmed by its participation in forums and international competitions. Such dynamism leads to the provision of many more than just local resources and draws on wide social networks within the business circles of the main benefactors as well as amongst international institutions. The expertise of the main actors in identifying and responding to the different calls for tender have been incomparable in drawing funds to the village in order to equip it, transform it, and install a certain level of comfort while respecting and maintaining its so-called 'values and traditions' which have been broadly (re)constructed.

These dynamics, successful in recent decades, today come up against the gradual weakening of both European and national frameworks. A new local administrative district is emerging following the Kallikratis Plan (Law 3852/2010) for territorial reform of 2010. In future it is these new bodies which will possess the means and the decision-making powers in fields of intervention such as that which, up to then, had enabled the development of Nymfaio. This administrative change, accompanied by a redistribution of local power, was received with a certain amount of disbelief by local councillors in Nymfaio who had, hitherto, been the kingpins and whose initiatives would now have to be submitted to third parties for approval. It is therefore the autonomy of the local authorities which is currently threatened by new forms not only of interdependence but also of control. Will this context of uncertainty, coupled with the current economic crisis, bring about a reconfiguration of those modes of action and networks whose functioning has already been briefly described? A village such as Nymfaio, with its homogenous residential profile and its well-managed economy, probably appears as an isolated figure in the critical situation in which Greece has found itself since the 2000s. Today, the time for 'projects' seems to be if not 'over' then at least subject to increased competition for the vital resource which is European and, even more so, national funding.

In this respect, the example of NGO Arkturos seems to speak volumes. If this latter occupies a special place in the revitalisation process in Nymfaio, it has also been affected by the changing context described above. Its reorganisation is fairly symptomatic of new logics of flexibility which are imposed on it. Founded in 1995 by the businessman Yannis Boutaris, Arkturos first and foremost entered the struggle to end the tradition of dancing bears that the Gypsies dragged from place to place. Yannis Boutaris used his relations in his native village to set up a 'sanctuary' where dancing bears could live out their last days in a vast enclosed park, home to about fifteen bears, and visited by more than 65,000 people per year. As Jean Gardin (2012) reminds us, the Arkturos experience is witness to an original alliance, in the person of Boutaris, between economic impact, power games, attachment to things local, and developmentalist logic. This son of a wine-merchant, born in Thessaloniki in 1942, became a renowned businessman at the head of the enterprise which bears his name, and an influential politician, elected Mayor of Thessaloniki in 2010 and 2014 with support from the left. In Nymfaio the importance of Arkturos is indisputable. It is quite significant, too, that, when a representative of the local council quotes the number of tourists to have visited Nymfaio, he bases the figure on the number of tickets sold to visit the bear sanctuary. However, over recent decades, Arkturos' activities have diversified. The isolation of the village of Nymfaio at an altitude of 1,300 metres does not permit any rapid or regular access to the far-distant Pindus or Rhodope mountain ranges. Furthermore, having to pass through Aetos to get up to Nymfaio is ample justification for pausing in this agricultural area in the plain, which is useful not only to tourists but also to Greek employees and volunteers and those from other European countries. Specialisation then takes place: on the plain are the technical and scientific activities, with the installation of the administrative headquarters of the NGO, and in Nymfaio the educational and recreational nature trail. The patrimonial village of Nymfaio seems to be serving as the nucleus from which regional development plans are radiating out: a reception centre for wolves has opened in the valley, in the village of Agrapidia, with a breeding centre for sheepdogs to protect flocks from larger predators. The site at Aetos is increasingly serving as both a reception centre and a locus for scientific activities (bedrooms, convention centre, laboratory, library). As we can see from this particular case, Nymfaio's role is strengthened, but it also seems to be sharing out the benefits… However, as a director of the NGO points out, the presentation of these spatial rearrangements according to a regional development plan should be seen in context: that of the territorial reform of 2010 which stripped all autonomy from the local council of Nymfaio to the benefit of a major ward in the valley, with Amyndaio at its centre.

> Twelve years ago we had the Kapodistria reform. This created some new wards but left some communities (*kinotitès*) autonomous (like that of Nymfaio). These communities retained their autonomy for political reasons … they were privileged: they had good political connections. It would have been better, nevertheles, if they had granted more power to the heads of these local communities in Kallikratis. Now, you need to go to the new central municipality in Amyndaio … bah! But my village is here! We are Vlachs, we are Pontic Greeks … We should be able to say 'We in this village wish to develop such and such a project … without having to get authorisation from another village'.

For Arkturos, two different periods seem to follow on from each other: firstly, for twelve years, Nikolaos Mertzos held three mandates as chief of the local council of Nymfaio, during which the village knew great financial autonomy, and the involvement of generous donors. There then followed a more troubled time due to the economic crisis and especially to the territorial reform in Kallikratis which deprived the *kinotita* of any real power, which thus passed into the hands of the authorities in a much wider area – an area which is much more heterogenous from both an economic perspective (Nymfaio seemed like a privileged enclave) – and, as suggested in some interviews, from an identificatory perspective, as Nymfaio is the only Aromanian village in the region. In fact, things began to get complicated for the association, especially as its founder, Yannis Boutaris, was elected Mayor of Thessaloniki and could no longer get involved as much as before in the local projects. Two of the driving forces in the development of Nymfaio were weakened through displacement: local power was devolved to a much wider community so that the village could not continue its projects for development; and the influence of the main benefactor and founder of the NGO found itself lost within the higher spheres of power on his becoming mayor of the second largest city in Greece. In this context, it is easy to understand why discourse and action were reoriented towards the development of the plain: for the ward to obtain authorisation or credit, the mayor himself must be made to understand how the activities would directly benefit the entirety of its administrative areas, and not just the village of Nymfaio.

The border as a new locus for resources?

The set-up which we have just presented around the village of Nymfaio is less than fifty kilometres from the border between Greece and the Republic of Macedonia. This remote location within Greek national space has today enabled local actors to take part in EU cooperative programmes, collaborating, notably, with the neighbouring country. Through this type of approach, a new way of accessing supportive resources emerges and reveals some of the effects of financing projects in a border context. The first programme of its type, the transborder cooperation between Nymfaio and the village of Malovishte in the Republic of Macedonia took place between January and December 2001 within the framework of the Programme of Community Aid to the Countries of Central and Eastern Europe. The aim of the project was to maximise the developmental potential of the village, building on its cultural heritage and on the ecological and environmental assets of the space. The idea was to set up a plan of action to determine the priorities should possible future opportunities for economic development materialise (Javourez 2017). With its forty or so inhabitants, Malovishte could, in principle, be seen as Nymfaio's 'double' in the Republic of Macedonia: the 'protected' mountain setting (Pelister Natural Park) and the village both offer the minority language and culture which is Aromanian.

Like Nymfaio, Malovishte is also known for its Vlach past, its pastoral specialisation, its crafts and its wool trade with the great cities of central Europe. With only a few families there nowadays, living principally from forestry, Malovishte, at the height of its activity, once had a population of up to 3,000 from the nineteenth century up until 1916. First the Balkan Wars

Figure 4.9 Malovishte: an aborted project?

and then the two World Wars dealt a fatal blow to the reach of the village, with the great trade families emigrating to Serbia, Greece or the neighbouring town of Bitola. However, the points of comparison stop there as, if Nymfaio is a 'model' village, Malovishte still gives a clear impression, even today, of having been disinherited. The village abounds in abandoned houses, often no more than ruins. The access road is too narrow for the bus to get through and there are no signs that any leisure activities or hotels have been developed to encourage tourism. If Malovishte is, in fact, in the same situation in which Nymfaio found itself before its successfully reclaimed heritage, reproducing the same outcome as the Greek village can not be taken for granted.... This first example of transborder cooperation could not be sustained: the Vlach international folk festival dreamed up for this project ground to a halt after several years and studies carried out within the framework of the cooperation have not yet been exploited. And the essence of this cooperation seems to be elsewhere for its principal instigators: transborder contact has been set up and has been exploited through other activities which are visibly more promising. Transborder cooperation has, effectively, enabled those from the village to benefit, through its partnership with Nymfaio, both from the expertise of Greek actors used to this type of project, and from access to

Figure 4.10 The town of Krushevo: a more reliable focus of cooperation

Nymfaio's networks with other Greek partners and with new EU sources of funding. We find once again the figure of Nikolaos Mertzos at the heart of this project in Malovishte; at the time president of the council of Nymfaio, he appears to have used his role as one of those responsible for getting the project work underway. The closeness of relations between the two villages, and in particular the support given to the Malovishte project by the Greek government, appears thus to have taken root in ancient links uniting the two places, and some of their inhabitants, which have, from 1997, been progressively renewed.

A second programme of cross-border cooperation was then signed between Nymfaio and the Macedonian town of Krushevo (5,000 inhabitants). Funded between September 2007 and March 2009 under the CARDS programme, this particular project aimed more specifically at the development of cooperation in the tourism sector. Just as in Malovishte, it was a question of exploiting the particularities of the site for tourism, and setting up bodies to oversee the promotion of the town and the organisation of this new activity. Officially the cooperation programme was designed to promote the town's architectural heritage and religious tourism, simply through putting the municipality of Krushevo in touch with its Greek partner. However, other actors more discretely supported these closer ties, especially the Agios Nikolaos association for friendship and cooperation between Krushevo and Greece. Founded in October 2009, this association organises course in Greek language for the inhabitants of Krushevo. It also arranges for children and adolescents following these courses to attend summer camp in Greece, and for students to gain bursaries to Greek universities. Although it does not wish to be known as a community association, as it accepts members from all ethnic groups in the region, Agios Nikolaos remains strongly linked to its Vlach component. Its founder claims to be Vlach and attaches great importance to this dimension of his identity, even though he only speaks basic Greek. However, the challenge of this cross-border cooperation and its relations with the municipality have encouraged the association to be open to all, even if some of the activities it proposes are reserved for its Vlach members only – as is the obtention of bursaries in Greece which are part of an official programme of the Hellenic Republic reserved for those of Greek ancestry (*Omogeneis*) from neighbouring countries (Javourez 2017). This is consistent with earlier years: when it came to establishing links between Nymfaio and Malovishte, this cooperation had been a determining factor in relations with the actors involved with these closer ties at the end of the 1990s and in the use of their networks within the Vlach community in the Republic of Macedonia (Blondel *et al.* 2013).

As the two examples above have shown, the affinities which certain groups from southern areas of the Republic of Macedonia have with Greece can still be seen today, though only marginally expressed. They are mainly evident in their occasional use of the Greek language, a skill which, in some cases, has been passed down to current generations, and which we find nowadays at the heart of this revitalisation of cross-border relations. These remains of a past, in which the town of Bitola was a stronghold of a Greekness accepted by the majority of the Aromanian population (Lory 2011), provided certain individuals with opportunities in the establishment of particular cross-border relations (Javourez 2017; Givre and Sintès 2015). Nevertheless, we cannot overlook the political dimension to this activity, in which Greek officials played a major role. The issue of the origins of the Vlachs and of their belonging to the Greek nation, which we have already seen in the case of the Vlachs in Albania (Sintès 2008b), is at the heart of some Greek representatives' involvement through the activation of these cross-border networks. Such a discourse is also promoted by actors from the Republic of Macedonia who are involved in these cross-border relations.

Geopolitics and cross-border cooperation

In these last examples, the revitalisation of heritage thus seems to be the conjugate product of a national policy, a local movement and an initiative by economically and socially powerful actors, who themselves have symbolic attachments not only to villages but also to influential networks, sometimes claiming an Aromanian heritage in this region. In the cases discussed as a whole, cross-border cooperation based on heritage and community, through membership of these communities – becomes an economic, symbolic and political resource. This history and memory-based community justifies, in a way, its involvement in cross-border relations by its efficiency. It is true that the link between Aromanians from the Republic of Macedonia and those from Greece is accepted as a natural fact, fruit of the region's history throughout previous centuries. As Guillaume Javourez's research shows (Blondel *et al.* 2013; Javourez 2017), this relationship is part of a cross-border regional identity which is expressed as much through its official contacts between cultural associations and the authorities, as in terms of interpersonal relations. Even so, it is really through initiatives from the Greek side that these relations have become possible. The first contacts between members of Vlach associations in the Republic of Macedonia and local actors in Nymfaio were established following a meeting with the leaders of Vlach organisations in Northern Greece under the auspices of the Greek diplomatic mission in Skopje (Javourez 2017). These examples show how cross-border or transnational activity can take the place, in a more subtle way, of relations between the official authorities of the two countries who, in this context, have been blocked by an international-level dispute over diplomatic issues (Givre and Sintès 2015).

However, if the mobilisation of the Vlach networks is ever-present in the two examples discussed here, it would be advisable not to over-estimate their reach. Even if the role of Greek officials still seems to be decisive, those elements put in place to set up networks are, on the other hand, very varied and nearly always seem to show a pragmatic fluidity. In order to fulfill the aims of creating such an association, of staging such a project, contacts and relations of cooperation can thus rely on other logics: the memory of population movements between the two countries at the time of the Greek civil war, the routes taken today by seasonal workers or even the ethnic lines of distinction we have just described – even all at once depending on their efficacy in the short term. The mobilisation of networks of Greek-loving Vlachs thus appears to be one of the dimensions which can be brought into play (amongst others) to set up this network of associations participating in the diffusion of the Greek language and ensuring, in a way, the promotion of Greece in a Republic of Macedonia with which official relations are still amongst the most complicated. In Krushevo, the geopolitical implications of these contacts may nevertheless raise questions about the reasons which convince a municipality led by the nationalist right, and Greek actors and institutions, to work together on such projects, so radically divergent are their opinions on the subject of regional geopolitics. The answer seems to lie once again in their pragmatism and in the particular advantages that each can draw from this cooperation. Financial support now being exceedingly rare due to the economic crisis, both sides are nevertheless able to gain access to hitherto un-hoped-for resources. In all talk of this cooperation, attachment to place and the desire to better the living conditions of the inhabitants are inexorably linked to cooperation with neighbouring partner countries. It is easy to see how the border currently constitues a reference space and a flexible area of action depending on the risks and especially the opportunities in this context of a somewhat conflictual interstate neighbourhood.

Nymfaio, Malovishte and Krushevo are interesting case studies of localities which are both peripheral to and involved in these conflicts. Through the intermediary of international heritage development programmes, we again found cases of recognition of communality across a disputed border. This recognition turns out, nevertheless, to be both occasional, situational and instrumental. The situation endlessly fluctuates between exceeding and reaffirming the cleavage of the border, based, amongst other things, on shrewdly selected patrimonial and historical arguments. Ratifying the 'authorised patrimonial discourse' (Smith 2006) of a locally shared space, however, is a good way to not 'lose face' in the struggles in which the two states are engaged in terms of cultural legitimacy. Significantly different from that which we saw in Thesprotia in Chapter 2, the 'status' of the transnational Aromanian community, well integrated here in both national frameworks, allows the affirmation of a sort of 'non-national' heritage at the border, which is less likely to stir up contentious issues ever-present in this region. This is actioned thanks to the initiative of a network of actors, situated on either side of the border, who benefit from a 'Europeanised' vision of the locality as proposed by the new frameworks – and new sources of funding. The transfer of a 'top-down' development 'model', even with sometimes very weak results, demonstrates the resources from which inhabitants of the Republic of Macedonia could benefit through relations with their Greek neighbours, who have a certain economic power and who remain often an obligatory route through which to access EU frameworks and funding. In the context of tense geopolitical relations between the two states, these cross-border cultural projects also show that this type of 'patrimonial diplomacy' (Givre and Sintès 2015) is seen as multilayered and especially flexible depending on the available opportunities. This is very obvious in light of the shifting of projects from the village of Malovishte to the town of Krushevo, which is economically more dynamic and, particularly, more eligible. Interest also comes from the fact that these initiatives strengthen the idea of a common cultural area on both sides of the border (Givre and Sintès 2015).

* * *

These different practices of cultural heritage in the North of Greece suggest that the sense of cultural heritage is a complex construction, deriving both from institutional frameworks and from local settings. They are thus witness to the new neighbourhoods and the conflicts which have affected these regions over recent decades. However, it is obvious everywhere that cultural heritage is not only used as a way of stabilising the border. Today there is a new vision of culture which would seem to allow the articulation of different narratives in a single space: amongst others a national narrative, a minority-group narrative, a new-resident narrative and an institutional-actor narrative, which are causing a rethink of relations between borders (political, geographical) and limits (cultural, symbolic) in a world where mobility has become the norm for many inhabitants. Of course, this plurality runs up against (or is the cause of) the conflicts of interest of national powers and many other power games. The 'cultural diplomacy' mentioned earlier is part of these new power relationships where Europeanisation is not necessarily contrary to renationalisation or, more widely still, to the implementation of cultural projects for much wider economic, social, political and national purposes. On the whole, however, these examples still question the outlines of what Balibar and Wallerstein (1988) call the 'Nation form', where the different local practices contradict the hypothesis that national discourse is monolithic in character. These cases in fact highlight the relations which are woven between identity networks activated by mobility (whether it be of migrants, as shown in Chapter 2, of institutional actors or of new residents), and which become firmly anchored in the local through varying displays about the characteristics of the place, often deploying cultural representations embodied in concrete elements of heritage. In light of this final section of the chapter, these direct links also seem to be deeply affected by the actions of international actors who produce discourses and instruments which, at least at first glance, can rise above those of the nation-state.

This tension between the state and a society made up of local networks could be perceived as nothing new when we speak of the Balkans (Prévélakis 1994). Nevertheless, it can seem particularly apt in the context of the spread of mobility behaviour. In Greece, the cases of Balkan and Albanian migration – as with the return of minorities which history paints as banished (Chams from Epirus, Sephardic Jews from the Dodecanese, and Turks or Slavs from

Macedonia) – can provide strong examples of the revitalisation of alternative memories through the development of geographic mobility. To broaden the perspective, this movement goes hand-in-hand with the strengthening of regional and local identities, such as the localism in Albania studied by Gilles de Rapper (2007) which we also find in Greece through the effects of migration from the 1990s (Papataxiarchis 2005). In the revival of this type of question, there is a strong likelihood that any modification of links with Europe and with the Balkans will play a vital role. According to Arjun Appadurai, care must be taken not to fall into the 'primordialist trap'; these different phenomena teach us, in fact, more about issues concerning contemporary societies than about a hypothetical constant of human behaviour which will make of a return to roots a sort of common tendency for all human destiny.

Chapter 5

Rescaling power in an era of globalisation

The various ethnographies presented in the previous chapters give a sense of the diversity within these situations. All those involved, whether economic migrants, networks based on memories of the diaspora, neo-residents of the borderlands or those involved in the re-evaluation of cross-border heritage, have their own distinct characteristics that give rise to these different situations. Nonetheless, these scenarios have elements in common that shed light on the larger dynamics of social transformation in contemporary Greek society, as well as trends that have a wider effect on Europe and the Mediterranean. These approaches have all the hallmarks of specific emerging identification discourses with a different emphasis to the more classical discourse of those nation-states from where the authors originate. Whether it is Jews from Rhodes, a minority who have vanished from the heart of the island where they have their roots, Albanian-speakers in Greece, confused with Albanian migrants who have been arriving since the beginning of 1990, or groups of Aromanians in the various regions of Macedonia or in Epirus, these affiliations all appear to be faced with new forces which, instead of creating a kind of global melting pot, stemming from the standardisation of lifestyles and identification, are instead leading them to affirm or re-affirm their particularity through the new channels of expression open to them.

In the same way, beyond the classic mechanisms of power, the different kinds of geographical mobility presented throughout this volume paradoxically seem themselves to foster a certain kind of social fragmentation. Cross-border relationships, suspended for nearly half a century in the shadow of the Iron Curtain, have now been reactivated and networks uniting people with different citizenships have been (re)formed from fields as diverse as trade, migrant networks and marriage. This reactivation has led to the promotion of an alternative or minority memory, along with a re-evaluation of traditional terms of legitimacy, thus linking the future of contemporary Greek society to that of its neighbours engaged in post-socialist rationales. More widely in the country, the oldest minority groups have been joined by more recent flows of migrants, leading to a marked revival of the minority claim and a significant shift in the prevailing social and political frameworks of coexistence. According to some commentators, this movement, connected to European politics on the protection of minority rights, could affect the stability of the country concerned (Riedel 2002). In actual fact, even if the different groups studied do not share the same attitude with respect to Greek nation-building, all of them invariably challenge its definition and treatment of 'otherness' in this country, and their fate enables us to consider the dynamics of identification in a global world on a bigger scale. Should we systematically see a connection between this movement and a general weakening of the position of the nation-state? Should we be thinking here in terms of a further consequence of European regional integration? To what extent is this a case of a new social construction of places in the Balkan region or in the Mediterranean? Answers to these questions can be found in the following pages in which some aspects discussed in Chapter 1 are revisited in order to show how these different scenarios reveal 'from below' some of the 'cultural dimensions of globalization' (Appadural 1996b) which, whilst creating phenomena of convergance and standardisation of lifestyles, paradoxically fosters (or provokes) a discourse of identification that makes these small groups stand out. Such discourses invariably rely here on a history, a past or a collective memory for confirmation of their legitimacy and for simply thinking about their role within space in a new way.

From roots to pastures new

Meeting diverse groups of people in Greece's border territories raises the issue of the link between the increased mobility of the people of this region and a more frequent recourse to a discourse on roots and origins, in order to explain the changes that have been happening there. The opening up of borders or efforts to ensure peace, in addition to the movement of assets and people which this made possible again, in effect allowed the inhabitants to (re)form links with citizens in neighbouring countries. Furthermore, as we have repeatedly seen in this volume, these 'newcomers' are not always considered as strangers, and their arrival no longer arouses feelings of something new. Rather, they engage in a kind of 'historic revival,' especially when they are determined to affirm that the troubled past of the border territories gives them the right to inhabit such spaces. It is interesting to note how changes to legal frameworks and the normalisation of inter-state relations desired by Nato or the European Union, today make it theoretically possible for people who emigrated during difficult times to return. This is manifestly the case for the Jews of Rhodes or the Chams of Thesprotia cited in the previous pages, but we should also remember, in relation to the Greek territory, the Slavic-speaking communities (Javourez 2017; Karakasidou 2002; Monova 2002), or even the descendants of Muslims affected by the population exchange of 1923 (Bayindir Goularas 2010). These different examples reinforce the fact that the fringe territories of Greece offer rich opportunities for studying this kind of memory-based mobility. More generally, these are also new relationships with places, driven by easier geographical mobility, which could be accused of actually leading to the reinforcement of these kinds of alternative identity. This is what is suggested by the example of migrant groups whose positioning with respect to the narrative of Greekness, although more conformist, is also based on the mobilisation of tradition and lived heritage from a much more local perspective, as observed in Thesprotia and Macedonia. Research carried out in Greece these past few years highlights the relationship between new spatial practices affected by mobility or migration, and the process of putting down new roots that is constantly informed by the past, a necessary justification for asserting the right to put down roots in these disputed border territories.

Recent social science studies on migration clearly show such connections between memory and mobility. For a long time, however, migrants seemed to have been officially condemned to forget, as a result of their long-term settlement in the country of immigration. This is the conclusion that could be drawn, for example, from reading Abdelmayek Sayad, when he investigated 'the three ages of Algerian migration to France' in 1977. The author presented migration in terms of successive phases, leading the migrant inevitably towards more or less successful integration into the host country, and the dissolution of links to his country of origin. This type of approach has been the source of long-standing typologies and classifications, based on migrants' underlying motivations for displacement (pioneer, labour and family migration). All implicitly suggest a teleological approach to migration, whose participants found themselves inexorably transformed, depending on the length of their stay, from a status as new arrivals to one of 'immigrants' joined by their families in the final phase of the migration process. This type of vision was a product of its time: the 1970s and 1980s saw the definitive closing of European borders, whilst foreigners, resettled at a time of economic reconstruction throughout the old continent, had little option but to integrate. As Dominique Schnapper (1992) points out, zero immigration policies and the closing of borders were, at the time, a corollary of the injunction that foreigners in France should integrate, as in the rest of Europe. In typical fashion, the paradigms that were then dominant in the field of Migration Studies largely portrayed the migrant either as an immigrant trying to integrate (often unsuccessfully), or as someone absent from his or her country of origin – which s/he, as an emigrant, was helping to develop. Only recently have contra-flows (both material and immaterial) become legitimate subjects for study, highlighting the relationship with the place of origin (Simon 1979). These are expressed partly by the comings and goings between the country of destination and that of departure, through the steady flow of remittances to families, and through the multitude of connections that technological progress has made more visible and more accessible, all creating *territoires de la mobilité* (i.e. 'territories of mobility') (Faret 2003), as opposed to a vision of migration flows as unidirectional. Finally, the often imaginary link with the country of origin has been able to evolve into a powerful point of connection for groups of people, within the framework of diasporas largely rediscovered at the end of the 1990s. The significance of the links created between places in the countries of departure and arrival has brought new themes into the study of migration, so much have they been seen as structural elements of contemporary migration. This kind of consideration has led to much greater attention being paid to social phenomena which bring into play issues of migrant identity and memory. My research on Albanians could become part of this development, so much did the relationship between discourses of identity and the creation of migrant networks become an accepted perspective relevant to analysing the practices of these migrants in Greece.

More widely, the mobilisation by some migrants of this discourse on origins appears today to lead to what could be called an 'age of return', as if origins have become such an accepted means of self-definition that migrants have adopted them both theoretically and practically – a sort of introspectif movement (a self-reflection) of one's routes, which encourages the migrant to think back to his own migration in order to highlight a history often unknown and neglected in official discourses. We saw above how this was true for the actions of Rodeslis scattered throughout many countries in the world, and also for the mobilisation of border identities connecting Albanian migrants to Greece. This return of the past can also be seen in the formation of new types of geographical mobility which, contrary to the initial migration, see the migrants (or their descendants) retracing their steps, returning to the places of origin for both repeat trips (holidays or dual purpose), or one-off journeys (a pilgrimage in search of identity or roots tourism). As in the previous period, the emergence of this new field of research cannot escape the context in which it emerged, under the influence of a two-fold dynamic which sees the questions of migration and of relationships with the past moving to the forefront of social, cultural and political issues (Lavabre 2006). During the

1990s, general political agendas on national group identity, and the way in which migrants could appear to either challenge or subvert them, were at the heart of the debate on migration issues in Europe and in a world affected by a return to theories of civilisation. It is no coincidence that, during this same period, the literature on diasporas increased considerably, testifying both to the change in the way in which the topic is covered and to our understanding of the issue of memory in migration. This memory seems to stretch a long way back, to be tenacious even, and migrants will not lose it so easily in the countries of settlement, since they do not actually settle there fully because they are in a situation of cultural hybridity – and not one of forgetting or transition, as described by Sayad (1977). This hypothesis is confirmed by the emergence of a new paradigm, in use for a time in Migration Studies, which hightlights circulatory patterns in migration flows.

This new vision of migration, at the risk of culturalising or essentialising it, leads to a fairly radical reconsideration of the migrant, who should now be understood as a member of a transnational community, whose experiences and behaviour could be explained by its generations-old history all the while the memory of it still exists and is active (or activated). More generally, it has to be said that the attention given to the memory of migrants is part of a wider movement of the time, the 'age of identity' according to Marcel Gauchet (1998), which sees a range of groups recollecting the past, sometimes from a need to confirm and legitimise their position. The proliferation of these processes and the emotional charge that accompanies them, sometimes leads to a sense of competition between memories in a more general social climate of 'a war of memories' from which few countries are immune, particularly in the Mediterranean space (Crivello 2010). The proclamation of all-encompassing supranational identities, like that currently promoted in Europe through EU policy, with its mythical accents and integrationist perspective, is, paradoxically, contemporaneous with the resurgence of memory-based claims, founded on the distinction to which the migrants themselves also firmly subscribe. Furthermore, since the beginning of the 1990s, the opening of Greece's borders to the other citizens of the Balkans and, *a fortiori* since the lifting of the Schengen visa requirement for those coming from countries bordering Greece (2007 for Bulgaria, 2009 for the Republic of Macedonia, 2010 for Albania), have made 'memory-based returns' so much easier – as shown for returning migrants – for all who have some family history on Greek territory. The fragmented representations of the past which commemorative events stemming from it the most often imply for Greece thus inevitably raise the issue, for the past as for the present, of how to live together.

Losing the border and regaining memory(ies)

In addition to sensitivity towards these new migration issues, the (long-)disputed nature of the Greek borders provides fertile grounds for the study of this type of 'memory-based mobility'. This is because of the complex allegiances brought about by the relatively recent disappearance from these regions of plural principles of social regulation from the Ottoman Empire, in favour of the more monovalent management of the nation-state. Moreover, if, by establishing controlled zones along the borders and monitoring who lives there, and by drawing up regulations prohibiting foreign nationals from owning property there, the state has long been protecting itself against the emergence or the return of (potentially irredentist) minority groups, then these different restrictions have been lifted as fast as Greek legislation has become aligned with the European Union frame. As we have seen, the current ease of displacement now also enables an original kind of visit to the border territories of Greece, undeniably introducing a new element which undoubtedly challenges some of the constructions of collective identity.

In this respect, the Rhodian Jewish case reveals the link between these new forms of mobility and the characteristics of the place of departure. For a long time, the Greek authorities seemed reluctant to help the resettlement of this kind of group on Rhodes, due to the peripheral nature of the islands of the Dodecanese and their position on the border with Turkey. As far as the Rodeslis are concerned, the memory of their homeland seems to have been strengthened by this deeply felt enforced alienation, both because of the historical circumstances in which the community disappeared during the Second World War and because of the suspicion displayed for so many years by the Greek authorities and the barriers which arose before these return visits. This element, which is due largely to the peripheral position of the island of Rhodes, would have contributed to strengthening the Rodeslis' discourse of belonging, paradoxically creating very favourable conditions for the revivification of memory of the Jewish presence on Rhodes now. This trend is the same for all those 'diaspora' groups who show a deep attachment to a homeland that was lost in very violent circumstances – to the extent that Michel Bruneau (2004) even made it a part of his definition of diaspora – and these groups are now becoming an even greater part of its economic or cultural development, contributing in the name of a belonging long-since denied to them. This type of connection again allows us to affirm the distinctive characteristics of the peripheral territories. Due to their historical trajectory, they have remained places that are more vulnerable to the current phenomenon of fragmentation suggested by the appearance of this type of group, particularly as today, as we will see later, these returnees are in a position to draw on the legitimacy that they lacked in their opportunistic use of certain aspects of the discourse about management in connection with tourism, the preservation of heritage and even with economic development. These returns, nonetheless, when felt as a threat, seem sometimes to create tension. This is the case, for example, if they are involved in disputes over property. Rhodes, Thesprotia and Macedonia are very much the types of place where these issues are either officially or informally raised by agents of memory-based mobility. These concerns contributed to a more general sense of uncertainty that affected the country in the 1990s, with the mounting regional tensions mentioned in the first chapter. The symbolic case of the Republic of Macedonia and the blocking of its constitutional name by the Greek authorities could be interpreted as a means of disrupting a supposed irredentism with its central issue of the dispossession of property after the civil war. The same applies to claims concerning Greater Albania 'until Preveza' (see page 57) – and the confiscations of property belonging to Albanian-speaking groups who lived in the border area until the Second World War. This feeling of insecurity dominated Greece in the 1990s and 2000s, no doubt triggered by memories of the Cypriot conflict in 1974 and the fear of contagion of a 'Yugoslavian' scenario. In Greece, as elsewhere in the Balkans, this climate enabled the confusion of minority claims with antipatriotic activity, as scholars have clearly shown for this decade in the whole region (Markou 2008; Séraïdari 2006, 2010; Skoulariki 2003; Tsitsélikis and Christopoulos 1997) and, as my own fieldwork has, on occasion, been able to confirm, by the reality of expressions of xenophobia targeted particularly at the groups under investigation.

Over and above the effects of the (not only economic) situation of the 1990s (or its traces during the following decades), we can also understand this rejection as a product of the gap between the nation-building frameworks and the contemporary logics of globalisation and immigration that currently affect the country. We can hypothesise in effect about the mismatch between this sort of reactivation of 'marginal identities' and the canons of national discourse, founded in Greece since the nineteenth century on the tensions between Hellenism and *Romiossini* (Herzfeld 1987), and focused on two aspects of identity – language and faith (Drettas 2003; Herzfeld 1995: 41–2). This definition often radically excludes minority groups from the national majority group for both religious and linguistic reasons. More precisely, during the centuries over which the modern Greek nation was forming, the assertion of 'genos' over 'ethnos,' as described by Georges Prévélakis (1997: 37), associated historically with the process of homogenisation of the population (Pierron 1996), also led to the rejection of all groups that did not have the characteristics required to be a member of the majority group. According to Georges Drettas, this confusion between religion and nation has remained a dominant feature across the entire post-Ottoman region of

Figure 5.1 Xenophobic expression in Greece *right* Desecration of the Rhodes monument (2012) *below* Anti-Albanian graffiti in Voha (October 2002) 'Albanians get out'

which Greece is a part, influenced by the social functioning of the various millets, or religious groups, which existed during the imperial period, and which would have had a profound influence on local political culture. This affirmation is reinforced by the assertion that not one of the states that came to power after the Ottoman Empire (at least, those in the Balkans) have any 'structural secularity', and religious groups still dominate, as we saw in the Yugoslavian conflict in the 1990s, providing the undisputed foundation for nationalities (Dimitrijevic 2000).

This is how minority religious groups in Greece potentially become ethnic or national minorities (Clogg 2002), in a country whose population is officially 97.6 per cent Orthodox Christian. Exclusion from (or rather non-membership of) the national community, evidence of which we have found traces amongst our research groups, is demonstrated by the fact that not one of the display boards in the Jewish museum of Rhodes was translated into Greek until recent times. This is also evidenced by some aspects of life for the Catholics in Tinos, whom we met in the course of another project (Sintès and Thuillier 2009). The confusion between nation and faith has been thoroughly written into the Greek Constitution, which declares that the official religion of the country is Orthodox Christianity and that other religions (inasmuch as they are recognised by the state), are only tolerated if they refrain completely from any proselytising activity, at the risk of prosecution. Setting the parameters in this way, the state formally bases its sense of national 'otherness' on ethno-religious identity and officially distinguishes those within the body of its citizens who have Greek heritage from those who do not. Any objections to this that might arise from non-Orthodox Greek citizens are explained thus: it was the Greek Orthodox millet that formed the nation-state such as it is presented, for example, in educational programmes (Fragoudaki and Dragona 1998).

This implacable logic is the social backdrop to all Greece's border territories where there are religious or linguistic minorities. The best known case in the academic bibliography is that of the Muslims of Thrace but the Jews of Rhodes and even the Albanian-, Aromanian- and Slavic-speaking people met in the course of this research could provide additional examples. In this ideological context, where religious or linguistic conformity has often been associated with loyalty, it is easy to see how suspicion, yet again, can surround the issue of minoritary identity in these regions, as my misadventures in Thesprotia described at the end of the second chapter illustrate. To highlight only those tensions that arise when the plural nature of the past is evoked in these marginal spaces runs the risk of giving only a partial account of what such an action involves. It would fit too neatly into a picture of national identity resisting globalisation, embodied here through international migration and transnational flows. My field research in Rhodes, Thesprotia and Macedonia alike has led me to see the subtleties involved in these situations. In effect, other factors can come into play which, over and above the simple rejection of minority groups, enable us to show how they fit in with contemporary and social processes.

From transformation in the ways of inhabiting place to the mobilisation of memory: territorial impact

The feelings of suspicion sometimes expressed in Greece towards these small groups in fact runs contrary to the great fluidity of discourses of identity frequently heard on the ground. This fluidity seems to enable some actors to escape the intense polarisation of political discourse in force in the 1990s and 2000s. This can be detected in the emergence of narratives which are more specifically local or regional, and much less exclusively 'national' in all senses of the word. In a way, it appeared that the resurgence in the visibility of minority memories was even enough to enable positive interaction with people in local society, with their discourses and their use of spaces. This is what examples of the expression of Jewish memory in Rhodes or of places in Thesprotia and the Vlach villages in Macedonia, and even of the cross-border networks involving Albanian migrants, have all shown. In all of these cases, the presence of new arrivals (or returnees) has even functioned as a kind of catalyser offering new channels for the expression of local identity. It has also been taken up by the inhabitants as a position from which to oppose the public authorities with whom they are in conflict, as on Rhodes, or in order to stake their claim to the rapid growth of funding for cultural projects -as described for the villages of Western Macedonia. It is interesting to note, in this respect, that some individuals – who, for decades, have either been in a weak position with regard to social development, like the inhabitants of the old town of Rhodes, who were traditionally the poorest in the town (Skevofylakas 1988), or were members of religious (like Jews or Muslims on Rhodes) or linguistic minorities (the Albanian-speakers of Epirus, Corinth and Attica, or the Slavic-speakers of Macedonia) – have demonstrated an ability to use certain elements of the current management discourse to uphold and legitimise their claims. To achieve this, they proclaim, loudly and strongly, that they conform to the financial rationale for tourism, to the best preservation of historical heritage and even to ethical respect for diversity as upheld by UNESCO and the European Union in their literature, and that they all demonstrate a certain integration of values, of hierarchies and of norms that, although initially introduced by public powers, are today used to defy authority. On Rhodes, the themes of tourism and minorities have been integrated into discourses of appropriation of local spaces, produced by the community of people involved with heritage issues, who thus draw a sense of legitimacy from these local references to a shared past.

In this respect, observation of processes of valorisation of heritage in the village of Sagiada, in Thesprotia enables completion of the picture. Here, too, the past has been evoked in order to strengthen the presence of certain groups. Beyond the conflicts of memory specific to this region, and still largely present both in discourse and on the ground, the diverse accounts tracing the origins of the actual village, its displacement since the Second World War, and even its first foundations on the little hill close by, are determining factors confirming the belonging of all its inhabitants – in the broadest sense of the word – to this community. This includes the descendants of emigrants who moved abroad or into the towns, and who are linked today with the village through various practices and journeys they make to it (second homes, holiday and weekend visits, taking part in village celebrations etc). Ease of travel gives these people the chance to be there in person several times a year, although their primary residence is elsewhere. This new ability seems to have accentuated their tendency to claim that they 'belong here', despite living some distance away. These spatial practices have also facilitated, for over a decade, the appearance of a new type of inhabitant – secondary residents who have made Sagiada their 'village of choice', and not only during the summer. These 'elective Sagiadanis,' have also appropriated the discourse of 'a return to the source', via the return to a more peaceful, more 'natural' life, a life closer to tradition, even if their family roots are not located in this region, and despite (or because of) the fact that this village is very marginal within Greece as a whole. 'Inhabiting' the space becomes linked to a whole range of justifications which emphasise traditions or the 'Tradition' of which heritage, and the special memory of this region, are important aspects of the alignment of the relationships that they have with these places. We are still far from coming up with rationalised justifications for the land-use development of the agricultural plains that testify to the presence of earlier generations, or even simply of consideration of the pleasant nature of such a tourist area. This tendency seems all the more striking when we think of the old villages abandoned by preceding generations, like those of the Mourgana Mountains. They are nostalgic places not only for those who lived there, but also for their descendants, regardless of status, who never cease to allude to their many qualities. These qualities, when lauded by the newly resident, are often in clear contrast to 'the ills of our society' and, as such, clearly constitute a 'heritage', a collection of values and traditions to preserve and pass on, with some local individuals going to considerable organisational lengths – as shown in Chapter 4 – when there is a celebration in the village or the travelling polyphonic festival. Construction of this locality, understood as a space that is lived, known and appropriated, does seem here to be determined by the values attributed to the place. These values go hand-in-hand with a narrative concerning the diverse historical layers in the planning, development and domestication of a border territory marked by disputes, with this no longer being seen as something completely taboo but rather as an eminently remarkable characteristic that is part of what defines the place.

These experiences of transformation (particularly the growth in experiences of mobility and migration) thus lend themselves to the emergence of pluralistic ways of living which, in return, enable the construction of new connections with places, for which re-creation of the past has become a frequent option. As has been asserted in other contexts, for example, in studies on gentrification led by Fabrice Ripoll (2006), recourse is frequently made to the discourse on preservation or on being true to the authenticity of people and places, in order to make sense of how space is used. To a certain extent, this discourse gives rise to the 'mega appropriation' that some writers have observed: 'After all, there is no better way of legitimising an appropriation and having grounds for ownership than filiation and heritage' (Gravari-Barbas and Guichard-Anguis 2003: 14). This kind of discussion over space enables new, recently arrived groups to define their identity through an affiliation forged by history, by heritage. 'Heritage, with its signs, emblems, and symbolic references' (Rautenberg 2003: 114), is an efficient tool for the marking and appropriation of space for these new arrivals. In the context of an institutional extension of forms of preservation and recognition of the built heritage, claiming ownership of an aspect of heritage also enables the newcomers to get involved in plans for these places, to acquire the right to engage, even to have some control over the future of these places … in brief, to 'make their mark' on the space where they live on a more or less regular basis. In this scenario, the disputed history of borders can now be seen, there, as an exceptional historical feature, to the extent that it is forging a tradition. On the other hand, as we have seen in the case of the Vlachs of Nymphaio, at a time of relative peace, historically, this kind of minority presence can even serve as a positive feature worth promoting openly, in order to attract the new resources that national and even international institutions are making available.

Using locality to gain 'roots and wings'

The scenarios described in the previous chapters are thus characterised by a plurality of ways of simultaneously living in a place and being on the move, which points to a significant redefinition of the relationship with places. On the basis of this research, we can question the 'schemes of territoriality' which are inseparable from these changing, fluctuating and mobile conditions of a world that is increasingly described as globalised and deterritorialised. Territory is defined here in the sense of social experience. Is the 'production of localities' (Appadurai 2001) now more constructed from the intersection of multiple scales (regional, national, global)? Today, mobility predominates (Clifford 1997), as it provokes the mutual presence (peaceful or conflictual) of diverse populations, each of which values localness differently. This mobility is not in fact inconsistent with autochtony, as it asserts itself as a way not only of 'belonging to' but also of 'creating' territory, within which different ways of living coexist. The issue of how localities are produced and, therefore, how a shared space is produced, involves the cohabitation of many values, identities and memories. In this way, the territory enables us to question the building of relationships between the social and the spatial which, at times, relies less on physical closeness than on reticular proximity (Lussault 2007). The critical factor in changes to the relationship with 'locality' and with living locally asserts itself if we refer back to '*polytopicité*' (Stock 2006), in other words living in a fluidity and plurality of places. The new reality of mobility is thus de-territorialising locality, understanding it less in terms of a spatial unit and more in terms of social habits. Since the 1990s, increasing enquiry into processes of globalisation has emphasised this notion of locality in terms of the experience of questioning – at a local scale – these new social links created by the diasporic phenomenon and the growing ease of displacement and communication (Appadurai 2001). Thus, 'space in hypermobile contemporary society is relative, relational and characterised by *cospatialité*', in other words, 'The capacity to enjoy, at one and the same time, several places of different sizes' (Lussault 2007: 63). Far from being a threat, these forms of '*plurilocalisation*', of being both from here and from there, here and from here, while simultaneously sometimes being from elsewhere, are a fundamental part of the experience of 'contemporary locality'. These processes are creating hybridity, especially in the possibility for both individuals and groups to become, simultaneously, both 'locals' and 'foreigners', 'tourists' and 'residents' or, in certain contexts, 'returnees' – even, for some, 'haunting spectres of the past'.

The scope of this study certainly presents a major challenge in the case of Balkan societies, frequently understood through the prism of attachment to microspatial areas that take the form of 'small homelands' (Prévélakis 1994: 93). The regional upheavals that occurred at the end of the Cold War, forcing the question of how local belongings are affected by, react to (or interact with) the geographic mobility and migrations that touched the entire region, evidently appear to be unsettling perspectives through the re-evaluation of contemporary ways of being 'from here' and/or 'here'. For example, this is how Giorgos Agelopoulos, looking at ways of self-identifying as 'local' in Florina (Greece), demonstrated that this issue is particularly unclear today, not only because it is rare to receive a definitive answer but also because the issue stems from a constant negotiation of belonging, of the fluctuating capacity to acknowledge the presence of 'others' in lived time and space (Agelopoulos 2005). One major research stream is to start by considering these terrirories (or places often thought of as exclusive) as narratives and as multiple experiences, negotiated and eventually fought over in space and time. The massive increase in migratory processes and in fluid uses of space, and the new scales for regional, national and transnational territories, contribute to the growth of self-narratives and changing relationships with spatial practices. The processes described earlier when discussing cross-border cooperation between the Republic of Macedonia and Greece, or the showcasing of heritage affecting the old town of Rhodes, express very succinctly how these movements do not simply depend on the geographic plurality of origins of their instigators but equally require a plurality of perspectives of history and memory – even of the 'value' of the lived places. Frequently set in motion during the production of contemporary 'locality', these processes are expressed, partly, through their capacity to create not only 'new links to old places' (Givre and Sintès 2013), but also renewed or unknown links between individuals whose local traditions might prove divergent and heterogenous. The borderlands of Greece highlight, in particular, the tension between the pluralisation of individuals' or minorities' stories of time and space which recent efforts to open them up have occasioned, and the monolithic, official or rigid visions often projected by political or institutional bodies aiming to nationalise these regions. This new plurality reveals the fundamental challenge presented by the forms of copresence, coexistence and cohabitation that make up contemporary 'locality'.

Whilst researching ways of inhabiting place within these mobile groups, the cases studies presented in this book draw upon the plurality of ways of living and appropriating space. These really varied approaches and research fields have also allowed me, from a more global perspective, to focus on some of the 'integral relationships' between the social and the spatial, to use Michel Lussault's expression (2007), if this author – who defines social space as 'all those phenomena which describe the social regulation of the distance between separate realities', and spatiality as 'all those uses of space by social operators' – is to be believed. Today, these relationships between the social and the spatial can not (or no longer) be seen as entirely congruent. It is no longer possible to neatly assign one social group to one particular place, in the same way that it is no longer possible to understand migration or mobility as simple flows travelling through space without having an effect. On the one hand, migration or mobility are constructed *in* certain places to the same extent that they construct them. In a context of increasing mobilities, we first need to acknowledge that these spatialities are not singular but multiple: we should talk more about living spaces in the plural or of synergistic ways of living (transnational and cross-border, regional, urban, rural, local…). On the other hand, within this set of examples, 'locality' becomes a good tool with which to reflect on relationships to places, constructed as much by a lasting presence over time as by the experience of change. In this world of mobility and reticularity, there is no one way of living, symbolised by a home and a fixed location, but different skills in, or ways of, living, born of the materially embodied experience of circulation and change, like the collection of objects which Dominique Bouiller (2011) calls '*habitèle*'. In their different forms, however, these ultra-modern ways of 'making the world' sometimes carry the hallmark of the past as a way of justifying the present. In any case, the degrees to which this past is evoked take us further and further away from homogenising narratives built into the nation-state's history. Throughout the diverse processes described in this volume, it is the plurality of narratives at play in today's Balkan societies in particular that has emerged and which intersects around two fundamental axes: space considered as 'home' – visible in the way it is lived, in its social relations and in its 'localities', which are (or are rendered) increasingly more complex – and also space as a territory shared, with others, through movement and, sometimes, appropriated from afar.

Effects of globalisation?

At the heart of this renewed diversity, the processes brought to light in the field reveal themselves as much through discourse as through the practices that distinguish them from the classic frameworks of expression of national identity in Greece. Such processes relate at times to the circumstances of a long-identified group of people whose characteristics distinguish them from the dominant profile of the country's other citizens. For others, the discourse confirms a more nuanced identity, enabling us to assert the existence of the 'in-between' types mentioned above, where difference is only partially or occasionally evoked, depending on the different space–time contexts in which it is expressed. Through the various examples of how solidarity can unexpectedly be activated between these groups and citizens of other countries, typically found on the other side of the limits of 'otherness,' ease of geographical mobility is clearly implicated in the revivification of minorities or of local groups, as much through transnational links as through the reinforcement of regional identities. However, apart from migrants or mobile actors in contemporary society, attention should perhaps also be paid to the role that institutional actors can play in these same processes, such as, for example, international management bodies, where the action is organised on a smaller scale but also impacts the same processes. Even if their influence is not always easily measured, they can also be seen as alternative guarantees to national frameworks through the various actions they suggest and the discourses they subscribe to. It is thus that I was able, on several occasions, to witness the influence of the new regulatory or incentivising measures promoted by these international institutions. Compliance with these frameworks thus enables some inhabitants on the fringes to confirm their more secure inclusion in the 'global hierarchy of value' mentioned at the beginning of this book, all the while keeping their distance *vis-à-vis* the dominant profile of the country's citizens. This is the case, for example, when the issue of the protection of minority rights is raised, or of migratory policies, the designation of heritage or the labelling of identities and regional products. In all of these cases, it seems possible to show that reference to the past, or to a certain kind of authenticity associated with it, can also be promoted by management regulations that have been introduced by institutional authorities. These regulations offer an alternative (and noticeably transgressive) discourse to that traditionally forged by the nation-state which, up to now, has viewed fringe territories and minority expression in a much more unequivocable way.

The field which normally deals with the construction and diffusion of official discourses on the past is one which is concerned with the relationship between power and history or, rather, between power and the narrative of history (seen more as *historia rerum gestarum* than as *res gestae*), a nuance that allows for an understanding of 'suspect time-spaces' in relation to the historicity of their development (Grataloup 2011). This is also what Michel-Rolph Trouillot's (1995) book *Silencing the Past* talks of, when he points to the distortions, in the case of Haïti, between official history and minority narratives whilst, at the same, demonstrating the need to 'track power' through relying on issues of power to expose the logics involved in this kind of discrepancy. If we follow this thread it seems, then, that discourses on the past must also be questioned with regard to the changing relationships between the levels of power that today affect the entire world. In fact, if the nation-state has been recognised as a dominant prescriber of the mobilisation of the past through the promotion of a hegemonic national narrative during the last century, as invoked, for example, in the work of Anne-Marie Thiesse (1999) and Eric Hobsbawm (Hobsbawn and Ranger 1983), things have been viewed as much more nuanced over the last few decades, with the assertion of a discourse pertaining to sub-national identity. In the Balkans, variations of this discourse (re)appeared during the 1990s, with the fall of political regimes from the Eastern bloc and the break-up of Yugoslavia; however, we need to realise that the roots of this movement also seemed to be more global. Thus, when history seems to be a permanent reinterpretation, the effects on the present of which are numerous and whose 'historical turn' in anthropological studies is designed to make things more transparent (Cornish 2013), perhaps the characteristics of past mobilisations should be considered in relation to the redeployment of institutional and political bodies, with respect to these themes, which derive only from historical factors unique to each region. Each of the territories discussed above leads us to believe in these processes of social fragmentation and geographical mobility in relation to such repositionings. This perspective, applied to the realities observed in Greece, enables a re-evaluation of the somewhat insubstantial evidence which claims that these scenarios of return of (or recourse to) the past, are not only determined by immanent (bottom-up) processes, but also emerge from new habits or new relationships to territory, initiated by local protagonists under the aegis of both migration and 'locality'. The examples of the 'small groups' studied in this monograph also need to be thought of through their inclusion in broader logics, where they submit to the injunctions (or more subtle suggestions) of agents involved in the discourse of management, often found at the supranational level.

Institutional back-up for an alternative recourse to the past

Such a viewpoint stems from the realisation that declarations of identification and territorial practice found in the field have often also appeared to be influenced by the activity of institutional operators. Albanian migrants, for example, are subject to Greek law on migration which forces them to adopt a clear position on Greekness, and enables a differentiation between the migrants. Jews from Rhodes saw their approach approved, and even supported, by the canons of patrimonial development, led by UNESCO's labelling of the old town of Rhodes and the touristic interest in this site. Concerns over the country's heritage promoted by international fora would appear to resonate in much the same way as the many schemes aimed at rebuilding, over the summer, the community of inhabitants of old Sagiada, as well as those in each of the villages in the surrounding mountains. These effects of administrative discourse are even more strongly felt in the forms of cultural cooperation entered into on either side of the border between the Republic of Macedonia and Greece. These examples are a reminder that the culture, authenticity and history to which the protagonists refer in the various fields in order to explain and formalise their practices are effectively a multifactoral and contextual construct of which institutional facilities are also a part.

In this respect, the development of the Jewish past in Rhodes is a good example which can be compared with other places in the Mediterranean where this type of regeneration has taken place. The originality of the various actors engaged in this work can thus be examined and some lessons learned. The development of the Jewish past in a place exists, for example, in a comparable manner in the 'Paths of Sepharad' in Spain, which aimed to promote the memory of Jewish communities which disappeared during the *Reconquista* in the different towns throughout the country (Lévy and Olazabal 2003).

Similar operations can also be found, since 1992, in the Comtat Venaissin (Southern France) based on the history of Jewish communities in Provence (Grange 2003). In the case of Rhodes, it is striking to note, however, that the main actors involved in the regeneration of the Jewish past are nearly always exclusively private, and that the local authorities in Rhodes only appear to be marginally concerned. In contrast, these sponsors appear to conform to memorial recommendations that UNESCO labelling has built into their management norms. On the other hand, it appears equally revealing that this putting in place of a patrimonial activity is not easy to impose and that tensions even arise between the holders of these memories, the descendents of Rhodian Jews who came to the region to honour together the memory of their ancestors, and the direct sponsors of commemorative activity which encourages a more mainstream promotion of the Jewish memory in Rhodes more suited to excursions and tourism. If this activity can be presented as a means of safegarding the threatened memory of the Rhodian Jewish community, it also leads to a desecration of this memory through the trivialisation of the journey and the mundaneness of its touristic exploitation. This is how the return trip can be deceptive for migrants faced with the reality of a place so long mythologised: 'Me, the *kai ancha*, I thought it was the Champs Elysées', or 'I don't remember the fountain being so small', said the older ones who left before the war; for the younger ones: 'I'm fed up with *mézé* (Greek appetisers), I want a real dish!', or 'In Israel there is a real fight, here there are only stones'. These different remarks show a revealing discrepancy in the tension between the 'imposition' of memory as perhaps suggested by the force of 'patrimonial concensus' (Bondaz *et al.* 2013), even it is only indirectly imposed in this particular case, and the group – object of this discussion – whose heterogeneity is revealed on this occasion.

As far as the exploitation of memory or of culture generally is concerned, the intervention of economic actors is quite usual when justifying and developing cultural and commemorative resources. For some, the commodification occurring through their intervention may turn out to be a particularly effective means of desecration. This relationship between commemorative discourse and economic interest is vital in the current deployment of Jewish memory in Rhodes, but it surfaces very clearly too in the heritage experiences observed in Macedonia and Epirus. It enshrines the general movement which has occurred over recent decades. If, effectively, the 1960s and 1970s were years of thought about development – in which cultural forms eventually appeared to be obstacles, the beginning of the twenty-first century saw the harnessing of culture through the economy, embodied, in part, by UNESCO's recognition in 2011 of the virtues of the 'purple' economy. Between cultural economy and the 'culturalisation of development' (Givre and Regnault 2015), culture even asserts itself as a field highly appropriate for economic dynamics, and even for reviving peripheral spaces, as a 'functional resource from which spaces relegated to the periphery can be socially and economically developed' (Amilhat-Szary and Fourny 2006). In spite of the rejection of what some descendants of Rhodian Jews expressed as the perversion of 'their' memory, the assertion of economic efficiency may prove to be decisive in this process of distinction through culturalisation found in peripheral groups, through imitation or even through the adoption, quite simply, of a dominant model. Such an element may also be at least as important in the establishment of such arrangements as the irrepressible desire to attest to a difference, to a particularity, which may be dear to them.

When considering more generally the connection with peripheral identities during the 1990s in Greece, the recommendations of the supranational institutional actors seem, effectively, to have acted in favour of the revitalisation of some minority discourses in the country. We can see this, for example, in the results of the Euromosaic project – its report on the production and reproduction of minority linguistic groups in the EU was submitted to the European Commission in 1996, as were those of the European Bureau for Lesser-Used Languages (EBLUL), which received a very mixed welcome in Greece. The only (tense) visit which its researchers made to the Arvanite villages led to pressure on them to leave the place quickly, demonstrating the sensitive nature of such a question (Williams 1992: 88). The case of the judgement rendered against the architect Sotiris Bletsas provides another example. In 1995, during the pan-Hellenic gathering of the Vlachs, this latter had, in fact, distributed a brochure by EBLUL showing a map of the areas where Aromanian, Bulgarian, Slavo-Macedonian, *Arvanitika* and Turkish are spoken on Greek territory. The scandal and complaints which followed saw Bletsas condemned to a heavy fine and 15 months in prison. On this occasion the president of the courts of justice even declared, echoing the feeling of much of the country, 'OK, all these things are perhaps spoken. But do we really need to refer to it?' (Sintès 2008b). In spite of the strength of these reactions, it would seem that intervention, even very indirectly, at the supernational level may enable the use of an alternative medium of expression to the usual national frameworks which are usually very unreceptive to this type of discourse. The links between the Greek Slavo-Macedonian party *Ouranio Toxo* and the European Parliament's European Free Alliance bear witness to this. Indirectly, as discussed in the first chapter of this volume, a reinforcement of 'ethnicisation' or at least a certain form of fragmentation can be seen as the result of top-down processes. As found in the works of Achileas Lazarou –an author who continuously affirms the 'hellenity' of these Greek Aroumanians –these new discourses, implicitly promoted at the European level, come up against national discourse in this case. The following reactions at the moment when the EU authorities recognised Aromanians from Greece as an official minority bear witness:

> There is no doubt that recent decisions made as much by the European Parliament as by the European Council, according to which the Greek Vlachs are a minority within their own country – under false pretences – will also result in failure. Due to the absence of official Greek representatives, these two decisions will not win the support of the Vlach population in Greece. On the contrary, they are claims by the agents of pre-war Romanian propaganda who were in fact born outside Greece, more precisely in Bulgaria (Dobroudja) and in Romania. Consequently, they can only represent themselves and a few pupils from Romanian schools of the same period or their descendants. In fact, it is only a question of around twenty very militant persons, small fry compared to the 200,000 Vlach whose conscience is fully Hellenic. (Lazarou 1998: 95–6)

'Glocalised' processes?

Such comments lead us to think that top-down processes must also be taken into account in understanding the logics of the situations presented in this book. The reference to the past can thus be understood as much in its relation to the appropriation of space stemming from the new mobility practices of its inhabitants as to a management or political discourse the application of which requires international institutions or social actors being inspired. The apparent contradiction which these discourses pit against the canons of the nation-state must also be highlighted, even if one should undoubtedly treat this last point more subtly. The heritage and cultural development highlighted in all of the studies in this book may appear to reveal the creation of a 'meta-ideology' (Olivier de Sardan 1995), in reply to questions posed in Chapter 1 about the position of the reference to the past in the 'global hierarchy of value'. Through these observations on the cases of Nymfaio or of Sagiada, as well as on the streets of the old town of Rhodes, the relations between enhanced (or enhanceable) cultural expression – even contrary to the canonical expression of national identity – and the implementation of public policies for economic development or urban planning are often in evidence.

At the international level, this culture–development nexus has received massive investment since the 2000s, as testifies UNESCO's 2001 Universal Declaration on Cultural Diversity, its recognition at the Johannesburg World Summit on Cultural Diversity as the fourth pillar of sustainable development in 2002, and UNESCO's adoption of the Convention on the Protection and Promotion of the Diversity of Cultural Expressions 2005. In 2004, the fact that the Annual Report of the UNDP was devoted to 'cultural freedom in a diverse world' has sanctioned the adoption of culture (or cultures) as a tool for economic development at a global level, confirming its endorsement as one of the United Nation's eight millennium goals in 2000. In Europe, more specifically, this movement has drawn states towards types of collaboration which take cultural issues into account. Since 2007, and the promotion of the 'European Agenda for Culture', cultural issues are amongst the main strategic priorities of the EU. In South-Eastern Europe, cultural policies are seen in border areas as potential factors of peace and reconciliation, the catalyst for a peaceful living together. As well as these goals of pacification or cohesion, culture is also increasingly considered as a potential economic resource thanks to the organisation of cultural events or the revitalisation of natural and cultural heritage, of craftsmanship or traditions, all judged to be potential sources of tourist development. Through all these examples, the assertion of cultural development as social project is required, constituting a breeding-ground well suited to the dynamics described in this volume.

The link between these previously described dynamics and the field of 'development' is thus crucial, given the economic lethargy of most of these peripheral spaces. The notion of the specific aim of social, political, economic and cultural transformation can be found very obviously in the description of the Nymfaio and Malovishte/Krushevo projects. The cultural dimension appears to have potential as an indiscutable local (re)qualification and developmental factor, built around historically and culturally shared features which add value over and above the cleavages illustrated primarily by the disputed political borders. But it is through recourse at many levels to polycentric forms of confirmation and legitimisation (from the inhabitants of these places to the European Community) that the 'local' is thus constructed and can draw the source of its eligibility from those formerly rejected (or at least 'diluted') particularities.

The frameworks within which these projects (programmes, packages, European funds, labels) reside prove eventually to be easily alterable and suitable for permanent reinterpretation according to contexts and usage. Focusing on the local, these projects are less embodied in administratively bounded physical territories and more in the 'eligible areas' of expandable or retractable 'projects' depending on the circumstances and the international calls for tender, which often seem to escape the direct control of state power. The final case study presented in Chapter 4 bears witness to the structure and cooperation of the European institutional packages and networks of actors (local, translocal and transnational) within the heart of these projects which may, in part, be qualified as the achievements 'of a community' or even 'of a minority'. In this case we are talking of the discussion about the 'Vlach presence' in the village of Nymfaio, so much does this belonging seem to easily find its place at the heart of a Europeanised local lifestyle, whereas it would seem to be concurrently losing its relevance at the regional or national level. Benefiting from a new lease of life following its participation in the framework of cross-border cooperation, does this inclusion demonstrate the 'Europeanisation' or 'globalisation' of 'ethnic powers' (Gossiaux 2002) or its simple adjustment to those conditions which are henceforth dominant?

Any description of this type of tension between local and international actors on the one hand and the nation-state on the other will recall the notion of glocalisation, which seems perfectly suited to the hierarchy of actors prevailing here. If this concept was initially used to invoke relations between world capitalism and the places of its incarnation (Ghorra-Gobin 2003), it can also be used to mean the congruence of local levels of power and international governance at the expense of the nation-state's territorial control (in the sense of its topographical metrics on a political space). The different schemes proposed below to illustrate the positionning of the actors involved in the examples of Albanian migrants in Greece or of the revitalisation of the Jewish past in Rhodes initially lead to this type of conclusion, and seem thus to respond to one and the same logic, which can be summarised in Figure 5.2.

However, as suggested, we must beware of the temptation to attribute only these different tendencies to purely global/local logics. This would inevitably lead to the cultural essentialism too often used to invoke the 'Balkans', focusing more on the supremacy of local or ethnic identities in the region than on the power of nation-states which are regularly perceived to be weak or weakened. Should these tendencies not be taken to be a form of instrumentalism or even of institutional coproduction (including that of the state or of regional and local authorities) by organisations which influence the exercise of power in different 'loyalties': kinship, ethnicity, political persuasion or 'national belonging (Gounaris and Frangopoulos 2009)? In effect, like 'Mediterranean societies', the forms of power in the Balkans are often perceived to revolve around patronage and clientelism (Campbell 1964). But rather than continuing in this vein, it would seem better to focus on the emergeance of a dispositive of power which involves, at different levels, influencial actors, organised communities and states which are 'bearers' or 'referees' of EU projects and programmes, and to affirm instead the importance of networks (topological spaces) in the production of social and political resources, as described above. In fact, to such an extent that it would not seem at all appropriate to approach transnational programmes as networks of actors independently of the related social and policital forms, the interlaced relations – themselves multilayered – which are reborn in the field as concrete projects or as effective actions. In their essential flexibility,

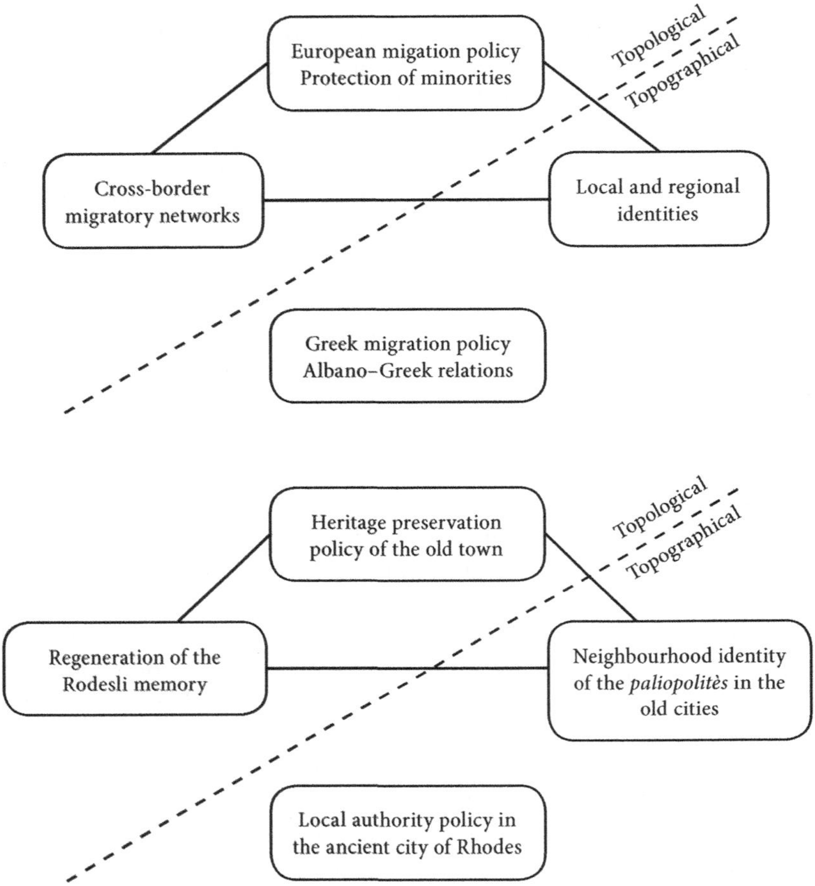

Figure 5.2 Links between actors in the examples of Albanian migrants' (above) and Rodeslis' returns (below)

the network practices which these examples suggest are characterised by their capacity to move from place to place, continually looking for the best position … which does not prevent them from fully occupying the strongest places when they find them. Observing such a trend leads us to question again the classic interpretation whereby the reinforcement of local or minority belonging is a sign of weak allegiance to the nation-state. This last question prompts wider reflection on the transformation in the levels of power on contemporary territories in order to include such observations within a broader interpretive framework.

Scales of globalisation in the Balkans

Since 1990 and the fall of marxist-inspired regimes, the important economic, political and social transformations which have affected all the Balkan countries seem to have upset relations between levels of power just when these latter were also changing at a world level. Such a process was accompanied by a switch to a market economy in most cases and, for countries like Greece and its Turkish neighbour, by the acceleration of state reforms imposed by international authorities, and in particular by the European Union. These different movements can nevertheless be seen as one single movement if one is to believe certain observers of the globalisation process. This is the thesis, for example, put forward by James Rosenau who, as early as 1992, conflated the fall of the Berlin Wall and developments in Western countries into one and a single movement. This latter was made up of 'turbulences and cascades' resulting from a transformation of relations between power and space, and from a stand-off between states and multicentred systems which benefited from technological transformations in communication and transport (Rosenau 1992). In their recent work many authors, (see, *inter alia*, Sassen 2007; Abélès 2008), situating their analyses at a much more global level than those shown in this volume, argue for increased attention to be paid to these changes in the role of states concerning issues of power and territory. This type of approach can thus serve as a framework for my fieldwork observation perspective.

In Greece, in effect, as in the other Balkan countries and in line with such analyses, the development of numerous parameters seems to have led to a questioning of traditional national allegiances – closely allied with the withdrawal of the nation-state from many areas of society, from both an economic and an ideological view point – what Saskia Sassen calls a process of 'denationalisation' (Sassen 2007). Here, as elsewhere, globalisation has favoured the promotion of new actors who are currently challenging the political omnipotence of the nation-state, in this way modifying the legitimacy of territorial regimes. Throughout the Balkans, too, from the 1990s, intervention by higher-level institutions, the reins of which are paradoxically state-held, confirmed the wavering of nation-states. The wars in the ex- Yugoslavian countries provided numerous occasions for this to take place, as, for example, in Kosovo, with the intervention of a coalition of countries under the authorisation of the United Nations in 1999 and the taking of control of the region in the framework of a civil administration in different guises (MINUK, EULEX). In every country of the peninsula, the EU often establishes itself as the most regular and efficient of these transformations via the different programmes it has led or still leads (PHARE, CARDS, OBNOVA, INTERREG, IPA). This same level of power can be found within the framework of policies of security and of regulation of migratory flows which stem from close cooperation between states and the EU (FRONTEX) but also from tensions – such as those with Turkey over readmission agreements. Numerous cooperation programmes now make the most of European policies in the region, and are working towards the goal of integration of every Balkan country into the EU. For the countries concerned, respecting these orders is vital as it directly affects their future integration into the international game. Funding for these different projects is granted on condition that the clauses set by international bodies are respected. For many years, the case of Serbia, whose accession to the European Union is linked to its close cooperation with the International Criminal Tribunal in The Hague, has been a shining example.

> We can thus see how instruments designed to prepare the membership of the Western Balkans become a political lever enabling the European 'core' to influence the 'outlying' Balkans. (Cattaruzza and Chaveneau-Le Brun 2007: 4)

This process affects a good number of sectors of Balkan society. Within the framework of the Association and Stabilisation Agreement (ASA), for example, and unlike what had previously been undertaken in preparation for EU enlargement to Central and Eastern Europe, the EU is responsible on its own terms not only for material aspects such as the rebuilding of infrastructures or the stimulation of the economy, but also for non-material elements like peacekeeping or identity reconstruction. Since the financial and economic crisis of 2008, the drive to bring Greece up to European standards can be compared to this movement, in as much as it shares the same spirit of control and validation by international bodies created on this occasion (demonstrating that lability is also common at this level). The strength of these recommendations on those elements 'which had once been integrated in the territories and institutional areas of the national' (Sassen 2007: 20) sits well with the process which we can call, in this region, 'EU-isation' or 'Europeanisation', so greatly does the European horizon seem to be the dominant influence on such changes. Through the broader modifications which affect institutions, ways of life, relations with places, and behaviours – these EU actions are in a strong position as instigators of new normative frameworks.

In light of these observations, one wonders if the Balkans will yet again show themselves to be a space where national powers are easily be controlled, where the 'great powers' can dictate the game, as has seemed to be the case in recent centuries. Would it not be better to consider that this weakening of the nation-state in certain spheres of power is nothing other than the outcome of a process which has also occurred in other world regions? Its more accomplished character instead confirms that the peninsula is at the forefront of a new form of governance which will open the way to new means of regulation between the different levels of power and will eventually resuit in the 'Balkanisation of the West' as prophesied by Stjepan Mestrović (1994). In this new context, any study of contemporary Balkan society must take into account the different levels of power, without, however, reifying an unstable reality and ressorting to the invocation of absolute determinants – tradition versus modernity, states versus local society, transnationalism versus nation – which would lead one to conclude on, no doubt too quickly, the strength of social or ideological inertia, pushing even more to 'imagine the Balkans' as a place set apart from modernity. On the contrary, as Saskia Sassen (2007) suggests, these levels of reality mean that globalisation processes need no longer to be thought of uniquely as strictly nested, as the different actors can draw on resources at varying levels to carry out their projects, as the numerous examples in this volume have shown. John Durham Peters explains this by pointing out that one of the main features of our time is the condition of 'bifocality' which enables the majority of social actors to be aware, at one and the same time, of both the local and the global scale (Durham Peters 1997).

From a geopolitical viewpoint, government use of international institutions to bolster their national interests provides a new example of the complexity of relations between the levels of power which do not systematically oppose the national and the supranational. This is the case when the Greek government, for example, threatens to veto Turkey's membership of the EU due to the non-application of readmission agreements signed by the two countries in 2001. It is also evident in the difference of opinion between Slovenia and Croatia over the Gulf of Piran. For the Slovenian state, integration at the higher level of the European Union appears to have provided the country with a new means to push its regional project in the Adriatic Sea; the same applies to the quarrel over the name of the Republic of Macedonia covered earlier in this volume. Instead of leading inexhorably to its weakening, the inclusion of a state at a supranational level can, on the contrary, enable it to reinforce its aims and objectives at the expense of another. Locally, the example of 'patrimonial diplomacy' described in the previous chapter confirms that supranational frameworks can also serve as spaces of expression for nation-state actors. The higher levels can also strongly intervene in the identificatory processes through their recognition or 'rejection': the slogan 'We are all Europeans' chanted in the streets of Tirana during the embassy crisis of 1990, which demonstrated the people's determination to be governed by a higher power which they perceived as fairer, and the Euroscepticism visible today in the Balkan countries, are two opposing examples of this. More deeply in society, we can nevertheless raise concerns once again about the reality of this supposed weakening of the state. To achieve this, we need simply to focus once again on the protagonists and situations described throughout the pages of this book. The formation of identity frameworks is achieved through diverse means (mobility, networks, heritage, culture) always located in a social space and which will become an integral part of the construction of both public space and the intimacy of family and private places. In the hands of sometimes now private or non-state actors, they can nevertheless today take on the mantle of social control which was once the role of the state. We should not, perhaps, see this process as disappearance but rather as redeployment, culminating in what Michel Foucault has labelled 'the statization of society' (Foucault 1978).

* * *

What emerges through these discussions is that closing the primordialist trap on those surveyed is avoidable if we recognise that the assertion of difference, through more frequent recourse to resurgeant characteristics from the past, may also be a complex product of our era. If the new mobilities and territorialities appear determining in any understanding of this resurgeance, the role played by the producers of official discourses must also not be overlooked, which is why it is at the core of my more recent studies of European programmes on the northern borders of Greece, presented in Chapter 4. The production of both identity and locality is thus confirmed as a complex process in which many different actors are involved. One of the most striking and note-worthy features to emerge is that these primordialist movements paradoxically co-exist elsewhere with an accrued individualisation of ways of thinking, of thinking of oneself, and of constructing one's spaces on the one hand, and the assertion of nationalist tendencies on the European political scene on the other.

Conclusion

My fieldwork in Greece in recent years has led me to study some of the logics of the mobilisation of the past in relation to the diversity or polyphony of memories in the country. Such mobilisations at present seem to be supported by processes such as the strengthening of transnational links enabled by the increase in mobilities and migration on the one hand, and their adaptation to a particular form of consensus concerning minority expression on the other. Over and above the prevailing situation at the heart of their nation-state, international political recognition effectively provides efficient support enabling local and minority expressions to be positioned within a set of norms henceforth seen as *a priori* legitimate. The permitted performance of these discourses of identification serves to strengthen their specular dimension for those who see themselves as part of these groups. The performance suggests (even obliges) a way of presenting – even thinking of – the self, of looking at the self as in a mirror; this appeared to me to apply particularly to the descendants of Rhodian Jews or to other groups encountered during my fieldwork. The last process, neverless, also undergoes a certain simplification, a normalisation of the expression of belonging based on codes suggested by some of its promoters. Such a movement occurs again at the expense of individual memories and their inevitable plurality, as evidenced by the disagreements between the various protagonists of these revitalisation projects over the best practices to adopt. No matter at which level it is planned, the institutionalisation of memory which these processes suggest goes through a stage of normalisation of space and practices, and the role of institutional actors does not appear to be of any importance in this latter trait.

And yet such a movement takes place on the ground with no obvious discrepancy with the development of nationalist discourses either in Greece or in neighbouring countries. This paradox inevitably brings to mind the remarks made by Ferdinand de Saussure on the evolution of languages, which would in effect be subject to two apparently opposing tendencies which he terms the '*force d'intercourse*', or pressure of communication (the gradual unification of particularities as the transfers and exchanges increase in number) and the '*esprit de clocher*' – individualism or provincialism – (the strengthening of regional particularities as a reaction to standardisation). What de Saussure had initially seen as contradictory he finally felt was moving in the same direction: a tendency towards standardisation, understood at different levels (1916: 282). The same applies to the memories of small communities in Greece. If the strengthening of national discourses takes the form of a net radicalisation of the whole of society as far as the themes of migration and 'otherness' are concerned, a radicalisation which often contradicts transnational, minority or local narratives through combatting their plurality, a comparable process can be seen at the very heart of those groups which make up this society – including those who consider themselves special within the national whole, leading them also towards a standardisation of discourses and representations in order that they conform to received canons of correct local or minority expression.

What is more, no matter the level of understanding, recourse to a renewed reference to bygone years has become a sign of our times, according to historian François Hartog. These observations refer to the conclusions drawn from his work on the 'regimes of historicity' and confirm the requirements of the present in the social use of the past, which he so eminently qualified as an 'infinite present' or as 'presentism' (Hartog 2003). Reinhard Koselleck (1990) described the same phenomemon when he alluded to the shortening of the distance between 'experience' and 'horizon of expectation'; imposing an imperative of emergency, the end of future prospects would therefore explain this 'return to the past' as the only possible outcome. Nevertheless, Moses Finley (with Harthog and Carlier) (1981), taken up by Marie-Claire Lavabre (2006: 10), had identified the limits of such theories, which were not sufficient to explain the widespread adoption by the majority of social actors of such a belief in the legitimacy of using the past in the present. From nationalist parties to representatives of ethnic minorities, why such unanimity? The preceding pages of this volume on the transformation of power relations seek to answer this question through analysis of the role of institutions in the spread of such representations. This is why, in order to explore this hypothesis more deeply, my more recent work has focused on the effects of the institutionalisation of memory via EU programmes to preserve both natural and cultural heritage within some outlying spaces of Greece. Reference to the past was boosted here by the use which these institutions proposed to make of it, investing in (by simplifying them) the sheer variety of memories in order to render them legitimate items for promotion and development. Relations between this legitimation and the propagation of the cultural economy also affect this mass phenomenon. Whatever the cause, such processes introduce a new way of thinking the world and of thinking of oneself in the world which, while purporting to control the course of time, contributes to the fragmentation of both societies and spaces.

The reflections which proceed from the studies set out above are woven together around issues which are often treated separately, and whose heterogeneity makes them hard to summarise (spatial mobility, migration, memory, heritage, cooperation, culture, development). They are the result of research experiences gained on different sites and purposes, but during which some common processes have come to light. Initially the observation of international migrations provided the opportunity to formulate some hypotheses which essentially underlined the extent of centrifugal phenomena and of the tendency towards social and spatial fragmentation which went with them in this context. These initial thoughts thus led to a more general consideration based on different contexts and different configurations (border zones, tourist regions, diasporic networks), of the dynamics which affect links with otherness and change in Greece, especially through the observation of situations involving memory or the heritage of 'small groups'. En route, these studies have allowed me to put together some thoughts about the mechanisms of globalisation in this region, focusing on the cultural dynamics and the rolling out of forms shaped by institutional, especially international, packages.

This broadening of my thematic perspective was accompanied by a methodological development to which the account of my research experiences in this text bears witness. The methods used turned out, over time, to be increasingly empirical. The hypothetico-deductive method which marked my earliest research has gradually faded away, enabling me to deal, in a way which seemed to be more efficient, with the thematic developments described in the previous paragraph. In this way, observation of the dynamics of memory and identity which took place in Rhodes, for example, and on the territories around the Greco-Albanian border, forced me to take more notice of the discourses and practices of the individuals involved, as they turned out to be sources of invaluable and sometimes surprising information. Already, in my doctoral work on the construction of migratory networks of Albanians in Greece, I was tempted to research, through patient observation, the sometimes unconscious practice behind formal discourses that can be revealed more in interviews than in media discourses or official statistics. Increasingly, the direction taken by this work led me to accept the 'passive' observation of the different configurations chosen for the study – 'idle' observation said some, when I was working in the sunshine of the Aegean Sea! This methodological flexibility translates in the writing of this book as the gradual lengthening of references to field observations, as well as the greater use of interview quotes reproduced verbatim, which sometimes gives to the last few pages the appearance of a narrative, a thick description. Through the use of such interview procedures, of analysis and restitution, this work refers to the developmental objective – even coproduction – of a comprehensive discourse on social processes. This explains why my enquiries are often more to do with every-day life and, even if the observation takes place within more particular media (European programmes) or at certain more exceptional moments such as village festivals or services of remembrance, it is always within the framework of daily lives which gives them meaning. The material produced through this type of enquiry (discourse and practices, mental constructions and concrete experiences), observed in the field, reveals as much the sum of the material elements which these social processes demonstrate as the mental package of coherence and legitimity which accompanies them. Such an approach stems from the mistrust of a scientific discourse which has universal pretentions. Even so, this wariness does not cancel out the tension produced by the concern over transferability or at least over analogy, so as not to confine the intention solely to the producing of a monographic study.

* * *

This methodological development answers two social science concerns which are well known today, and which I will only bring up briefly. Firstly, the intention to do away with the 'colonial paradigm' which will involve constructing a system of understanding from the outside (Collignon 2007). On the contrary, the issue here is to give voice to those interviewed who are not necessarily in a position of power, but in a 'subaltern' one, as it is more commonly said in English (Spivak 2010). This preoccupation goes hand-in-hand with my curiosity about a geography which attempts to explain the logics of social domination, which stimulates my interest in the study of minorities or small groups caught up, at least partially, in contexts of subordination. The other concern, more epistemological in the sense that it involves the techniques and practices of scientific production, is that of the adoption of social contructivisim as introduced by Berger and Luckmann (1966), and which is consistent, in my case, especially with the deconstruction of mainstream narratives, i.e. the questioning of nation-state discourses in order to reveal social polyphony. This sensitivity leads, over and above the study of minority situations, to the giving of value to the flexibility of identities seen as discursive products largely conditioned by the contexts of their utterance. I am here referring essentially to the theories of interactionism which, on other subjects, have been influenced by the work of Erving Goffman (1975), even if I often consider levels of social aggregation greater than the individual, and to Fredrik Barth's (1969) analyses of ethnic boundaries. With its more direct links to the Balkans, the work of Jean-François Gossiaux (2002) has also played a decisive role in the manner in which transformations of Greek society have been envisaged in this book. Finally, the issue of the incorporation and especially of the performance of identity (Butler 2009; Butler and Jami 2003) or of culture (Dimitriadis 2009; Kirshenblatt-Gimblett 1998) appears to be an efficient prism through which to understand the logics of certain processes. Due to these influences, and in spite of the thematic flexibilities presented above, my approach has almost always focused on the geographical margins rather than on the centre, being more interested in the excluded or the peripheries, and in the processes which lead to the reproduction of this marginality rather than to its results – as the latter are never more than the transitory state of an ever-changing reality.

Secondly, the work presented in this volume raises the issue of the continental position occupied by South-Eastern Europe (Cattaruzza and Sintès 2012). This approach also aims to enhance our understanding of the current transformations in this region by analysing, on the one hand, the role played by outside forces (the development of exchanges, migrations, economic convergence and the standardisation of forms of governance), and local dynamics too commonly associated with issues of permanence or of tradition, on the other, which often leads to the Balkans being held up as a space of ethnicisation of society, of conservatism and of widespread antisocial practices. My studies, due to their level of understanding, aim to show, on the contrary, that these logics overlap and that their dynamics are often heterogenous, and even sometimes paradoxical. They also, in particular, leave protagonists some room for manoeuvre and negotiation. This last statement in no way seeks to deny that the processes in question are deployed in societies, built up over a long period in relation with the historical specificity of the region, in which the formation of social groups based on their linguistic or religious characteristics can be seen as a recurrent and distinctive feature. Even so, I maintain that this kind of construction of otherness is today continually updated, in relation to more global, institutional and, of course, economic processes. Within this framework, it seems to me that, for better or worse, the growing importance accorded by institutions to cultural factors, even to their development and application, encourages frequent recourse to ethnic or cultural explanations in the interpretation of social transformation, and clearly affects the positioning of the different participants in the social games documented in this volume.

* * *

In fine, this work aims to distance itself from an interpretation of South-Eastern European societies as subject to the more-or-less successful transfer of a set of standards (those of the European Union or of the 'Western world') at the cost of a 'traditional society' which would not be to their advantage. My approach instead draws inspiration from studies which have shown how these processes of social transformation brought about by globalisation can live side-by-side with processes which appear to derive from tradition, lineage and locality (Agier *et al.* 1987; M'Bokolo and Amselle 2005), and which in no way lead to a downgrading of the second by the imposition of the first. During my research, especially in the particular cases of processes of revitalisation of the social memories of small groups, it has been possible for me to understand how these very contemporary dynamics were involved in the timely and valuable mobilisation of the past: Albanian migrants whose migratory network has become a memory-making machine, Rhodian Jewish networks caught in their practice of identity-based mobility towards the land of their ancestors and groups of inhabitants along the northern border of Greece implementing displays for the institutionalisation of local memory (relying on associations, national public administrative authorities, international groups etc.).

In each of these cases, the marketing and politicisation of identity or culture serve as a backdrop to 'configurations of memory' observed on the ground. Study of them initially raises the eminently geographical question of relations between power and places – echoing the work of Claire Andrieu on the second half of twentieth-century France – 'Is central power (i.e. the nation state) losing its symbolic power? (…)'. If Andrieu concludes in her case-study that 'the mirror of the nation-state maintains its ultimate identity function' (Andrieu 2006: 17), what about early-twenty-first-century Greek society? Now that the crisis is in full swing, on what basis can consensus be forged? We cannot help but notice that, in recent years, in their provocatory verbal (and occasionally physical) invectives, neo-Nazi members of the Greek parliament regularly address those on the left, reminding them of the battles lost by communist fighters during the civil war. It is this lack of consensus borne by the past which nourishes the current animosity, a sort of reversed 'guerre des mémoires' ('memory war') which is not based on a conflictual interpretation of the past but where the tensions of yesteryear enter the controversy to give some sense to those of today. As we have seen in other Mediterranean countries, '(…) political and commemorative conflicts obviously interact, and political instability prevents any possibility of calming memories' (Crivello 2010: 26).

Already in 1925, Marc Bloch reminded us of the social function of memory, which would allow change while giving the illusion of continuity. Nevertheless, to authorise such an operation, a veritable '*travail de mémoire*' (public gesture of remembrance) as put by Maryline Crivello (2010) is called for, in particular in the Mediterranean region which, without being an exception in the world, demonstrates an incredibly high number of traces of the past in the present (to the point of provoking, in some American or Japanese tourists, mental disorders, indicative of this physical over-presence of vestiges of the past). In this regard, Greece, the Balkans and all the countries of the Mediterranean appear as laboratories relevant to the analysis of past/present relations: 'From the Balkans to the Near-East, via the Maghreb, the incompatibility between the different scales of memory (official, collective, individual) only serve to exacerbate inter- or intracommunity antagonisms which transform conflictual memories into a central issue in all conflicts of identity' (Crivello 2010: 14). Nevertheless, one of the objectives stemming from this research is the conciling of this observation with the necessary enlarging of our view of these spaces, in order to demonstrate how they are at the heart of the more global processes which they reveal. Use of the past fits in well, in effect, with the wider movement which is that of the 'culturalisation' of contemporary societies and more especially the strengthening of links and social networks which base their legitimacy on a common past which binds them. Through these different works, I am effectively seeking to illustrate the processes currently taking place in today's world, by analysing them from the perspective of the special relations between dynamics of identity and of social space.

Glossary of ethnonyms and other specific terms

Aromanians: Speakers of a romance- or Latin-based language related to Romanian and spoken in the south of the Balkan peninsula by groups of herdsmen who have long been semi-nomadic known sometimes as Vlachs or Tsopani, which signifies 'shepherd' in Turkish. The literature on relations between Vlachs and Greece is sparce, and yet those works which do cover this topic highlight the sensitive aspect of some issues, so virulent are the stances taken over the origins and the affiliations of this group. Many texts published in Greek uphold the hypothesis that the Aromanians are linked to Hellenism through carnal or blood ties, and by politics as they would have been affected by national Greek sentiment to the point of being one of the most active groups in the edification of modern Greece in the nineteenth and twentieth centuries. This hypothesis stems from the more general notion that all Aromanian speakers in the Balkans are true Greeks, sharing with the other inhabitants of Hellas the same ethnic belonging and the same national consciousness.

Arvanites: An Albanian group from the south of the Balkan peninsula. They settled in the region in the thirteenth century at a time when social upheaval had forced them to flee their territories of origin (Ducellier *et al.* 1992). These Albanian or *Arvanitika* speakers have remained in Greece, even though their linguistic specialism has lessened over the years (Guefou-Madianou 1999). Historically, they were to be found in the regions of Argolis, Boeotia and Attica, in South Euboea and on the islands of the Gulf of Saronikos. Some even go so far as to date their presence on Greek soil back to the eighth, and even, for Peloponnesian Albanian speakers, to the sixth century AD. They would have arrived on the tail of the Avar invasions or, more peacefully, during their wanderings as shepherds. However, the major waves of settlement of Albanian speakers on Greek territory come later – in effect, we find them in Thessaly between 1290 and 1350. Large groups soon followed, by invitation of the Despot of Mystra in the Peloponnese, between 1341 and 1355, and then between 1460 and 1470 in the islands of Hydra, Poros and Spetze and on the east coast of the Peloponnese. However, as the different meanings of the term 'Arvanite' found in the field show, it is difficult to get a true picture of this groups, whose contours are as loose as the definition of the term used to define them…

Epirus: Epirus is a region on the eastern flanks of the Pindus mountains. Meaning 'continent' in Greek, this mountainous region takes its name from the realm of of King Pyrrhus in the second century BC. The region now overlaps the border between Greece, where it is an administrative division (prefecture, then *périphéria*), and Southern Albania. Traditional representations of Southern Albania in Greece set the northern border at the River Shkumbi, which flows through central Albania. This region, known as Northern Epirus, has long been claimed by Greece (officially up until the Protocol of Katshtica in 1920) and Greek troups were able to partially occupy the territory (1913, 1914–1916, 1941). This prompted the birth of a short-lived secessionist state – the Autonomous Republic of Northern Epirus, created and dissolved in 1914. The region shelters a strong Greek-speaking community which both states recognised in the 1914 Protocol of Corfu.

Kalantzides: A professional group from the mountainous Mourgana region mentioned in Filiates as having existed up until World War II, before the great waves of population relocation which followed this conflict. The Kalantzides were itinerant tinsmiths who travelled as far afield as Thessaly to find work even though their main residence was in these mountain regions. They are an interesting example of ethnicisation of a professional group as they are often attributed ethnic characteristics, a common origin and a language – the *Kalantzitika* – which is in fact Greek slang.

***Kinotita, dimos, nomos, périphéria*:** terms used for Greek territorial entities in order of priority, translating as: commune, municipality, department and region. Since 1997 and the Kapodistrias Reform, a decentralisation took place which merged the 441 *dimi* and 5,382 *kinotites* into 900 *dimi* and 133 *kinotites*. In 2010, a new law came into force – the Kallikratis Plan, named after the architect who designed the Parthenon – was applied to consolidate this movement, replacing the 54 prefectures by 13 administrative divisions (*périphéria*), reducing the number of *dimi* to 370 and doing away with the *kinotita*.

Ladino: Ladino (mainly used in the liturgy), also known as Judezmo or Judaeo-Spanish when talking of the spoken language in daily use, derives from mediaeval Spanish and confirms the historic link with the Al Andalus communities. It also borrows many words and phrases from the languages where these communities have lived, as well as from Hebrew.

Macedonia: Macedonia is a region which is currently split between Greece, the Republic of Macedonia and Bulgaria (to which we should add several Slavic-speaking villages surrounding the Great Lake Prespa in Albania). I have chosen in this volume to call the state arising out of the Yugoslav Republic of Macedonia by its constitutional name of the Republic of Macedonia – using the name which the inhabitants of the country themselves used, even though France recognises it as the Former Yugoslav Republic of Macedonia – like the United Nations. After the Prespa agreement with Greece, signed in June 2018, the country changed its name to the Republic of North Macedonia.

***Omogeneia*:** Like other countries of massive emigration, the laws which govern access to Greek citizenship are based on ius sanguinis, or blood right. The term is used to designate members of this Greek ethno-national community as it signifies 'of the same birth'. As Georges Prévélakis explains, this administrative term reflects awareness of a homogeneous cultural body, Hellenism, with its centuries-old history and the universal vocation of its religion – both dominant features of modern Greek identity (Prévélakis 1997: 36, 37). Without entering into the detail of the different elements which make it up, this identity implies that all the children of Hellenism can recognise each other and receive protection from the current Greek state. Through this logic, the laws of the land have recognised the entire Greek diaspora as an integral part of the Greek population, in whichever country its members may find themselves and the political stance of that country towards the diasporans. Even so, around the middle of the 1970s Greek-speakers from Albania and Turkey were already granted special rights. Just like political refugees, they could apply for a Greek passport if the country of origin refused to grant them one. Such a law is intended to accord a legal status to those who were stateless, those rare fugitives who secretly escaped from hermetically sealed countries. Today the situation has considerably changed. Since 1989, several hundreds of thousands of natives of former people's democracies and of Albania have been able to claim that they are of Greek origin because, according to some estimates, there are around 300,000 settled in their 'mother country'.

Rodeslis: The self-designation of 'Jews from Rhodes', even if these people were not all necessarily born on the island. The name Rodesli is applied to survivors of the holocaust, together with their families, but also (and especially) those branches of the Jews from Rhodes dispersed across those regions to where their parents and grandparents migrated. In French, they call themselves, somewhat indifferently 'Rodesli' or 'Rhodiotes,' a name derived this time from the Greek word, meaning Rhodians. In some contexts, such as in Brussels, the designation 'Sephardi' was given to Jews from the Ottoman Empire (from Turkey and from Egypt) amongst whom the Jewish descendands of the community of Rhodes made up a very significant group.

Romaniots: Groups of Greek-speaking Jews from the south of the Balkan peninsula. Their presence there dates back to Antiquity, pre-dating the arrival of the Sephardim from Spain after their expulsion in 1492. These latter had a considerable influence on the Romaniots, both from a cultural and a ritualistic point of view.

Sarakatsani: Like the Vlachs, the Sarakatsani are transhumant shepherds from the south of the peninsula. However, unlike the Vlachs, they were characterised by their exclusive use of a Greek dialect and, occasionally, by their completely nomadic lifestyle, without even a place of temporary residence. These groups are found today mainly in Greece and Bulgaria and the majority now lead sedentary lives.

Chams (Çam in Albanian, *Τσάμηδες* in Greek): An Albanian-speaking group from the North-West region of Greece and in the region of Konispol in Albania, between the River Acheron and the archeological site of Butrint, in the Chameria region – Çamëria in Albanian, Tchamouria in Greek. Since World War II the area has been known as Thesprotia, after the name of the ancient tribe who lived there (the Thesprotians) and is used to designate the administrative subdivision of the prefecture in the port of Igoumenitsa. This Greek territorial adminstrative body disappeared in 2010 through its integration into the territory of the Epirus periphery. In Greece it is customary to say that the Chams are distinguishable by their practice of the Muslim religion, yet old travelogues show this to not always be true. In the early eighteenth century, Athanasos Psalidas described the region, saying that it was peopled with Greeks and Albanians: 'The first are more numerous, and the second divided between Christians and Muslims' (cited in Dalamankas 2002: 95–7). We are, therefore, talking of a linguistic rather than of a religious community. After World War II, and accused of collaborating with the occupying Italian and German armies and of support in the carrying-out of massacres, most Chams either fled the region or were expelled (Kretsi 2002; Péchoux and Sivignon 1989). And yet some Albanian-speakers were able to remain in the region, though these were mostly of the Orthodox faith. Of the twenties of thousands of Albanian-speakers in pre-war Greek Epirus, only 11,000 remained in 1951. According to the Greek census, it was mainly Muslims who left the country. Given the propensity to associate the Greek identity with Orthodoxy in the border regions it is not surprising that, because of their religion, these people were more willing to be known as Greeks than as members of a 'minority' group of national traitors.

Vlachs: see Aromanians.

Bibliography

Abélès, M. (2008) *Anthropologie de la Mondialisation*. Paris: Fayard.

Agelopoulos, G. (2005) 'Autochtones et anthropologues: expériences ethnographiques en Macédoine occidentale', *Ethnologie Française*, 35(2): 305–16.

Agelopoulos, G. (2006) 'Όψεις των Ανθρωπολογικών μελετών της μετανάστευσης στην Ελλάδα', *Κοινωνία και Ψυχική Υγεία, Τεύχος* 6: 106–12.

Agier, M., Copans, J. and Morice, A. (1987) *Classes Ouvrières d'Afrique Noire*. Paris: Karthala.

Alhadeff, V. (1998) *Le Chêne de Rhodes: Saga d'une Grande Famille Sépharade*. Paris: Paris-Méditerranée.

Amilhat-Szary, A.-L. and Fourny, M.-C. (2006) 'Introduction: territorialité et nouvelles évolutions de la frontier', in A.L. Amilhat-Szary and M.C. Fourny (eds) *Après les Frontières, Avec la Frontière: Nouvelles Dynamiques Transfrontalières en Europe*. La Tour d'Aigues: Editions de L'Aube, pp. 7–20.

Amselle, J.-L. (2010) *Rétrovolutions. Essais sur les Primitivismes Contemporains*. Paris: Stock.

Andrieu, C. (2006) 'Introduction: le pouvoir central en France et ses usages du passé, de 1970 à nos jours', in C. Andrieu, M.-C. Lavabre and D. Tartakowsky (eds) *Politiques du Passé*. Aix-en-Provence: Presses Universitaires de Provence, pp. 15–26.

Angel, M.-D. (1998) *Jews of Rhodes: The History of a Sephardic Community*. New York: Sepher-Hermon Press.

Angelidou, A. (2008) 'Migrations in the "neighborhood": negotiations of identities and representations about "Greece" and "Europe" among Bulgarian migrants in Athens', *Balkanologie* 11(1–2). Online at: http://balkanologie.revues.org/1152 (accessed 30 May 2015).

Anteby-Yemini, L., Berthomière, W. and Scheffet, G. (eds) (2005) *Les Diasporas: 2,000 Ans d'Histoire*. Rennes: Presses Universitaires de Rennes.

Appadurai, A. (1991) 'Global ethnoscapes: notes and queries for a transnational anthropology', in R. Fox (ed.) *Recapturing Anthropology: Working in the Present*. Santa Fe: School of American Research Press, pp. 191–210.

Appadurai, A. (1995) 'The production of locality', in R. Fradon (ed.) *Couterworks: Managing the Diversity of Knowledge*. New York: Routledge, pp. 204–25.

Appadurai, A. (1996a) 'Sovereignty without territoriality: notes for a postnational geography', in P. Yaeger (ed.) *The Geography of Identity*. Ann Arbor: University of Michigan Press, pp. 40–58.

Appadurai, A. (1996b) *Modernity at Large: Cultural Dimensions of Globalization*. Minneapolis: University of Minnesota Press.

Appadurai, A. (2001) 'Grassroots globalization and the research imagination', in A. Appadurai (ed.) *Globalization*. London: Duke University Press, pp. 1–19.

Appadurai, A. (2006) *Fear of Small Numbers: An Essay on the Geography of Anger*. Durham NC: Duke University Press.

Arrehag, L., Sjöberg, Ö. and Sjöblom, M. (2005) 'Crossborder migration and remittances in a post-communist society: return flows of money and goods in Korçë district, Albania', *South Eastern Europe Journal of Economics*, 3(1): 9–40.

Arrehag, L., Sjöberg, Ö. and Sjöblom, M. (2006) 'Postcommunist cross-border migration in South-Eastern Albania: who leaves, who stays behind?', *Journal of Ethnic and Migration Studies*, 32(3): 377–402.

Athanassopoulou, A. (2005) 'Nos Albanais à nous: travailleurs émigrés dans une communauté arvanite du Péloponnèse', *Ethnologie Française*, 35(2): 267–78.

Athanassopoulou, E. (1997) 'Blessing in disguise? The Imia Crisis and Turkish-Greek relations', *Mediterranean Politics*, 2(3): 76–101.

Balabanian, O., Bouet, G., Delondes, O. and Lerat, S. (1991) *Les Etats Méditerranéens de la CEE: Espagne, Italie, Grèce, Portugal*. Paris: Masson.

Baldwin-Edwards, M. (1998) 'When free markets reign: aliens in the twilight zone', *South-European Society and Politics*, 3(3): 1–15.

Baldwin-Edwards, M. and Salifios-Rothschild, C. (1997) 'Immigration and unemployment in Greece: perception and realities', in N.-G. Bermeo (ed.) *Unemployment in Southern Europe: Coping with the Consequences*. London: Frank Cass, pp. 212–23.

Balibar, E. and Wallerstein, I. (1988) *Race, Nation, Classe. Les Identités Ambiguës*. Paris: La Découverte.

BALKABAS, in press, *Les Balkans Par Le Bas*. Paris: Karthala.

Baltsiotis, L. and Embirikos, L. (2007) 'De la formation d'un ethnonyme. Le terme Arvanitis et son évolution dans l'Etat hellénique', in G. Grivaud and S. Petmezas (eds) *Byzantina et Moderna: Mélanges en l'Honneur d'Hélène Antoniadis-Bibicou*. Athens: Alexandria, pp. 417–48.

Barth, F. (1969) *Ethnic Groups and Boundaries: The Social Organization of Culture Differences*. Oslo: Universitetsforlaget.

Bayindir Goularas, G. (2010) 'Vers les terres natales, vers les terres des ancêtres', *Téoros, Revue de Recherche en Tourisme*, 29(1): 31–6.

Benatar, J. and Pimienta-Benatar, M. (2000) *De Rhodes à Elisabethville: l'Odyssée d'une Communauté Sépharade*. Paris: Siiac.

Benbassa, E. and Rodrigue, A. (2002) *Histoire des Juifs Sépharades, de Tolède à Salonique*. Paris: Le Seuil.

Berger, P.-L. and Luckmann, T. (1966) *La Construction Sociale de la Réalité*. Paris: Armand Colin.

Béteille, R. (1974) Les Aveyronnais: Essai Géographique sur l'Espace Humain. Poitiers: University of Poiliers, unpublished PhD thesis.

Bieber, F. (2007) 'Less diversity, more integration: interethnic relations in the contemporary Balkans', *South-Eastern Europe*, 32(31): 23–38.

Bloch, M. (1925) 'Mémoire collective, tradition et coutume. À propos d'un livre récent', *Revue de Synthèse Historique*, 40(118–20): 73–83.

Blondel, C., Javourez, G. and Stojanova, M. (2013) 'The European cross-border cooperation in the Balkan countries: marking space and the multi-scalar production of locality', in N. Bardhoshi, G. de Rapper and P. Sintès (eds) *Social Practices and Local Configurations in the Balkans*. Tirana: UET, pp. 97–120.

Bocquet, D. (2004) 'Rhodes 1912: Les mésaventures du Général d'Ameglio', *Cahiers de la Méditerranée*, 68: http://cdlm.revues.org/667?lang=en (accessed 25 August 2015).

Bondaz, J., Isnart, C. and Leblon, A. (2013) 'Au-delà du consensus patrimonial. Résistances et usages contestataires du patrimoine', *Civilisation*, 61(1): 9–22.

Bossuet, L. and Sotiropoulou, E. (2007) 'Charme rural et renaissance villageoise', in Y. Luginbühl (ed.) *Nouvelles Urbanités, Nouvelles Ruralités en Europe*. Brussels: Peter Lang.

Bougarel, X. and Clayer, N. (2001) *Le Nouvel Islam Balkanique: Les Musulmans, Acteurs du Post-Communisme 1990–2000*. Paris: Maisonneuve et Larose.

Bouiller, D. (2011) 'Habitèle virtuelle', *Urbanisme*, 376: 42–4.

Bouskari, E. (2009) *Η Οθωμανική αρχιτεκτονική στην Ελλάδα*. Athens: Ministry of Culture, Directorate for Byzantine and Post-Byzantine Antiquities.

Brah, A. (1996) *Cartographies of Diasporas*. London: Routledge.

Braudel, F. (1977) *La Méditerranée: l'Espace et l'Histoire*. Paris: Flammarion.

Brettell, C. (2003) *Anthropology and Migration: Essays on Transnationalism, Ethnicity and Identity*. New York and Oxford: Altamira Press.

Brubacker, R. (2001) 'Au-delà de l'identité', *Actes de la Recherche en Sciences Sociales*, 139: 66–85.

Bruneau, M. (ed.) (1998) *Les Grecs Pontiques: Diaspora, Identité, Territoires*. Paris: CNRS.

Bruneau, M. (2004) *Diaspora et Espace Transnationaux*. Paris: Economica.

Burawoy, M. (ed.) (2000) *Global Ethnography: Forces, Connections and Imaginations in a Global World*. Berkeley: University of California Press.

Burawoy, M. and Verdery, K. (eds) (1999) *Uncertain Transition: Ethnographies of Change in the Postsocialist World*. Lanham, MD and Oxford: Rowman and Littlefield.

Butler, J. (2009) *Ces Corps qui Comptent. De la Matérialité et des Limites Discursives du 'Sexe'.* Paris: Editions Amsterdam.

Butler, J. and Jami, I. (2003) 'Considérer le problème plus que l'identité', in *Pensées Critiques. Dix itinéraires de la revue Mouvements 1998–2008*. Paris: La Découverte, pp. 117–30.

Butler, R. (2003) 'Relationships between tourism and diasporas: influences and patterns', *Espace, Populations et Sociétés*, 21(2): 317–25.

Campani, G. (1992) 'L'Italie et les Albanais', *Hommes et Migrations*, 1155: 38–43.

Campbell, J.-K. (1964) *Honour, Family and Patronage. A Study of Institutions and Moral Values in a Greek Mountain Community.* Oxford: Clarendon Press.

Candau, J. (2005) *Anthropologie de la Mémoire*. Paris: Armand Colin.

Castles, S. and Miller, M. (1993) *The Age of Migration: International Population Movements in the Modern World*. London: Macmillan.

Cattaruzza, A. (2010) *Territoire et Nationalisme au Montenegro*. Paris: L'Harmattan.

Cattaruzza, A. and Chaveneau-Le Brun, E. (2007) 'Ni voisins, ni membres. La "périphérisation" des Balkans occidentaux *via* le processus d'adhésion à l'UE', *L'Espace Politique*, 2. https://espacepolitique.revues.org/619 (accessed 28 August 2015).

Cattaruzzza, A. and Sintès, P. (2012) *Atlas Géopolitique des Balkans*. Paris: Autrement.

Cavounidis, J. and Chatzakis, L. (2000) *Αλλοδαποί που Υπέβαλαν Αίτηση για Κάρτα Παραμονής*. Athens: EIE.

Cela, E. and Moretti, E. (2008) 'L'immigrazione albanese in Italia: 1990–2005', in L. Di Comite, O. Garavello and F. Galizia (eds) *Sviluppo Demografico ed Economico nel Mediterraneo*. Bari: Cacucci Editore, pp. 351–74.

Charbit, Y., Hily, M.-A. and Poinard, M. (1997) *Le Va et Vient Identitaire: Migrants Portugais et Villages d'Origine*. Paris: INED–PUF.

Ciarcia, G. (2011) *Ethnologues et Passeurs de Mémoires*. Paris and Montpellier: Karthala.

Clifford, J. (1994) 'Diasporas', *Cultural Anthropology*, 9(3): 302–38.

Clifford, J. (1997) *Routes. Travel and Translation in the Late Twentieth Century.* Cambridge, MA: Harvard University Press.

Clogg, R. (ed.) (2002) *Minorities in Greece: Aspects of a Plural Society*. London: Hurst.

Cohen, R. (1997) *Global Diasporas: An Introduction*. London: Routledge.

Coles, T. (2003) 'Diaspora and the mediation of vacationscapes: some lessons from enticing Jewish-Americans to Germany', *Espace, Populations et Sociétés*, 21(2): 327–40.

Collignon, B. (2007) 'Note sur les fondements des *postcolonial studies*', *EchoGéo*, 1. http://echogeo.revues.org/2089 (accessed 28 August 2015).

Collignon, B. and Staszak, J.-F. (eds) (2003) *Espaces Domestiques. Construire, Habiter, Représenter.* Paris: Bréal.

Conti, C., Natale, M. and Strozza, S. (2003) 'Le rimesse degli immigrati: determinanti, modalita di invio e aspettative di impiego', in N. Acocella and

E. Sonnino (eds) *Movimenti di Persone e Movimenti do Capitali in Europa*. Rome: Il Mulino, pp. 289–365.

Cornish, H. (2013) 'The life of the death of "the fighting fairy woman of Bodmin": storytelling around the museum of witchcraft', *Anthropological Journal of European Cultures*, 22(1): 79–97.

Crivello, M. (ed.) (2010) *Les Echelles de la Mémoire en Méditerranée*. Arles: Actes Sud/MMSH.

Cvijić, J. (1917) 'Les mouvements métanastasiques de la péninsule balkanique', *Monde Slave*, 1: 1–15.

Dakhama, H. (2005) 'La présentation de soi au pèlerinage de Rabbi Hahya Lakhdar (Maroc)', in S. Chiffoleau and A. Madoeuf (eds) *Les Pèlerinages au Maghreb et au Moyen-Orient. Espaces Publics, Espaces du Public*. Beyrouth: Ifpo, pp. 39–58.

Dalakoglou, D. (2017) *The road. An ethnography of (im)mobility, space, and cross-border infrastructures in the Balkans*. Manchester: Manchester University Press.

Dalamankas, A. (2002) *Ήπειρος, παρελθόν παρόν και μέλλον*, Athens: Koultoura.

Dallègre, J. (ed.) (2011) *La Grèce Inconnue d'Aujourd'hui: De l'Autre Côté du Miroir*. Paris: L'Harmattan.

Damianakos, S. (1996) *Le Paysan Grec*. Paris: L'Harmattan.

Damianakos, S. (2001) 'Espace urbain et espace rural: fiction statistique et observation sociologique (1961–1991)', in G. Burgel and Z. Démathas (eds) *La Grèce Face au Troisième Millénaire: Territoire, Economie, Société, 40 Ans de Mutations*. Athens: Laboratoire de Géographie urbaine de Paris X, pp. 121–38.

Deets, S. (2006) 'Reimagining the boundaries of the nation: politics and the development of ideas on minority rights', *East European Politics and Societies*, 20(3): 419–46.

Dépret, I. (2005) 'L'Église Orthodoxe de Grèce et le "combat" des cartes d'identité (2000–2001)', *Archives de Sciences Sociales des Religions*, 131–2: 27–46.

de Rapper, G. (2004) 'Les Guègues et les Tosques existent-ils? L'opposition Nord/Sud en Albanie et ses interprétations', *Espace, Populations, Sociétés*, 4: 625–40.

de Rapper, G. (2007) 'The Greek–Albanian border and its impact on local populations', in R. Morrissey (ed.) *Cahiers Parisiens/Parisian Notebooks 3*. Paris: University of Chicago Press in Paris, pp. 566–75.

de Rapper, G. (2008) 'Looking for Europe on the borders of Albania'. Athens: Panteion University, paper given to the international conference *Europe At, Across and Beyond the Borders*, 27–29 November.

de Saussure, F. (1916) *Cours de Linguistique Générale*. Paris: Editions Payot et Rivages.

di Meo, G. (ed.) (1996) *Les Territoires du Quotidien*. Paris: L'Harmattan.

Diminescu, D. (2005) 'Le migrant connecté: pour un manifeste épistémologique', *Migrations/Société*, 17(102): 275–92.

Dimitriadis, G. (2009) *Performing Identity/Performing Culture: Hip Hop as Text, Pedagogy, and Lived Practice*. New York: Peter Lang.

Dimitrijević, D. (2000) 'De l'utilisation idéologique de la notion de culture en général et dans les Guerres en ex-Yougoslavie en particulier', *La Lettre de l'ARA*, 44: 11–14.

Dimitrijević, D. (2004) *Fabrication de Traditions, Invention de Modernité*. Paris: Editions de la Maison des Sciences de l'Homme.

Dimitrijević-Rufu, D. (1998) 'Identité contextuelle: le cas d'une communauté roumaine de Serbie', *Les Oubliés des Balkans, Cahiers Balkaniques*, 25: 165–74.

Doménach, H. and Picouet, M. (1987) 'Le caractère de la réversibilité dans l'étude de la migration', *Population*, 42(3): 469–84.

Drain, M. (1990) *La CEE Méditerranéenne: Dossiers des Images Economiques du Monde*. Paris: SEDES.

Drettas, G. (2003) 'Pour une anthropologie religieuse de la Grèce contemporaine', *Messogeios*, 20–1: 21–41.

Ducellier, A., Doumerc, B., Imhaus, B. and de Miceli, J. (1992) *Les chemins de l'exil, bouleversements de l'Est européen et migration vers l'Ouest à la fin du Moyen-âge*, Paris: Armand Colin.

Dufoix, S. (2003) *Les Diasporas*. Paris: Presses Universitaires de France.

Durham Peters, J. (1997) 'Seeing bifocally: media, place, culture', in A. Gupta and J. Ferguson (eds) *Culture, Power, Place: Explorations in Critical Anthropology*. Durham NC: Duke University Press, pp. 75–92.

Emke-Poulopoulou, H. (1986) *Προβλήματα Μετανάστευσης: Παλλινόστησης*. Athens: IMEO–ΕΔΗΓ.

Emke-Poulopoulou, H. *et al.* (eds) (2007) *Οικονομικές Μετανάστριες στην Ελλάδα: Διαπολιτισμικότητα και Εκπαίδευση*. Athens: Gutenberg.

Fabre, D. and Iuso, A. (2011) *Les Monuments Sont Habités*. Paris: Éditions de la Maison des Sciences de l'Homme.

Fakiolas, R. (2003) 'Regularising undocumented immigrants in Greece: procedures and effects', *Journal of Ethnic and Migration Studies*, 29(3): 535–61.

Faret, L. (2003) *Les Territoires de la Mobilité: Migration et Communautés Transnationale entre le Mexique et les Etats-Unis*. Paris: Editions du CNRS.

Finley, M.I., Hartog, F. and Carlier, J. (1981) *Mythe, Mémoire, Histoire. Les Usages du Passé*. Paris: Flammarion.

Fintz-Menascé, E. (1991) *Gli Ebrei a Rodi*. Milan: Guerini.

Foucault, M. (1978) 'La gouvernementalité', in M. Foucault, *Dits et Ecrits, T. III*. Paris: Gallimard, pp. 635–57.

Fragoudaki, A. and Dragona, T. (eds) (1998) *Τι Είναι η Πατρίδα μας;» Εθνοκεντρισμός στην Εκπαίδευση*. Athens: Alexandria.

Franco, H.-M. (1994) *The Jewish Martyrs of Rhodes and Cos*. Harare: Harper Collins.

Gardin, J. (2012) 'Gestion de la grande faune: vers un sauvage équipé? Le cas de l'Ours grec', in Groupe Oblomoff (ed.) *Le Monde en Pièces. Pour une Critique de la Gestion: 1 - Quantifier*. Paris: La Lenteur, pp. 87–123.

Gauchet, M. (1998) *La Religion dans la Démocratie: Parcours de la Laïcité*. Paris: Gallimard.

Gedeshi, I. (2006) 'From brain drain to brain gain: mobilising Albania's skilled diaspora', in K. Tamas and J. Palme (eds) *How Migration Can Benefit Development*. Stockholm: Institute for Future Studies, pp. 113–32.

Ghorra-Gobin, C. (2003) 'De la métropolisation et de la glocalisation: l'impact des discours des chercheurs américains', *Espace, Populations, Sociétés*, 21(1): 43–50.

Giordano, C. (2001) 'Mobilizing history: the politics of time in European societies', in Z. Smitek and B. Brumen (eds) *Kulturno Antropologijo, Zemljevidi Casa – Maps ot Time*. Ljubljana: Zupanjceva Knjiznica, pp. 171–92.

Givre, O. (2008) *L'Evénement (Changer de Système)*. Marseille: Aix-Marseille University, BALKABAS Working Paper.

Givre, O. and Regnault, M. (eds) (2015) *Patrimonialisation Croisée, Jeux d'Echelles et Enjeux de Développement*. Lyon: Presses Universitaires de Lyon.

Givre, O. and Sintès, P. (2013) 'Nouveaux liens à d'anciens lieux: patrimoine et tradition pour (ré)habiter la localité dans deux espaces frontaliers (Grèce–Albanie, Bulgarie–Turquie)', in G. de Rapper and P. Sintès (eds) *Social Practices and Local Configurations in the Balkans*, Tirana: UET Press, pp. 233–58.

Givre, O. and Sintès, P. (2015) '"Européaniser" le local par-delà la frontière? Projets patrimoniaux et de développement entre Grèce et République de Macédoine', in C. Chavarochette, M. Demanger and O. Givre (eds) *Faire Frontière(s). Raisons Politiques et Usages Symboliques*. Paris: Karthala, pp. 191–206.

Glick Schiller, N., Basch, L. and Szanton Blanc, C. (eds) (1992) *Towards a Transnational Perspective on Migration: Race, Class, Ethnicity, and Nationalism Reconsidered*. New York: New York Academy of Science.

Glick Schiller, N., Basch, L. and Szanton Blanc, C. (eds) (1994) *Nations Unbound: Transtational Projects, Postcolonial Predicaments, and Deterritorialized Nation-States*. Basel: Gordon and Breach.

Goffman, E. (1974) *Les Rites d'Interaction*. Paris: Editions de Minuit.

Goffman, E. (1975) *Stigmate: Les Usages Sociaux des Handicaps*. Paris: Editions de Minuit.

Gogonas, N. (2009) 'Language shift in second generation Albanian immigrants in Greece', *Journal of Multilingual and Multicultural Development*, 30(2): 95–110.

Gossiaux, J.-F. (2002) *Pouvoirs Ethniques dans les Balkans*. Paris: Presses Universitaires de France.

Gounaris, V. and Frangopoulos, Y. (2009) 'La quête de la nation grecque moderne et le cas "grec" comme un cas paradoxal de la construction du fait national contemporain', *Socio-Anthropologie*, 23–4: 115–53.

Grange, S. (2003) 'Le patrimoine juif comtadin. Un enjeu de développement local?', *Les Cahiers Espaces*, 80: 105–8.

Grataloup, C. (2011) *Faut-il Penser Autrement l'Histoire du Monde?* Paris: Armand Colin.

Gravari Barbas, M. (1997) 'Le «sang» et le «sol»: le patrimoine, facteur d'appartenance à un territoire urbain', in J. Bonnemaison, L. Cambrezy and L. Quinty Bourgeois (eds) *Le Territoire, Lien ou Frontière? Identités, Conflits Ethniques, Enjeux et Recompositions Territoriales.* Paris: ORSTOM, pp. 55–67.

Gravari Barbas, M. and Guichard-Anguis, S. (2003) *Regards Croisés sur le Patrimoine dans le Monde à l'Aube du XXIe Siècle.* Paris: Presses Universitaires Paris-Sorbonne.

Grendi, E. (1977) 'Micro-analisi e storia sociale', *Quaderni Storici*, 35: 506–20.

Guefou-Madianou, D. (1998) 'Η χώρα του πνεύματος και η χώρα του οινοπνεύματος', *Συνχρόνα θέματα*, January–March: 104–15.

Guefou-Madianou, D. (1999) 'Cultural polyphony and identity formation: negotiation tradition in Attica', *American Ethnologist*, 26(2): 412–39.

Guentcheva, R. (2008) 'Les mobilités internes en Bulgarie, 1989–2005', *Balkanologie*, 11(1–2), online at: http://balkanologie.revues.org/1473 (accessed 1 June 2015).

Gupta, A. and Ferguson, J. (eds) (1997) *Anthropological Locations. Boundaries and Grounds of a Field Science.* Berkeley and Los Angeles: University of California Press.

Hartog, F. (2003) *Régimes d'Historicité. Présentisme et Expériences du Temps.* Paris: Seuil.

Hasson, A. (1974) 'The Sephardic Jews of Rhodes in Los Angeles', *Western States Jewish Historical Quarterly*, 6(4): 241–54.

Hasson, A. (1996) 'The Los Angeles Rhodesli Sephardic Community', in W. Kramer (ed.) *Sephardic Jews in the West Coast States. Vol. 2: The Los Angeles Sephardic Experience.* Los Angeles: Western States Jewish History Association, pp. 383–95.

Hasson, A. (2012) *A Guidebook to the Jewish Quarter of Rhodes.* Los Angeles: Rhodes Historical Foundation.

Hatzidaki, A. (2005) 'Models of bilingual behaviour in Albanian pupils' families: empirical research findings', *Epistimes Agogis*, 3: 79–102.

Hatziprokopiou, P. (2005) *Globalisation, Migration and Socio-Economic Change in Contemporary Greece: Processes of Social Incorporation of Albanian and Bulgarian Immigrants in Thessaloniki.* Amsterdam: Amsterdam University Press.

Hersant, J. (2001) 'La minorité musulmane en Thrace et l'intégration européenne de la Grèce', *Revue des Etudes Turques et Ottomanes, Documents de Travail du Centre d'Histoire du Domaine Turc*, 9–10: 113–31.

Hersant, J. (2008) 'Surveillances croisées et rivalité gréco-turque en Thrace occidentale: entre coercion et contrôle social', *European Journal of Turkish Studies*, 8, https://ejts.revues.org/2693 (accessed 6 October 2015).

Hersant, J. and Yatropoulos, N. (2007) 'Mobilisation identitaire et représentation politique des "Turcs" en Thrace occidentale: les élections législatives grecques de mars 2004', *European Journal of Turkish Studies*, 7, https://ejts.revues.org/1342 (accessed 6 October 2015).

Herzfeld, M. (1987) *Anthropology Through the Looking-Glass. Critical Ethnography in the Margins of Europe*. Cambridge: Cambridge University Press.

Herzfeld, M. (1995) 'Les enjeux du sang, la production officielle des stéréotypes dans les Balkans: le cas de la Grèce', *Anthropologie et Sociétés*, 19(3): 37–51.

Herzfeld, M. (1997) *Cultural Intimacy: Social Poetics in the Nation-State*. New York and London: Routledge.

Herzfeld, M. (2004) *The Body Impolitic: Artisans and Artifice in the Global Hierarchy of Value*. Chicago: University of Chicago Press.

Hirschon, R. (2005) 'Jews from Rhodes in Central and Southern Africa', in M. Ember, C.-M. Ember and I. Skoggard (eds) *Encyclopedia of Diasporas, Immigrant and Refugee Cultures Around the World*. Dordrecht: Kluwer Academic, pp. 925–34.

Hobsbawm, E. and Ranger, T. (eds) (1983) *The Invention of Tradition*. Cambridge: Cambridge University Press.

Iosifides, T. and King, R. (1998) 'Socio-spatial dynamics and exclusion of three immigrant groups in the Athens conurbation', *South-European Society and Politics*, 3(3): 205–29.

Javourez, G. (forthcoming) La Recomposition des Relations Frontalières dans les Balkans: l'Exemple des Régions de Bitola (République de Macédoine) et Florina (Grèce). Marseille: Aix-Marseille University, unpublished PhD thesis.

Kapplani, G. and Mai, N. (2005) '"Greece belongs to Greeks!" The case of the Greek flag in the hands of an Albanian student', in R. King, N. Mai and S. Schwandner-Sievers (eds) *The New Albanian Migration*. Brighton: Sussex Academic Press, pp. 153–72.

Karakasidou, A. (2002) 'Cultural illegitimacy in Greece: the Slavo-Macedonian "non-minority"', in R. Clogg (ed.) *Minorities in Greece: Aspects of a Plural Society*. London: C. Hurst and Co, pp. 122–64.

Karamanli, M. (2013) *La Grèce: Victime ou Responsable?* Paris: L'Aube.

Karydis, V. (2004) 'Το ζήτημα της δεύτερης γενιάς: εγκληματικότητα και μετανάστευση', in M. Pavlou and D. Christopoulos (eds) *Η Ελλάδα της Μετανάστευσης: Κοινωνική Συμμετοχή, Δικαιώματα και Ιδιότητα του Πολίτη*. Athens: Kritiki–KEMO, pp. 205–32.

Kasimati, K. (1984) *Μετανάστευση–Παλλινόστηση: Η Προβληματική της Δεύτερης Γενιάς*. Athens: EKKE.

Kasimati, K. (1993) *Πόντιοι Μετανάστες από την Πρώην Σοβιετική Ένωση: Κοινωνική και Οικονομική τους Ενταξη*. Athens: Panteon University and Secrétariat Général de l'Hellensme en Diaspora (ΓΓΑΕ).

Kasimis, C., Papadopoulos, A.-G. and Zacopoulou, E. (2003) 'Migrants in rural Greece', *Sociologia Ruralis*, 43(2): 167–84.

Kaufman, V. (2008) *Les Paradoxes de la Mobilité: Bouger, S'Enraciner*. Lausanne: Presses Polytechniques et Universitaires Romandes.

Kaurinkoski, K. (2008) 'Le "retour" des Grecs de l'ex-Union soviétique: politiques d'accueil et stratégies des migrants dans l'agglomération athénienne', in W. Berthomière and C. Chivallon (eds) *Les Diasporas dans le Monde Contemporain*. Paris: MSHA–Karthala, pp. 283–300.

Kayser, B. (2004) *Ils ont Choisi la Campagne*. Paris: Editions de l'Aube.

Kearney, M. (1995) 'The local and the global: the anthropology of globalization and transnationalism', *Annual Review of Anthropology*, 24: 547–65.

Kerem, Y. (1997) 'The settlement of Rhodian and other Sephardic Jews in Montgomery and Atlanta in the twentieth century', *American Jewish History*, 85(4): 373–91.

King, R. (2005) 'Albania as a laboratory for the study of migration and development', *Journal of Southern Europe and the Balkans*, 7(2): 133–55.

King, R. and Mai, N. (2004) 'Albanian migrants in Lecce and Modena: narratives of rejection, survival and integration', *Population, Space and Place*, 10(6): 455–77.

King, R. and Mai, N. (2008) *Out of Albania: From Crisis Migration to Social Inclusion in Italy*. London: Berghahn.

King, R. and Vullnetari, J. (2006) 'Orphan pensioners and migrating grandparents: the impact of mass migration on older people in rural Albania', *Ageing and Society*, 26(5): 783–816.

King, R. and Vullnetari, J. (2009) 'The intersections of gender and generation in Albanian migration, remittances and transnational care', *Geografiska Annaler B, Human Geography*, 91(1): 19–38.

King, R., Iosifides, T. and Myrivili, L. (1998) 'A migrant's story: from Albania to Athens', *Journal of Ethnic and Migration Studies*, 24(1): 159–75.

Kirshenblatt-Gimblett, B. (1998) *Destination Culture*. Berkeley: University of California Press.

Kivisto, P. (2001) 'Theorizing transnational immigration: a critical review of current efforts', *Ethnic and Racial Studies*, 24(4): 549–77.

Knafou, R. (ed.) (2004) *La Planète 'Nomade': Les Mobilités Géographiques Aujourd'hui*. Paris: Belin.

Kokkali, I. (2008) 'Spatial proximity and social distance: Albanian immigration in Thessaloniki, Greece'. London: LSE, 3rd LSE PhD Symposium on Modern Greece, 14–15 July 2007. Online at: http://www.lse.ac.uk/europeanInstitute/research/hellenicObservatory/pdf/3rd_Symposium/PAPERS/KOKKALI_IFIGENEIA.pdf (accessed 1 June 2015).

Kollarou, T. and Moussourou, L. (1980) *Παλλινόστηση*. Athens: Centre d'Etudes et de Recherché Humaines.

Kollias, E. (2001) *Μεσαιωνίκη πόλη Ρόδου : έργα αποκατάστασης* (1985–2000). Rhodes: Ministry of Culture, Office of Works of the Old Town of Rhodes.

Kolodny, E. (1985) *Η Σαμοθράκη στις Οχθες του Νέκαρ: Έλληνες Μετανάστες στη Στουτγάρδη*. Athens: EKKE.

Kontiadis, X. and Papatheodorou, T. (eds) (2007) *Η Μεταρρύθμιση της Μεταναστευτικής Πολιτικής*. Athens: Papazisis.

Konuk, N. (2008) *Midilli, Rodos, Sakız ve İstanköy'de Osmanlı Mimarisi*. Ankara: Centre des Recherches Stratégiques.

Koselleck, R. (1990) *Futures Past: On the Semantics of Historical Time*. Cambridge, MA: MIT Press.

Kretsi, G. (2002) 'The secret past of the Greek-Albanian borderlands. Cham Muslim Albanians: perspectives on a conflict over historical accountability and current rights', *Ethologia Balkanica*, 6: 171–95.

Kretsi, G. (2007) *Verfolgung Und Gedachtnis in Albanien: Eine Analyse Postsozialistischer Erinnerungsstrategien*. Berlin: Otto Harrassowitz.

Kristeva, J. (1988) *Etrangers à Nous-Mêmes*. Paris: Fayard.

Kule, D., Llaci, S. and Memaj, F. (2004) 'Businessmen, migration and socio-economic impact', *Economy and Business Review*, 1(15): 7–16.

Kyprianou, P. and van Boeschoten, R. (2006) 'Οι μετανάστες στα θρανία: Η κοινωνική ένταξη περνά από το σχολείο'. Athens: KEMO, paper presented at the conference *Διεπιστημονικές Προσεγγίσεις του Μειονοτικού και Μεταναστευτικού Φαινομένου*.

Labrianidis, L. and Hatziprokopiou, P. (2005) 'The Albanian migration cycle: migrants tend to return to their country of origin after all', in R. King, N. Mai and S. Schwandner-Sievers (eds) *The New Albanian Migration*. Brighton: Sussex Academic Press, pp. 93–117.

Labrianidis, L. and Lyberaki, A. (2004) 'Back and forth and in-between: Albanian return-migrants from Greece and Italy', *Journal of International Migration and Integration*, 5(1): 77–106.

Laliotou, I. (2006a) *Διασχίζοντας τον Ατλαντικό: Η Ελληνική Μετανάστευση στις ΗΠΑ Κατά το Πρώτο μισό του Εικοστού Αιώνα*. Athens: Polis.

Laliotou, I. (2006b) 'Κινητικότητα, μετανάστευση και υποκείμενο μεταξύ ανατολικής και δυτικής Ευρώπης', *Σύγχρονα Θέματα*, 92: 82–6.

Lauth Bacas, J. (2002) 'Greece and its new immigrants: features and consequences of the recent immigration to Greece', *Ethnologia Balkanica*, 6: 197–208.

Lavabre, M.-C. (2006) 'Introduction', in C. Andrieu, M.-C. Lavabre and D. Tartakowsky (eds) *Politiques du Passé*. Aix-en-Provence: Presses Universitaires de Provence, pp. 7–11.

Lazaridis, G. and Poyago-Theotoky, J. (1999) 'Undocumented migrants in Greece: issues of regularization', *International Migration*, 37(4): 715–40.

Lazarou, A.-G. (1998) 'Valaques de Grèce', *Cahiers Balkaniques*, 25: 61–98.

Le Breton, E. (2004) 'Mobilité, exclusion, marginalité', in S. Allemand, F. Ascher and J. Lévy (eds) *Les Sens du Mouvement*. Paris: Belin, pp. 117–23.

Legrand, C. (2006) 'Tourisme des racines et confrontations identitaires dans l'Irlande des migrations', *Diaspora, histoire et société*, 8: 162–71.

Levitt, P. (2004) *Transnational Migrants: When 'Home' Means More Than One Country*. Washington DC: Migration Policy Institute, online at: http://www.migrationpolicy.org/article/transnational-migrants-when-home-means-more-one-country (accessed 2 June 2015).

Lévy, J. (1994) *L'espace Légitime*. Paris: Presse de la Fondation Nationale des Sciences Politiques.

Lévy, J. and Olazabal, I. (2003) 'Les routes juives d'Espagne réveillent une mémoire oubliée. L'exemple de Gérone', *Tourisme de Mémoire: Les Cahiers Espaces*, 80: 59–65.

Lewkowicz, B. (2000) 'After the war we were all together', in M. Mazower (ed.) *After the War was Over: Reconstructing the Family, Nation, and State in Greece, 1943–1960*. Princetown: Princetown University Press, pp. 247–72.

Lianos, T. (2008) *Δημιουργία Μηχανισμών για την Αποτελεσματική και Βιώσιμη Υλοποίηση των Συμφωνιών Επανεισδοχής μεταξύ της Αλβανίας, της Ε.Κ. και ενδιαφερομένων τρίτων χωρών*. AENEAS European programme.

Lory, B. (2011) *La Ville Balkanissime: Bitola 1800–1918*. Istanbul: Isis.

Lussault, M. (2007) *L'Homme Spatial. La Construction Sociale de l'Espace Humain*. Paris: Seuil.

Luttrell, A. (2006) *The Town of Rhodes: 1306–1356*. Rhodes: City of Rhodes Office for the Medieval Town.

M'Bokolo, E. and Amselle, J.-L. (2005) *Au Coeur de l'Ethnie: Ethnie, Tribalisme et Etat en Afrique*. Paris: La Découverte.

Ma Mung, E. (2000) *La Diaspora Chinoise: Géographie d'une Migration*. Paris: Ophrys.

Mai, N. and Schwandner-Sievers, S. (2003) 'Albanian migration and new transnationalisms', *Journal of Ethnic and Migration Studies*, 29(6): 939–48.

Manousou-Ntella, K. and Ntellas, G. (2007) 'Αρχές αποκατάστασης-ανάσδειξεις των μνημείων της μεσαιωνικής πόλης της Ρόδου', in *15 χρόνια έργων αποκατάστασης στη Μεσαιωνική Πόλη της Ρόδου*. Rhodes, pp. 49–63.

Manta, E. (2004) *Οι Μουσουλμάνοι Τσάμηδες της Ήπειρου (1923–2000)*. Thessaloniki: Idrima Meleton Chersonisou Tou Aimou.

Margaritis, G. (2005) *Ανεπιθύμητοι Συμπατριώτες*. Athens: Vivliorama.

Markou, K. (2008) 'De la minorisation des Pomaques à la reconnaissance de la pomacité dans le contexte grec', in G. de Rapper and P. Sintès (eds) *Nommer et Classer dans les Balkans*. Paris, de Boccard, pp. 133–9.

Maroukis, T. (2012) *The Number of Irregular Migrants in Greece at the End of 2010 and 2011*. Athens: *ELIAMEP Briefing Note* 21/2012, https://www.google.ch/search?client=safari&rls=en&q=The+Number+of+Irregular+Migrants+in+Greece+at+the+End+of+2010&ie=UTF-8&oe=UTF-8&gfe_rd=cr&ei=9EUVVpOeLarC8gfX8ZnQAg (accessed 6 October 2015).

Martucelli, D. (2004) 'Les revers de la mobilité généralisée', in S. Allemand, F. Ascher and J. Lévy (eds) *Les Sens du Mouvement*. Paris: Belin, pp. 99–108.

Marvakis, A., Parsanoglou, D. and Pavlou, M. (eds) (2001) *Μετανάστες στην Ελλάδα*. Athens: Ellinika Grammata.

Mavromatis, G. and Tsitselikis, K. (2004) 'Η εκπαίδευση των μεταναστών στην Ελλάδα (1990–2003)', in M. Pavlou and D. Christopoulou (eds) *Η Ελλάδα της Μετανάστευσης: Κοινωνική Συμμετοχή, Δικαιώματα και Ιδιότητα του Πολίτη*. Athens Kritiki–KEMO, pp. 121–40.

Memaj, F. (2008) 'Fuga de cervelli: il caso dell'Albania', in R. Devole, F. Pittanau, A. Ricci and G. Urso (eds) *Gli Albanesi in Italia: Conseguenze Economiche e Sociali dell'Immigrazione*. Rome: Centro Studi e Richerche IDOS, pp. 101–12.

Memaj, F., Dika, I. and Mullaj, K. (2003) 'Intellectual migration and intellectual labour market in Albania', *Economy and Transition Review*, 2: 55–65.

Mertzoz, N. (2004) *Νυμφαίο η αναγέννηση του σε εικόνες*, Municipality of Nymphaion.

Mestrović, S. (1994) *The Balkanization of the West: The Confluence of Postmodernism and Postcommunism*. London: Routledge.

Meyer, H.-F. (2007) *Blutiges Edelweiss. Die 1. Gebirgs-Division im Zweiten Weltkrieg*. Berlin: Links-Verlag.

Michail, D. (2008) 'Albanian immigrants in Western Macedonia–Kastoria Greece: a challenge for rethinking Greek nationalism', in E. Marushiakova (ed.) *Dynamics of National Identity and Transnational Identities in the Process of European Integration*. Newcastle: Cambridge Scholars Publishing, pp. 138–53.

Michas, T. (2002) *Unholy Alliance: Greece and Milošević's Serbia*. College Station: Texas A&M University Press.

Michel, I. (2006) 'Le paradigme de la transition: chronique d'une fin annoncée. Le cas de l'Europe centrale et orientale', *Revue d'Etudes Politiques et Constitutionnelles Est-Européennes*, 2(1): 25–34.

Miletitch, N. (1998) *Trafic et Crimes dans les Balkans*. Paris: Presses Universitaires de France.

Miller, D. (ed.) (2001) *Home Possessions. Material Culture behind Closed Doors*. Oxford and New York: Berg.

Mintz, S. (1998) 'The localization of anthropological practice: from area studies to transnationalism', *Critique of Anthropology*, 18(2): 117–33.

MIT (2000) 'La mise en tourisme des lieux: un outil de diagnostique', *Mappemonde*, 77(1): 2–6.

Monova, M. (2002) 'De la logique de retour à la logique d'établissement: le cas des réfugiés de la guerre civile grecque en République de Macédoine', *Etudes Balkaniques*, 9: 73–92.

Morokvasic-Muller, M. (2001) 'Balkans: les exclus de l'élargissement', H*ommes et Migrations*, 1230: 81–93.

Morokvasic, M. (2002) 'Ouverture des frontières à l'Est', *Les Cahiers Français–La Documentation Française*, 307: 24–39.

Moussourou, L. (1991) *Μετανάστευση και Μεταναστευτική Πολιτική στην Ελλάδα και Στην Ευρώπη*. Athens: Gutenberg.

Nestoropoulou, A. (2008) 'L'altérité dans la presse régionale: l'exemple du département d'Imathias', in G. de Rapper and P. Sintès (eds) *Nommer et Classer dans les Balkans*. Paris: de Boccard, pp. 169–87.

Nestoropoulou, A. and Sintès, P. (2007) 'Une diaspora de l'intérieur? Le discours d'une association *vorioépirote* à Athènes', *Revue d'Etudes Comparatives Est-Ouest*, 41(4): 201–24.

Nitsiakos, V. (2010) *On the Border: Transborder Mobility, Ethnic Groups and Boundaries along the Albanian–Greek Frontier*. Berlin: LIT Verlag.

Olivier de Sardan, J.-P. (1995) *Anthropologie et Développement. Essai en Socio-Anthropologie du Changement Social*. Paris: Karthala.

Orgocka, A. and Jovanovic, J. (2006) 'Identity exploration and commitment of Albanian youth as a function of social opportunity structure', *European Psychologist*, 11(4): 268–76.

Paleologou, N. (2004) 'Intercultural education and practice in Greece: needs for bilingual intercultural programmes', *Intercultural Education*, 15(3): 317–29.

Panopoulos, P. (2005) 'Retour au village natal. Associations locales et renouveau culturel', *Ethnologie Française*, 35(2): 243–54.

Papailias, P. (2007) *Αφηγήσεις Μέσα από το Φωτογραφικό Αλμπουμ: Πόζες, Μνήμες, Βλέμματα*. Volos: University of Thessaly, Literature review for the PYTHAGORAS programme; *Μφυλες Διαστάσεις της Μετανάστευσης στη Νοτιοανατολική Ευρώπη: Εργασία, Ένταξη και Διαπολιτισμική Επικοινωνία*. Volos: University of Thessaly, PYTHAGORAS programme.

Papataxiarchis, E. (2005) 'La Grèce face à l'altérité', *Ethnologie Française*, 2: 203–12.

Papataxiarchis, E. (ed.) (2006) *Περιπέτειες της Ετερότητας: Η Παραγωγή της Πολιτισμικής Διαφοράς στη Σημερινή Ελλάδα*. Athens: Alexandria.

Papataxiarchis, E., Topali, P. and Athanassopoulou, A. (2008) *Κόσμοι της Οικιακής Εργασίας. Φύλο, Μετανάστευση και Πολιτισμικοί Μετασχηματισμοί στην Αθήνα του Πρώιμου 21ου Αιώνα*. Athens: University of the Aegean: Alexandria.

Parant, A. (2005) *Migrations, Crises et Conflits Récents dans les Balkans. Acte du colloque de Belgrade de l'Association Demobalk*. Volos: Presse de l'Université de Thessalie.

Pavlou, M. and Christopoulos, D. (eds) (2004) *Η Ελλάδα της Μετανάστευσης: Κοινωνική Συμμετοχή, Δικαιώματα και Ιδιότητα του Πολίτη*. Athens: Kritiki–KEMO.

Péchoux, P.-Y. (2002) 'Evangélos Bakayannis: souvenir d'une enfance ballotée aux portes de la guerre, Epire, 1939–1944', *Géocarrefour*, 77(4): 335–42.

Péchoux, P.-Y. and Sivignon, M. (1989) 'L'éviction des Tchamidès d'Epire occidentale en 1944', *L'Ethnographie*, 85(2): 113–19.

Pelossof, N. (2007) *Nisso: d'Une Île à l'Autre*. Amiens: Encrage-Picardie.

Petronoti, M. (1998) *Το Πορτραίτο μιας Διαπολιτισμικής Σχέσης*. Athens: UNESCO–EKKE.

Petronoti, M. and Triandafyllidou, A. (2003) *Σύγχρονα Μεταναστευτικά Ρεύματα στην Ελλάδα*. Athens: EKKE.

Picciotto-Fargion, L. (1991) *Il Libro della Memoria*. Milan: Centro di Documentazione Ebraica Contemporanea.

Pierron, B. (1996) *Juifs et Chrétiens de la Grèce Moderne: Histoire des Relations Intercommunautaires de 1821 à 1945*. Paris: L'Harmattan.

Pignataro, L. (2011) *Il Dodecaneso Italiano 1912–1947*. Chieti: Solfanelli.

Piore, M. (1979) *Birds of Passage*. London: Cambridge University Press.

Prévélakis, G. (1994) *Les Balkans: Culture et Géopolitique*. Paris: Nathan.

Prévélakis, G. (1997) *Géopolitique de la Grèce*. Paris: Complexes.

Prevelakis, G. (2011) 'La Grèce: trois décennies d'anesthésiant européen', *Géostratégiques*, 31: 97–109.

Ptéroudis, E. (1996) 'Emigrations et immigrations en Grèce: évolution récente et questions politiques', *Revue Européenne des Migrations Internationales*, 12(1): 159–89.

Ragaru, N. (2007) 'Repenser la politisation des identités: les engagements militants dans les Balkans d'aujourd'hui', *Revue d'Etudes Comparatives Est-Ouest*, 38(4): 5–28.

Rahmani, M. (2000) *Rhodes, Un Pan de Notre Mémoire*. Paris: Romillat.

Rautenberg, M. (2003) *La Rupture Patrimoniale*. Paris: Editions de la Croisée des Chemins.

Ripoll, F. (2006) 'Réflexion sur les rapports entre marquage et appropriation de l'espace', in T. Bulot and V. Veschambre (eds) *Mots, Traces, Marques: Dimension Spatiale et Linguistique de la Mémoire Urbaine*. Paris: L'Harmattan, pp. 15–36.

Rosenau, J. (1992) *Turbulence in World Politics*. Princeton: Princeton University Press.

Rosenthal, E. (1963) *Rhodesian Jewry and its Story*. Harare: Zimbabwe Jewish Board of Deputies.

Rumelili, B. (2004) *The European Union's Impact on the Greek-Turkish Conflict*. Birmingham: University of Birmingham, EU Border Conflicts Studies Working Paper, http://www.birmingham.ac.uk/documents/college-social-sciences/government-society/polsis/research/eu-border-conflict/wp06-eu-impact-on-the-greek-turkish-conflict.pdf (accessed 6 October 2015).

Rumelili, B. (2007) 'Transforming conflicts on EU borders: the case of Greek–Turkish relations', *Journal of Common Market Studies*, 45(1): 105–26.

Saïd, E. (1978) *Orientalism*. New York: Pantheon Books.

Sarra, G. (2001) *Μνημες της τραγικης Περιοδου 1936–1945*. Athens: Magazine Spiritual Life.

Sassen, S. (2007) *A Sociology of Globalization*. New York: W.W. Norton & Company.

Sayad, A. (1977) 'Les trois âges de l'émigration algérienne en France', *Actes de la Recherche en Sciences Sociales*, 15(1): 59–79.

Sayad, A. (1999) *La Double Absence, des Illusions de l'Emigré aux Souffrances de l'Immigré*. Paris: Le Seuil.

Schnapper, D. (1992) *L'Europe des Immigrés*. Paris: François Bourrin.

Schwandner-Sievers, S. (1999) *The Albanian Aromanians' Awakening: Identity Politics and Conflicts in Post-Communist Albania*. Flensburg: European Centre for Minority Issues Working Paper No. 3.

Segaud, M. (2007) *Anthropologie de l'Espace. Habiter, Fonder, Distribuer, Transformer*. Paris: Armand Colin.

Séraïdari, K. (2006) 'Grecs Orthodoxes et Grecs Catholiques, ou comment définir son identité par la religion', *Mésogeios. Méditerranée, Histoire, Peuples, Langues, Cultures*, 28(1): 67–92.

Séraïdari, K. (2010) 'Compétition entre Orthodoxes et Catholiques: la production du sacré dans une île grecque', *Ethnologie Française*, 40(1): 151–60.

Shain, M. and Mendelsohn, R. (2008) *The Jews in South Africa: An Illustrated History*. Johannesburg: Jonathan Ball.

Simon, G. (1979) *L'espace des Travailleurs Tunisiens en France: Structures et Fonctionnement d'un Champ Migratoire International*. Poitiers: University of Poitiers.

Simon, G. (2002) 'Penser globalement les migrations', *Projet*, 272: 37–45.

Simon, G. (2008) *La Planète Migratoire dans la Mondialisation*. Paris: Armand-Colin.

Sintès, P. (2002) 'Immigration, réseaux et espace métropolitain: le cas athénien', *Les Cahiers de la Méditerranée*, 63(1): 311–29.

Sintès, P. (2003) 'Les Albanais en Grèce: le rôle des réseaux préexistants', *Balkanologie*, 7(1): 111–33.

Sintès, P. (2005) 'Les Albanais en Grèce: Mobilités, Réseaux et Territoires. Nice: University of Nice Sophia-Antipolis', unpublished PhD thesis.

Sintès, P. (2007) 'Les mobilités des travailleurs balkaniques en Grèc : migration de travailleurs ou circulation régionale?' *L'Espace Géographique*, 36(4): 353–65.

Sintès, P. (2008a) 'Lire les résultats du recensement grec de 2001: tendances du peuplement et pratiques sociales de l'espace en Grèce', *L'Espace Géographique*, 37(3): 253–69.

Sintès, P. (2008b) 'Les Valaques de la région de Gjirokastër et la Grèce', in G. de Rapper and P. Sintès (eds) *Nommer et Classer dans les Balkans*. Paris: de Boccard, pp. 23–43.

Sintès, P. (2010a) *La Raison du Mouvement: Territoires et Réseaux de Migrants Albanais en Grèce*. Paris: Karthala.

Sintès, P. (2010b) 'Construction des discours d'appartenance en migration: l'exemple des Albanais en Grèce', *ANATOLI*, 1(1): 195–213.

Sintès, P. (2010c) '"Mi akodro de Rhodes": paroles d'une communauté juive de la mer Egée entre mémoire et actualité', in M. Crivello (ed.) *Les Echelles de la Mémoire*. Arles: Acte Sud/MMSH, pp. 75–107.

Sintès, P. (2010d) 'Retrouver Rhodes', *Téoros*, 29(1): 37–45.

Sintès, P. (2011a) 'Manœuvres politiques et discours de l'urgence: la frontière égéenne de la Grèce au cœur d'enjeux nationaux et européens', in N. Ribas-Mateos (ed.) *El Rio Bravo Mediterráneo: Las Regiones Fronterizas en la Epoca de la Globalización*. Barcelona: Bellaterra, pp. 375–90.

Sintès, P. (2011b) 'A qui Rhodes? Discours d'appropriation et de mise en valeur touristique dans la vieille ville de Rhodes', in L. Bourdieu and S. Chassé (eds) *Tourisme et Site du Patrimoine Mondial de l'UNESCO*. Quebec: Presses de l'Université de Laval, pp. 1096–108.

Sintès, P. (2013) '(Re)construire la Juderia de Rhodes', *Ethnologie Française*, 43: 19–30.

Sintès, P. and Thuillier, G. (2009) 'Des résidents occidentaux en Mer Egée: le case de l'île de Tinos', *Méditerranée: Revue Géographique des Pays Méditerranéens*, 113: 79–89.

Sivignon, M. (2001) 'L'automobile en Grèce: à la source d'une nouvelle relation entre villes et village', *Strates*, 10: 51–8.

Skevofylakas, G. (1988) *Κοινωνιολογική Μελέτη παλιάς πόλης Ρόδου: Ποιότητα ζωής*. Rhodes: Report on a joint study commissioned by the archeological services and the city of Rhodes.

Skordas, A. (2002) 'The new immigration law in Greece: modernization on a wrong track', *European Journal of Migration and Law*, 4: 23–48.

Skoulariki, A. (2003) 'La crise macédonienne (1991–1995) et la question des slavophones en Grèce', *Balkanologie*, 7(1): 137–46.

Smith, L. (2006) *The Uses of Heritage*. London: Routledge.

Sotiropoulou, E. (2007) 'Tourism, village space and the re-appropriation of rural: towards a new social organisation of the countryside', *Tourismos: An International Multidisciplinary Journal of Tourism*, 2(2): 113–28.

Spivak, G.C. (2010) 'Can the Subaltern Speak?', in R. Morris (ed.) *Can the Subaltern Speak? Reflections on the History of an Idea*. New York: Columbia University Press, pp. 21–78.

Stiliou, L. (2004) 'Greek employers and Albanian domestic cleaners: "we" and the "others" in the space of house'. Volos: Paper given to the conference *Gender, Migration and Transnational Communication*, 6 November.

Stiliou, L. (2007) 'Bulgarian migrant women working as live-in caregivers of the elderly: reflections on "domestic" and "public"'. Mytilene: Paper presented to the international conference *Gender, Work and the Household: Comparative Perspectives*, 30–31 March.

Stock, M. (2004) 'L'habiter comme pratique des lieux géographiques', *EspacesTemps.net*. Online at: http://www.espacestemps.net/articles/habiter-comme-pratique-des-lieux-geographiques/ (accessed 3 June 2015).

Stock, M. (2005) 'Les sociétés à individus mobiles: vers un nouveau mode d'habiter? L'exemple des pratiques touristiques, *EspacesTemps.net*. Online at: http://www.espacestemps.net/en/articles/les-societes-a-individus-mobiles-vers-un-nouveau-mode-drsquohabiter-en/ (accessed 3 June 2015).

Stock, M. (2006) 'L'hypothèse de l'habiter poly-topique: pratiquer les lieux géographiques dans les sociétés à individus mobiles', *EspacesTemps.net*, http://www.espacestemps.net/en/articles/lrsquohypothese-de-lrsquohabiter-poly-topique-pratiquer-les-lieux-geographiques-dans-les-societes-a-individus-mobiles-en/?output=pdf (accessed 27 August 2015).

Thanopoulos, J. and Walle, A.-H. (1988) 'Ethnicity and its relevance to marketing: the case of tourism', *Journal of Travel Research*, 26(3): 11–14.

Thiesse, A.-M. (1999) *La Création des Identités Nationales: Europe, XVIIIe–XXe Siècle*. Paris: Seuil.

Todorova, M. (2009) *Imagining the Balkans*. New York: Oxford University Press.

Topali, P. (2005) 'Εκεί ηρωίδα, εδώ Φιλιππινέζα: γυναικεία μετανάστευση και εργασία στο δημόσιο λόγο', *Σύγχρονα Θέματα*, 82: 72–83.

Topali, P. (2006) 'Ασύμπτωτες σχέσεις: Φιλιππινέζες οικιακές βοηθοί και Ελληνίδες εργοδότριες στην Αθήνα', in E. Papataxiarchis (ed.) *Περιπέτειες της Ετερότητας: Η Παραγωγή της Πολιτισμικής Διαφοράς στη Σημερινή Ελλάδα*. Athens: Alexandria, pp. 297–323.

Topali, P. (2008) *Σιωπηρές Σχέσεις, Διαπολιτισμικές Επαφές: Η Περίπτωση των Φιλιππινέζων Οικιακών Βοηθών στην Αθήνα*. Athens: University of the Aegean–Alexandria.

Tratnjek, B. (2014) 'Mémoricides dans les espaces post-yougoslaves: de la destruction de la mémoire à la réécriture d'une mémoire excluante', in G. Cattanéo (ed.) *Guerre, Mémoire, Identité*. Paris: Nuvis, pp. 215–38.

Triandafyllidou, A. and Veikou, M. (2002) 'The hierarchy of Greekness: ethnic and national identity considerations in Greek immigration policy', *Ethnicities*, 2(2): 189–208.

Trouillot, M.-R. (1995) *Silencing the Past: Power and the Production of History*. Boston: Beacon Press.

Tsitsélikis, K. and Christopoulos, D. (1997) *Το Μειονοτικό Φαινόμενο Στην Ελλάδα*. Athens: Kritiki.

Tsogas, G. (2009) *Η Σαγιάδα: Η Ιστορική Αρτυριές Και Αφήσεις*. Athens: Dodoni.

Tsokalidou, R. (2005) 'Raising "bilingual awareness" in Greek primary schools', *International Journal of Bilingual Education and Bilingualism*, 8(1): 48–61.

Vaïou, D. (2002) 'In the interstices of the city: Albanian women in Athens', *Espace, Populations, Sociétés*, 3: 373–85.

Vaïou, D. (2007) *Διαπλεκόμενες Καθημερινότητες και Χωροκοινωνικές Μεταβολές Στην Πόλη*. Athens: Presses de l'Ecole d'architecture.

Vaïou, D. and Kalandides, A. (2009) 'Cities of "others": public space and everyday practices', *Geografica Helvetica*, 1: 11–20.

Van Boeschoten, R. (2006) '"Είμαστε ξένοι εδώ": μετανάστευση, φύλο και στρατηγικές της καθημερινής ζωής'. Athens: Panteion University, Paper presented to the international workshop *Multiculturalism and Migration*, 23–24 October.

Van Boeschoten, R. (2007) 'Gendered memories: From communist past to migrant present'. Volos: Paper presented to the conference *Gendered Aspects of Migration in South Eastern Europe*, 30 November.

Ventura, L. (1994) *Μετανάστευση και Έθνος. Μετασχηματισμοί στις Συλλογικότητες και τις Κοινωνικές Θέσεις*. Athens: Mnimon.

Ventura, L. (1999) *Έλληνες μετανάστες στο Βέλγιο*. Athens: Nefeli.

Verdery, K. (1996) *What Was Socialism and What Comes Next?* Princeton NJ: Princeton University Press.

Vergeti, M. (1991) 'Pontic Greeks from Asia Minor and the Soviet Union: problems of integration in modern Greece', *Journal of Refugee Studies*, 4(4): 382–99.

Vermeulen, H. (1990) *Έλληνες στην Ολλανδία*. Athens: EKKE.

Vertovec, S. (1999) Conceiving and researching transnationalism', *Ethnic and Racial Studies*, 22(2): 447–62.

Vertovec, S. and Cohen, R. (eds) (1999) *Migration, Diasporas and Transnationalism*. Cheltenham: Edward Elgar.

Vgenopoulos, C.-G. (2000) 'Migrants and refugees in modern Greece', in C.-G. Vgenopoulos (ed.) *Population Movements and Development*. Athens: EKEM, Hellenic Centre for European Studies, pp. 87–104.

Voutira, E. (1991) 'Pontic Greeks today: migrants or refugees?', *Journal of Refugee Studies*, 4(4): 400–20.

Wihtol de Wenden, C. (2001) 'Un essai de typologie des nouvelles mobilités', *Hommes et Migrations*, 1233: 5–12.

Williams, C. (1992) 'On the recognition of minorities in contemporary Greece', *Planet*, 94: 82–90.

Wimmer, A. and Glick Schiller, N. (2002) 'Methodological nationalism and beyond: nation-state building, migration and social sciences', *Global Networks*, 2(4): 301–34.

Yérasimos, S. (ed.) (2002) *Le Retour des Balkans, 1991-2001*. Paris: Autrement.

Index

Printed and bound by CPI Group (UK) Ltd, Croydon, CR0 4YY

13/09/2026

14961099-0001